Praise for B.D. ~~~~

"This man has seen it all."
- 20/20

"I couldn't put it down."
- Chicago Sun-Times

"I found it absolutely hysterical!"
- Today Show

"Cruise Confidential is a deliciously addictive read..."
- Travel Channel

"...Ship for Brains is a fine pick, not to be missed."
- Midwest Book Review

"This is a very funny, behind-the-scenes exploration
of a cruise ship."
- Booklist

"Bruns doesn't hold back..."
- Thomas Cook Magazine (UK)

HIGH SEAS DRIFTER

Cruise Confidential
Vol. 4

B.D. BRUNS

World Waters

Las Vegas • Ottawa

Cover design by Brian David Bruns

Interior art by Brian David Bruns

Interior layout by Steven Urban

www.BDBruns.com

Library of Congress Cataloguing-in-Publication Data
        Bruns, Brian David
        Bruns, B.D.
        1st ed.
        Produced by World Waters

ISBN (print edition): 978-0-9856635-6-8
Library of Congress (PCN):

1. Cruise   2. Mediterranean

HIGH SEAS
DRIFTER

World Waters

Las Vegas • Ottawa

Table of Contents

PART 1: THE BAD GOODBYE

Santorini, Greece	7
Portoferraio, Elba	25
Porto Vecchio, Corsica	47
Venice, Italy	65
Corfu, Greece	83
Valletta, Malta	99
Tunis, Tunisia	119
Hvar, Croatia	139
Pompeii, Italy	161
Monte Carlo, Monaco	181
Wind Surf	201

PART 2: WHODUNIT

Cannes, France	225
Casablanca, Morocco	241
Tangiers, Morocco	261
Sete, France	279
Malaga, Spain	299
St. Tropez, France	319
Marrakech, Morocco	337
Ibiza, Spain	357
Transatlantic	377
Epilogue	397

APPENDIX

Ode to Bianca	
Rogue's Gallery	407
Rumble Yell: Training on Planet Vegas	413
Rumble Yell: Meet Cheek	427
Map of the Mediterranean Sea	445

HAPPINESS

cannot be given,
though it must be accepted.

— *B.D. Bruns*

PART 1
THE BAD GOODBYE

EVERYTHING

has its wonders,
even darkness and silence,
and I learn, whatever state I may be in,
therein to be content.

— Helen Keller

SANTORINI
GREECE

THE HEADLINE WOULD read "DEATH BY ASS." The newsprint already blazed across my imagination: text bold, black, and all caps. I would have preferred less brevity and more dash. Maybe "Local Man Succumbs to Killer Foreign Ass." Astonishingly, Mom saw this one coming. She always warned me I would die some horrible, unforeseen death if I dared leave my native Iowa. Or the house. I thought she was just being overprotective, yet here I was, thirty years and six thousand miles away, proving her right.

Twenty minutes ago things were going fine. Romantic, even. Not the good kind of romance—another item on Mom's list of Dangerous Don'ts—but the kind of romance that only the sea can invoke, a sea plied by ships of tall sails and peopled with men of courage, curiosity, lust for life. I had once counted myself among their number.

Nine hundred feet below us, cool mist lazed atop the gently lapping waters of the Aegean, pulsing to the sea's mysterious, ancient rhythm. Between us and hazy, smoking Fire Island lolled a small yacht, sails furled, barely seen but for a mast piercing the shroud. The mist did not blanket so much as bunch at the cliff's base, perhaps afraid to near that rumbling heap of ash and molten rock rising from the center of the sunken caldera. And fear it should. Such were the still restless remains of a destroyer: the very volcano that in one angry outcry slaughtered the entire Minoan civilization—even as it gave birth to the legend of Atlantis.

Had Poseidon himself been looking from that steaming rock, across his cerulean home and up above the cowering mist, past the satisfying contrast of chestnut brown cliffs, he would have delighted at the shock of whitewashed cottages and sky blue doors. The tiny geometries of man spread liberally atop the brown: thick and wavy like frosting smeared carelessly atop a cupcake, clumps bunching high in some areas, in others threatening to tumble over the steep sides in a sticky white avalanche. Spread, as it were, by the hand of the gods born of this land millennia ago. Long ago the gods destroyed the men living here, even as long ago men destroyed the gods. Man himself was responsible now for the wonder of Santorini.

"And a fine job he has done," my tall companion agreed.

I hadn't meant to speak such wonders of time aloud, being loathe to sound like a poet and stuff. He adjusted his eyeglasses and smiled in his slight, Dutch manner. "The gods were capricious, were they not? But man muddles through and, sometimes, wonders happen."

"Man muddles all right," I agreed, rather petulantly. I had been petulant a lot lately. Ardin lowered his sizable camera to better regard me. Considering what I knew of him, this was a large expression.

"You don't sound very American," he observed.

I dismissed any implied question with a chuckle and said, "I'm just getting a little tired of muddling."

"Aren't we all," Ardin agreed, hefting his camera once more.

He leaned his tall, lanky frame forward, into the wind. After a few crisp clicks, Ardin used the telephoto lens to illustrate the magnitude of the panorama before us: a broken ring of thousand-foot rock rising from a vastness of sea and sky, the point of merging blues indeterminate. "Look at that down there. If you can't appreciate that, you can't appreciate anything."

"I'll appreciate getting down there without dying," I commented drily, clutching tightly to the horn of my saddle. Beneath me, my mount shifted. This nameless beast, who was to be my ride down the nearly vertical cliffs of Santorini, puffed and fussed as much as nearby Fire Island. This was my first mule ride, and I was both surprised and intimidated by the power this humble animal exuded. I felt no safer than had I been straddling the raw power of the volcano. I hoped my beast of burden was not as capricious as the gods.

"If you can drive on American highways," Ardin quipped in his direct, Dutch manner, "surely you can handle a one mulepower vehicle."

My reply was a snort and a smart remark. "Don't you mean one asspower? It's okay. I'm used to flying by the seat of my pants."

"I can't drive!" trilled a voice behind us. "Can we walk?"

I turned in my creaking saddle to view our third companion. A delicate young Asian man clung to his saddle fearfully, skinny knees shifting along the beast's flanks in search of better purchase. With bone-white knuckles gripping the saddle horn, he had difficulty keeping his hair out of his eyes. He shook his head feverishly to keep too-long bangs clear.

"Time to learn," Ardin stated blandly.

That was the umpteenth time Ardin had said such that day, and I noted the rigid Dutchman had not even bothered to turn and look at our fretting companion. Though his posture indicated otherwise, I sensed Ardin sighing and drooping somewhat whenever our charge spoke. Waryo, an Indonesian assigned to replace Ardin as ship's photographer, acted precisely like the large eyed village boy far from home that he was. But his whimpering became simpering sometimes, leaving us to wonder whether he was merely naive or being coy. If the latter, he exhibited it in a most unusual manner.

"If you can't handle your saddle, Yoyo," Ardin continued, still not looking at the Indonesian, "Be reassured by the presence of an actual American cowboy."

Yoyo looked to me longingly for guidance and comfort. I snorted louder than my mule.

When the three of us had departed our ship to enjoy the port of Santorini, we had left the marina via funicular. Ascending to the city so far above was a matter of minutes by mechanical means. But going back we opted for something more... romantic. Despite my recent drop into apathy, I still found the desire to do what the locals had done since antiquity: making the nine-hundred foot traverse on muleback. I would have felt guilty letting the animals labor through the ascent—courtesy of my Catholic upbringing which imbued a sense of guilt over everything —and had therefore suggested we only ride the animals down. Yoyo agreed, if only in order to postpone an action he feared. Ardin, descendent of more practical stock, just shrugged at our foibles.

Dug into the overhanging edge of the cliffs was a corral. It smelled of animals steaming in the late June heat. We had descended an ancient stone ramp and into the striped shade under a roof of unpainted wooden slats. The shadows were not particularly deep, but the outside sunshine was bright enough that our eyes adjusted slowly. We approached several dozen quiet mules, most napping on their feet, a few watching us with large, brown eyes. The flicking of long ears and longer tails was the only movement in this lazy, warm place, barring the occasional snort or shaking head. After a while we found their keeper hidden among them, also mule napping.

The bored Greek came alive when he spied our approach. He rushed over, scraping a sweaty hand through thinning, wind-blown hair, and gleefully took our money. Then he promptly returned to sleeping on his feet.

"No instructions in the seat-back in front of us," I groused. "I have to endure being taught how to use a seatbelt every damn flight of my life, but when first dealing with live transportation, I'm on my own."

We waded into the mass of shifting animals, each man seeking his preferred mount. All were dressed in the

11

same worn saddles atop fraying blankets. Yoyo held his arms in so close as to hug himself, terrified of touching a flank. Selecting our animals at random, we struggled into the saddles. This was a new maneuver for me, but my decent height aided the ascent. Ardin, taller than me at nearly six foot four, had no difficulties whatsoever. Alas, Yoyo was a comical tangle of extremities flashing over the wide barrel of his mount's body. He finally lurched atop the saddle, panting.

"In the deserts and ghost towns of Nevada I've seen lots of wild burros," I observed. "And they look just like this. So are these burros or mules? I always pictured donkeys thinner, for some reason. And what the hell is an ass?"

Yoyo exploded into hysterical giggles. Ardin and I both creaked in our saddles to give him dubious looks. Yoyo clammed up. The effort apparently made him woozy, as he swayed atop his mule dangerously. No doubt his nerves were making him giddy. I just hoped he didn't pass out!

To our right rose a wall some twenty feet high, capped by buildings no doubt boasting a whitewashed balcony like every other building on Santorini. Before us dropped the only path, snaking downward at an alarming angle before curving out of sight. It was so steep, in fact, that the road was actually a series of steps. To our left, separated by only a three-foot stone wall, the land sheered away.

"No reins," Ardin noted.

Ardin looked ludicrous atop his mule. In his practical, worn travel clothes and hat he would have cut an impressive figure—almost Indiana Jones-esque—had he been on horseback. Instead, his feet extended far below the useless stirrups and his long, lanky form swayed above the bulk of animal like a lone reed buckled by the wind. Had he a lance, Ardin could have been Don Quixote; a whimpering, Asian Sancho Panza trailing uselessly behind.

"How we start these?" Yoyo asked. His English was not accented so much as broken. He was hesitant to use it and frequently omitted words, but when he did speak his delicate voice rang crystal clear and with excellent pronunciation. Ardin, on the other hand, spoke the superb English of a Dutchman. Next to him, even my native tongue sounded lethargic.

Ardin slapped his mule firmly on the rump and the entire herd began to shift in an organic, pulsing wave. The mass of animal flesh elongated until eventually one third of the nearly three dozen mules broke free of the corral and began descending. Those joining us without riders looked bored, perhaps wanted some exercise, or possibly a change of view. There were only two places in the lives of these animals: top or bottom, with one road between. Two shaggy, happy dogs also joined our procession. The clops of hoof upon stone were softly muffled. It was surprising to see such a large mass moving so quietly.

The quiet did not last long.

What I had assumed would be a leisurely ride was anything but. The nervous anticipation of climbing atop the mules in the corral was not unlike climbing into the car of a roller coaster, the slow start like rising to the first drop. The descent was sheer terror—and without the assurance of a safety harness. After the first bend the ribbon of wriggling road dropped so steeply, so quickly, I seriously thought we were leaping into the blue abyss. My stomach flipped as the herd recklessly plunged with the curves, seemingly out of control but moving ever downward, ever faster. Yet the 'joy ride' was just beginning.

Yoyo's shriek shattered the quiet. The effect was nothing less than the shot starting a race. The dogs began gamely yipping and nipping at the heels of the mules, which began shoving each other with great heaves of bulk. The chaotic mass plunged along the cliffside at a frantic pace. I had never felt so helpless in all my life. I gripped the saddle horn as my mule rammed his way through the crowd directly towards the cliff edge. I felt like I was driving on sheet ice down a steep hill into traffic: no brakes, no steering wheel. The protective wall barely came to my knees while standing, let alone on muleback. The collision felt nothing short of leaping over. I may have succumbed to an unmanly squeal.

My mule remained at the outside of the road for a while, and there I cruised, uncontrolled, just above the wall. I was given a respite as the majority of animals moved inward, to the cliffside, slamming Ardin and Waryo against the wall. The two men were ground against the rough stone, pressed by the sheer tonnage of mule flesh. Ardin prudently kept his elbows in and quietly endured the mauling of his knees, whereas Yoyo squealed bloody murder and flailed everything flailable. Their mules tried unsuccessfully to push away from the cliff, but seemed unable to do so against the might of the others. After several heart—and extremity—rending moments, the beasts flattened their ears, girded their loins, and surged away from the cliff wall. The herd thundered outward, towards the cliff's edge.

Towards me.

My mount took the crush bodily, ears flattened back and head down. His bulk and momentum were forward. Mine were not. I was nearly jettisoned from the saddle when the impact ripped my hands loose. For one horrific moment I looked straight down, down to the tiny waves breaking upon tiny rocks below—waves and rocks I knew damned good and well were not tiny at all. Both feet remained in the stirrups, just barely, which kept me atop the animal.

I had lived a long time with a swelled sense of adventure. I was a happy-go-lucky guy. But this whole thing was shockingly unsafe. Maybe the Greeks felt selecting the muleback ride over the cheaper funicular was self-censoring, or that people were responsible for their own safety. Maybe they just didn't care about safety because they didn't know anybody who had gone over a cliff. But I did.

My friend Will, a teacher famous for offering new students cans of Spam and using Spam haiku to teach math, had gone over a cliffside trail. He free fell the first thirty feet to land on his head upon solid rock. He then rolled down loose scree and rubble to the bottom of a ravine a hundred feet further. Will's head had broken open, and he lay there for hours with his brain exposed. The final protective layer had not been breached, but his right eye had literally been found on the back of his smashed head. Will's unconscious body was so difficult to extract that even the rescuer lowered from a helicopter broke his own leg in the process.

Will's survival had been a miracle by any standard, let alone his full recovery. Luckily his body had been unscathed, but half a dozen experts had to be flown in to literally reassemble his face. They started with his jaw—the only bone in his head unbroken—and reconstructed from there. They lost count of screws after one hundred. Astonishingly, a few weeks later Will was laughing again. In fact, he was even teasing the doctors about how they 'forgot to use a compass' on his tear duct, which had ballooned because it was reoriented incorrectly and tears didn't release outward. One year later he was back in his math room with his beloved pyramid of Spam on the desk. He had a long, thin scar under his hairline, but no other sign of trauma. He joked that his only worry now was receding hairline.

So Will's story had a happy ending. That mountainside had been nearly two hundred feet. I knew it well: I even used to run along its trail! But this was four times higher. I just hoped that Ardin's mount remained on the inside track. Without stirrups I truly feared for his life.

Several hundred vertical feet were traversed in this white-knuckle, gasp-inducing manner. Then suddenly all motion ceased. The herd came to a gentle halt halfway down the cliff. We panted and glanced about, stunned. The excitement was over. The mules, for their part, seemed completely at ease. Heat rose from their bulk. Flies descended. All was calm. Our thumping hearts and sweaty palms were the only evidence of recent chaos.

Ardin gave his mule a decisive spank, but this time it reacted in much the same way as my ex-wife: looking back at him with an expression that plainly said, 'you wish.'

"What now?" I asked, peering tentatively over the edge of the cliff.

"We wait," Ardin replied, gently probing his camera bag for indications of broken equipment within.

"We walk now?" Yoyo whimpered.

"You want to be on the road when the herd decides to resume its descent?" Ardin asked tersely, scrutinizing his lenses.

Yoyo's whining promptly quieted to a low mewl. Until a few moments later, that is, when he suddenly cried out in horror, "I broke a nail!"

"Good," Ardin replied tartly. "Now cut the other one."

I was left to ponder that odd rebuke when Ardin suddenly pointed his telephoto lens downward and began snapping photos. I followed his sight and noted the distinctive masts of our cruise ship, hundreds of feet below: our ship, our home, the Wind Surf.

The *Wind Surf* was an unusual cruise ship, to say the least. She was tiny, compared to the mega-liners that plied the world's seas, but also unique. She was an actual sailing vessel. Or, rather, a hybrid. Unlike the windjammer cruises, wherein guests pay for the privilege of handling the sails, the Surf was a luxury vessel with hydraulic, computer-driven sails unfurling at the touch of a button. She was designed to reach higher speed under sail than under motor propulsion. And was she ever a sight to behold.

"A ship at sea in God's way," Ardin murmured.

"Getting religious now that our lives are on the line?" I remarked rather insensitively.

Ardin answered with a kind expression. "My grandfather used to say, 'Under sail we went to sea God's way, the way God made the oceans and the winds; we were a part of it. Modern motor vessels fight the sea and the wind.'"

"Your grandfather was a sailor, then?" I asked, impressed. "Old school, with sails and all? My father spent four years in the U.S. Navy but was stationed in the middle of the desert in New Mexico, if you can believe that. He only went to sea one day. Of course, he still got a sailor's tattoo."

"Of course," Ardin repeated with a slight grin. "Both my father and grandfather loved being sailors. They loved being a living part of our heritage as the world's great seafarers. My grandfather started on sailing vessels when he was fourteen years old. Some were still hauling cargo as late as the war, but were phased out because they couldn't outrun U-boats."

"Incredible," I said. "I thought the age of sail was gone way, way back."

"Mostly," Ardin agreed. "My grandfather would tell me stories about it. Usually he was even more pragmatic than my father, rarely finding the beauty in anything. But not when it came to life under sail. He would get poetic about how they lived balanced between air and water, one with the elements. Their schedules were as unpredictable as the weather. In good wind they would sometimes sail around the clock, even up to a week. Everyone worked four hour shifts, one off and one on, for twenty four hours a day. Other times it would lay up in a calm for days on end, with nothing to do but wait. Not very practical in a modern business world. But then, there are always seafaring entrepreneurs in Holland. My father was in shipping, too, and wanted me to follow, but I'm artistically inclined. Serving as photographer on the world's largest sailing vessel seemed like a good medium."

"The *Wind Surf* is the world's largest sailing vessel?" I asked, surprised. Having only met Ardin the day before, I sure was learning a lot from him. A pragmatic artist was someone I wanted to get to know.

"She and her sister Club Med 2," Ardin said. "They displace 15,000 tons. Some of the replicas of big ships look a lot bigger with all their sails aloft, but they are in fact far lower and lighter. Most are less than half the weight, which is actually all that counts."

"Still the biggest ship I saw," Yoyo breathed.

"For being 10,000 kilometers from home," Ardin said drily, "You haven't been around much."

"How about you, Yoyo? Any sailors in your family?"

"No," he answered simply. He did not elaborate.

"I will miss the romance of being under sail," Ardin continued. "I was happy on *Wind Surf*, but will be happier at home with my wife in Vietnam."

"Your wife is Vietnamese?" I asked, surprised. Ardin's great height must tower over an Asian body! But I understood the burning, consuming desire for something different. It burns hot. It burns out. But I focused on the positive by saying, "That's my favorite thing about working at sea. It breaks down boundaries completely."

"My future wife is foreign," Yoyo popped up.

"Future wife?" I repeated, somewhat dubiously. "That's the phrase I use regarding Angelina Jolie."

Yoyo glanced up and down the steep road, but all was quiet. No stampede seemed eminent, so he awkwardly fished from his pocket a folded, dogeared photo. He reached out across the shifting mules to show me.

"She's gorgeous!" I complimented upon sight of the young vixen. She was a petite Asian with a round face and dark, beautiful eyes.

"She lives in China," Yoyo said, replacing the photo. "We met online."

Ardin tried unsuccessfully to hide a harrumph. Fortunately Yoyo was too preoccupied with saddle maneuvers to hear him.

"And you, Brian?" Yoyo eventually asked.

"The whole reason I'm at sea was to be with a woman," I replied from habit. While true, there seemed to be a whole lot more to the story now, a whole lot more I didn't want to talk about. I glanced down at the *Wind Surf*, reflecting on how so very, very tiny it looked. It looked equally tiny even close up. "We were here in Greece together just a week ago. I proposed to her here, in a manner of speaking. She even said yes."

"So she'll be joining you soon, then!" Yoyo exclaimed.

"Ships are no place for couples," I said rather sharply. More softly I explained, "She's vacationing with her parents in Romania."

"Romania?" Ardin repeated with evident surprise. It was perhaps the most emotion I had seen since meeting him.

"Yes," I said. "Transylvania. Beautiful country."

He paused before responding, then politely said, "I'm sure."

I chuckled at his obvious effort at restraint. He looked slightly relieved and added, "There's a Romanian woman on Surf you'll meet soon. She's... something else."

"A more qualified statement has rarely been uttered," I said.

Ardin's face blanched a bit, no doubt recalling an unpleasant memory, before returning to his usual neutrality. "She hates me, so do yourself a favor and don't mention my name."

"Oh? Why is that?"

"I won't give her what she wants," Ardin said simply. His lips quivered into a hint of a smile and he added, "Ask her if she's found her socks yet."

I was about to inquire further, but was distracted by a visitor from above. A shaggy, brown dog of monstrous proportions came running pell-mell down the road, barking furiously. Even before he met up with our herd, the mules decided this was the catalyst for resuming the descent.

Onward and downward we spiraled to the *Wind Surf*.

***

The small tender boat muscled through the waves with noisy purpose. I was pressed against the scratched window because both Ardin and Waryo shared the two-seat bench with me. Such was the lot of crew: we were given the tiny bits of space the passengers didn't want. I stared at the crystalline waters, wondering why their soothing blueness did not soothe. The mist had burned off, letting the sun stab as deep as it cared to. My gaze followed the shimmering spears of light down, down into the darkness. It was very conducive to reflection.

I tried to be as enthusiastic about the Surf as Ardin. I really did. But where he saw a glorious handful of tall masts I saw a measly handful of passenger decks. That's it. Not thirteen decks, each spanning a whopping 120 feet in width, but just six, measuring a mere 66. Ardin was an artist, so money did not concern him much. I was an art dealer, so money concerned me greatly. In my business, bodies equaled money, and Surf didn't carry many. To date I had been modestly successful at my job working on ships. Within a couple months of starting I had been given a ship with 3,000 passengers. Now I got 300.

What was I doing here?

The answer, of course, was that my priority had never been my career and it finally caught up with me. I had come to sea three years ago for one reason: to be with my girlfriend. Ships were her game, so they became mine. She was that magnetic. Bianca was a vivacious and vigorous woman the sun itself set for, seemingly humbled by her excitement at returning to her element of choice, the night.

At night she could dance and drink freely, well into the small hours, until exhaustion overcame her. Only then did the sun dare venture back over the world. Bianca's proximity had always been how I gauged my success. Needless to say, my employers had different criteria. I had pushed things too far, too long. Fate finally pushed back, and nobody can out-muscle life.

Suddenly the entrancing light was cut off. I looked up as the shadow of *Wind Surf* overcame all.

I'd already slaved below decks as a lowly waiter and enjoyed the high life as a three stripe officer, honorary as the rank may have been. What new could *Wind Surf* teach? Turns out, quite a bit. Crewing the world's largest sailing vessel was a completely new experience. Because she was so small compared to the mega cruise ships—over a thousand officers and crew on those—interaction here with officers was far more often and far more intimate—as were the difficulties among the crew. For the first time my job and personal goals were trumped by my surroundings.

Wind Surf was not merely a floating resort staffed by cheap labor for mass consumption, oh no. She was akin to the fabled sailing life of old. And thusly, perhaps inevitably, she defined my entire outlook as a sailor. I, too, became of the sea.

It didn't start that way, of course. My big ship experiences had to be expunged, a process both painfully fast and thoroughly disheartening. But once freed of stresses regarding my career or my relationship—both obviously now over—once I became of the sea, like the Surf herself, I soared on the wind. I learned new things every single day, about the ship, about the world, about myself. Life was as good as I could possibly imagine it, my highest of highs.

Yet *Wind Surf* would be my last ship. Our parting was not a good one. It wasn't just the lawsuit that haunted me after leaving, though that ran into five figures. What made my end at sea so heart wrenching was the humiliation, the indignation. The betrayal. The sea lives up to her notoriety as a harsh mistress. I am ever invigorated by her. I am forever haunted by her.

PORTOFERRIAO
ELBA

DIRECTLY BEHIND *WIND Surf*'s small reception desk in the stern, port side, lay the Photo Gallery. Such galleries on big ships leaned towards large affairs with numerous spotlights, but little Surf's was only a glorified corridor accessing the aft pool. The entire back wall and door were glass. The early morning sunlight shot through horizontally like a floodlight, turning displayed photographs into checkered, blinding panels of glossy squares.

"You're late," Ardin admonished, not even bothering to raise his gaze from a glass display counter of photo albums.

"Good morning to you, too," I replied, amused.

Ardin's head snapped up, eyeglasses catching the sun with a flash. I had to look away from the brilliance. The Mediterranean sun was amazingly direct—very different from the ambling, moisture-laden light of the Caribbean I knew so well.

"My apologies," he said. "I thought you were Yoyo. I didn't expect anyone else here this early."

"Haven't seen him," I muttered before launching into complaint. "Is it always this hot in here?"

"Now you sound American," Ardin deadpanned. I was in no mood for it, and said as much.

"It was not a rebuke," he defended lightly, "Rather an observation. Americans place a premium on comfort, even at any given moment. By this afternoon it will feel like I'm in Vietnam a week early."

His nod indicated the back wall, where scratches and whorls blazed with snagged light. The door leading to the pool deck was merely an uninsulated panel of glass. Worse, it was warped to prevent fully closing. Humidity wafted in almost visibly. Should the need for battening down the hatches arrive, the photos had much to fear.

Ardin shook his head ruefully and added, "I wonder if I should stay on Surf, though. I don't know how my little brother is going to survive."

"I thought your wife was Vietnamese," I said, frowning. "Isn't Yoyo from Java?"

Ardin smiled, apparently enjoying a fleeting thought of his beloved. "She is. I was not implying Yoyo is related to her. God no. But we're all family here."

"Here," I repeated warily. "On the Surf, you mean."

"*Wind Surf* is not like other ships," Ardin agreed.

I was beginning to chafe at reminders of how this ship was so different from the norm. Ardin was easily the fourth person I'd heard make such a comment. It made me even more anxious to get back to the big ships, to resume my life. I changed pitch by nudging, "Yo's that bad?"

Ardin grimaced. "He has no concept of selling to his audience. Have you seen his fingernails? Or nail, rather, courtesy of a mule. Most westerners live in a homogenous culture. Yoyo becomes the curiosity. You don't want the guest focusing on the salesman, but rather what he's selling. It is my responsibility to ensure my replacement is up to the task. He is woefully inadequate."

"If he was a good photographer it wouldn't matter, but...," Ardin continued, gesturing to the panel of photographs. "Guess which are his."

A mere glance clearly revealed Ardin's meaning. Ardin's portraits showed guests standing straight, smiling into the camera, the gleam of joy crisp and clear. The latter images were almost entirely out of focus. Yet this was a good thing, for blurry faces maintain anonymity. Far more damning was the guests' lack of forewarning. The result was that Yoyo created an exhaustive—if fuzzy—visual library of embarrassing facial expressions. It was a veritable doctoral thesis on mouths agape, each blur a new and interesting hole in someone's head. One man was even picking his nose.

"You mentioned we would see something worthy this morning?" I asked, presuming it was not that last, hideous photo.

"Ah, yes," Ardin said, stepping from around the counter. A turquoise polo shirt struggled on his tall, spare frame. It was obvious that a ship of Surf's size did not have the abundant resources to anticipate a man of Ardin's stature. "We will meet the *Wind Star* this morning."

"And?"

"And that is rare," he explained. "There are only three ships in the fleet."

"And?"

Ardin paused to regard me. With his thick glasses, hands clasped behind his back, and greater height bending down to look over me, he evoked a scolding teacher.

"Because we are not as big as other fleets does not imply we are lesser," Ardin chided gently. "Indeed, I say it promotes value. There are only three small ships plying all seven seas. Meeting up with a sister is cause for celebration."

He then added, most gravely, "Live a little."

Ardin gathered up his camera and bag of lenses, then gestured to the glowing door. He said brusquely, "Yoyo can find us if he wants to learn his job."

I followed him past the pool and up to the top level, the Star Deck. I was still unused to seeing the two sides of the ship so very close together. Three classic Cadillacs, bumper to bumper, were literally the same width. Compare that to *Carnival Ecstasy*, which parked classic cars on the promenade as mere decorations! Until I set foot on a real sailing vessel, with necessarily narrow beam, I hadn't realized just how much modern cruise liners felt like hotels.

"Elba," Ardin said, gesturing to the nearing island of low mountains, abundant flowers, and piles of orange-tiled houses.

"Elba?" I repeated. "As in 'Napoleon's exile' Elba?"

"Yes," he said. "When he escaped here, he went on to ravage the whole of Europe. We will pass directly beneath the smaller of his two palaces here."

The waters narrowed as the island's rugged flanks closed in to form a natural harbor. To our right, past the deep blue, past a slight ribbon of translucent blue-green, then finally past a shifting of sand, rose Elba. Atop a rise and nestled among snarls of vibrant green zig-zagged a centuries-old perimeter of stone. The wall of twenty or more feet hugged the island's edge closely, rising with it to cap a hill at the bay's entrance. From our vantage on deck six, we could just barely see past the wall and into the compound. The garden inside was laid in the forced symmetry the French preferred, enclosed by a cream-colored two-story building and attendant wings. Orange tiles capped all.

"Napoleon's house," Ardin observed. His camera clicked away.

"This is where he was exiled?" I repeated, stunned. "Guess I'm damned with freedom."

Ardin grinned and said, "Royalty live on another plane entirely from us mere mortals. We'll tour his palace later. You'll be fascinated to see his personal furniture and wardrobe. His famous French Marshal's hat is there. You'll see all manner of his things."

"Not his penis, though."

Ardin slowly lowered his camera to look at me. An eyebrow raised.

"It's in New Jersey," I explained helpfully.

Seeing that Ardin was not, in fact, satisfied with my clarification, I continued. "A urologist there has it in his private museum. Saving body parts of great men was in vogue in the 1800's. What, you think I'd make something like that up?"

Ardin's expression was unreadable.

"I mentally file away things like that for moments such as this," I continued into the conversation's sudden vacuum. Then hastily added, "I'm great at parties."

After a further moment of processing, Ardin just shrugged and said, "I can't compete with your connection to Napoleon's penis, but I do have a connection. He gave my family our name."

"What do you mean?"

"When Napoleon occupied the Netherlands, we had no surnames. We all knew who we were—it's a small country—but the invading French couldn't keep track of us. So at his orders they assigned us family names. Before was 'Bob, son of Frank,' and after it became Bob Frankson. That would have been fine, but they also just made things up at random. My family was henceforth known as Prein. Do you know what Prein means? It's the sole of a shoe."

"And people whine about today's politicians," I mused.

"Look," Ardin said, indicating the opposite direction with his camera. "*Wind Star* approaches."

Off the port stern an approaching ship cut cleanly through the water, low and sleek and glistening white. Though she moved towards the harbor mouth under motor power, her magnificence as a sailing ship was undeniable. She had a gentle, curving line that rose in the bow and the stern, that classic deck line of tall ships called the sheer. *Wind Star's* sheer rose up in front with a subtle and compound curve, up and out of the water, to flatten and sharpen into a classic pointed clipper bow. She cut the blue like a swordfish leaping atop the waves, with the unmistakable grace of wind ships of yore.

For *Wind Star*, though built in 1986, was of those romantic tall ships. She was envisioned by a savvy

Scandinavian whose family had been tall ship owners since time immemorial in the cold, glacier scarred granite islands of the Baltic, designed from the keel up by the old school shipwrights of the Wärtsila Shipyard in Helsinki, and finally assembled by the craftsmen and polytechniciens of the ACH shipyards in Le Havre on the Normandy coast. She looked nothing like a modern cruise ship, with squared bulk muscling under orders through the water at a criminal twenty-plus feet per gallon of fuel. *Wind Star* danced for the pure joy of it.

Yet *Wind Star* was also a modern ship, the first full-sized sailing vessel built in generations. The French designed computer programs to unfurl her sails and orient her booms so she could react to dangers at sea faster than any crew. And, unimaginable to her predecessors, her computers were designed to operate with a panic threshold of merely eight degrees angle of heel. To yachtsmen, such a heel is utterly insignificant, but modern psychological studies had identified that any angle steeper than eight degrees set off visual alarms in the average passenger's brain that the ship was going over. Thus *Wind Star's* computers never allowed her to go over that heel, even when tacking the wind.

"Did you know that under *Wind Star's* main mast is a U.S. silver dollar from 1889?" Ardin asked. "That's an old shipbuilding tradition. I'm impressed they remembered, considering it was the first tall ship built in two generations."

"How on Earth do you know that?" I asked.

"I'd imagine the same way you knew about Napoleon's penis," Ardin said. Then he mused, "I wonder if *Surf* has one, too."

"No, ships are girls."

31

Ardin wisely ignored my dick joke.

Surf slowed to allow Star to pull up along side. Both sisters slipped into the harbor of Portoferriao, side by side and sails full, with nary a dozen feet between. Together they passed the ancient city, dazzling the locals observing from shore. Old men watched silently, sitting heavily on benches, whereas boys squawked like birds atop stone walls clambered upon for a better view. Both ships loosed blasts from their air horns in greeting. The blares bounced off the flanks of Elba in sodden echoes. The unexpected baritones brought even more people out to look. Excitement was in the air.

The closest point of contact between the ships, the wings of both bridges, slid ever closer to each other. Suddenly two lone, white-clad officers stepped out onto the respective wings. Closer, ever closer, then closer still, they came. Had their bridges been on comparable decks the captains could have shaken hands. Alas, *Wind Star's* bridge wing was thirty feet above the waterline and *Wind Surf's* closer to forty. The captain of the Star looked up stiffly as his counterpart on *Surf* looked down. As one, they saluted each other. Cameras bristled. Cheers sounded. I yawned.

The captains then disappeared back into their vessels and readied to dock. *Surf,* having arrived first, once again pulled ahead and led the way. As the ships turned, the still-rising sun decided to enter the play. The silhouette of *Surf's* sails projected onto Star's, shadow upon white, triangle upon triangle.

Ardin raced off to capture the moment, leaving me to ponder whether or not I was impressed by any of it. No doubt alone of the thousand combined souls on the two ships, I was not. I was mentally and emotionally done with ships—certainly done with this one even before I started.

A renewed flash of officer's whites upon the bridge wing caught my eye. I recognized the strong build of Barney. At least my sense of humor wasn't completely gone: meeting Barney a few days ago still brought a chuckle. It had been the strangest meeting of an officer in my three years at sea.

It had not begun with Barney, however, but rather a bratty youth named Jeff. He was the departing art auctioneer I was sent to replace on über-short notice. It had not been an auspicious beginning. Indeed, it had the distinction of being the shortest handover in my company's history.

I had signed on in Pireaus, the port of Athens. Before both my feet had left the metal gangway at the waterline, Jeff had already cajoled the security guard into handing him my luggage to expedite things. So encumbered, he was not able to accept the handshake I offered. Jeff's sunburned face flushed under the load of my baggage—he was a small man—but he managed to excitedly wheeze, "I'll show you your cabin."

Without a further word he rushed down the corridor, knocking my garment bag upon each and every door along the way. A dozen heads popped into the corridor, looking about in confusion. I felt naughty as a flock of children knocking on neighborhood doors and fleeing. We descended one deck and strode a mere hundred feet before he stopped up short. In one hurried motion he unlocked a door, dropped my bags within, closed the door, and resumed his 'tour' of the ship. Seconds later we were on the main deck beside the ship's small casino. Jeff nodded to a set of metal double doors even as he dropped keys into my palm.

"There," he panted. "Most of the art's in there. Some's

33

in your cabin. Supplies are in a hidden locker by the central stairs. You'll find it. I'm outa here!"

Jeff skipped away. I was so surprised, and he so fast, he crossed half the lounge before I called after him.

"What?" I shouted. "You're leaving? I just got here!"

"Small ship," he called back, only half turning to answer. "Go to the bridge for your paperwork."

He resumed his departure.

"We haven't done the inventory," I reminded him. "We haven't done the handover documents. We haven't done anything!"

"Sundance can stick it up their ass!" he screamed back. An elderly couple relaxing in a nearby booth nearly tumbled out of their seats in surprise.

"Hey!" I reprimanded angrily, striding across the lounge to catch him. "What's the matter with you?"

Jeff retreated with an almost pathological desire for escape. I caught up to him, grabbed his arm, and demanded again, "What's the matter with you?"

"I hate this job and I hate this ship!" he snapped, wiggling free of my grip. "Put whatever you want on the handover report, 'cause I quit!"

I said nothing, knowing well how the stress of the job caused art auctioneers to snap. I had seen better and more seasoned men than this kid crack under the pressure. My very first auctioneer—rookie of the year, no less—had first gone alcoholic, then ulcerated, then impotent, and then bananas. It had taken only two contracts. The second auctioneer and his wife had nearly divorced before quitting. The third went on vacation to Thailand and literally disappeared. An auctioneer trainee friend of mine, so nerve-wracked that she chewed her fingertips to bloody stubs, had nearly endured an emotional breakdown on my last handover. The fact that I hadn't broken yet was clearly a testament to how stupid I was.

"Fine," I finally said. I understood. My first sight of *Wind Surf* had been so disheartening I had nearly gotten back into my taxi with orders to the airport. "Whatever. I'll walk you to the gangway and you'll answer my questions for at least that long, okay?"

Jeff nodded. He calmed upon realization that I wasn't going to force him to stay any longer.

"You didn't even show me the purser," I began, resuming our walk.

"Go to the bridge for all that," Jeff said quietly.

"Where's the handover documentation? You know, your business plans and schedules?"

"I didn't do any. Doesn't matter. Every cruise is totally different: new ports every day, new homeports in new countries every week. No employees. No auctions. No sales. Ever."

I stopped up short. "What?"

"Get used to it. Wait'll you hear about the auctioneer before me," he said derisively. "It'll blow your God damn mind."

"We're here," Jeff said brightly. It had only been one minute. The *Wind Surf* was truly one tiny ship!

"So no advice at all, then," I said bitterly, succumbing to the sickening knot tightening in my stomach.

"Yeah," he said, jumping onto the sunlit gangway. "The tour bitch is psycho."

And he was gone.

To say it was a disheartening introduction was an understatement. My mind reeling, I left to find the bridge. I had never been on a ship's bridge before. Having joined ships after the terrorist attacks of 9/11, bridges had been strictly off limits to unnecessary personnel. Barring the extraordinary revenue we generally secured, art auctioneers were surely the least necessary persons on board.

The search for *Wind Surf's* bridge did not take long. With only three decks of public space, and one clearly labeled Bridge Deck, even Yoyo would have found it proficiently. I approached from an outside deck, nerves growing more taut by the minute. Gathering sign-on paperwork seemed far too trivial a task to be bothering the bridge officers. Small ship or not, these men were responsible for the very lives of hundreds of people. Squinting against the glare, I stepped through the wide, open doorway.

The bridge was a long, wide chamber extending the length of *Wind Surf's* beam, excluding the outside walkway and bridge wings. To the fore was an entire wall of glass stretching above an entire wall of electronics. The panels were only sparsely populated with gauges and buttons, reminding me of the low budget bridge set from the original Star Trek. The back of the room was uneven with nooks for reading paper charts, if officers were so inclined, and racks of clipboards and duty rosters and maintenance schedules and such. Overall, the bridge was spacious and bright, clean and airy. Only one man was posted inside. He wore officer's deck whites, which on the *Surf* meant a white dress shirt with epaulets over white shorts.

And he had a guitar.

The officer—second officer, as denoted by his epaulettes—sat upon a stool with his feet propped onto the electronics. He hunched forward and gazed down at his acoustic guitar. Forehead creasing above Oakley sunglasses, he concentrated on placing his fingers properly upon the strings.

I stepped up to introduce myself when he suddenly threw his head back and belted out, "SHOT THROUGH THE HEART!—AND YOU'RE TO BLAME—darlin' you give lo-ove... a bad name!"

His guitar thrummed into the opening riff of the Bon Jovi classic. The sound filled the chamber beautifully. I stood there, immobile and listening, astounded the song continued beyond the opening. After several minutes a slight, handsome man in a stained boiler suit entered from the opposite entrance. He stepped up behind the singer, gave me a smile, and listened along for a moment. Finally he tapped the officer on the shoulder.

The second officer, whose name tag read 'BARNEY', ceased playing immediately. Barney did not rise, however, but merely craned his head back to look upside-down at his visitor.

"We're done painting the rails," he said. "I'll be in the engine room."

"Aye aye," said Barney, even as the other man departed.

With a big grin, Barney looked back at me. "Good morning. What can I do for you?"

"Signing on," I replied. "I'm the new art auctioneer."

"Oh, okay," he said, jumping gamely to his feet. Though we were both over six feet in height, his build was significantly huskier. Offering his hand he said, "Welcome to the family! I'm Barney, Second Officer."

"Brian," I said, shaking his hand. I smiled and teased, "I'm sorry to interrupt your important business."

"Bon Jovi is important," Barney agreed. "We're in port anyway, so there's not much to do. Still, one of us needs to man the bridge. Come on, I'll get you squared away."

That had been several days ago. Since then I had discovered *Wind Surf* was indeed a laid-back ship. No name tags were fine, as were shorts, sandals and no shaving. Hats were fine, too, which I was informed of several times with a rather unusual emphasis: Barney saying cryptically, "Please, man, no more duck hats. I miss hunting and I just wanna grab for my shotgun."

Returning mentally to the present, I saw Ardin speaking with the hotel director, Francois. The Frenchman had distinctly skinny limbs that looked out of place emanating from a middle thickened with age. A bowling ball with sticks. His round head had features rather pinched together and was topped with thinning, oily hair a bit too black to be natural. Dangling from his wrists were several gold chains. His mannerisms were subtly flamboyant, just enough to hint he was probably gay.

"Brian, perfect!" Francois called excitedly with a thick accent. He was so enthusiastic he even clapped his hands together. "You're as big as two Asians. I want to see you in a T-shirt, on the pier, in ten minutes."

"Sure," I said, somewhat hesitantly. I didn't have a chance to ask him why, for he strode away briskly, shaking a fist at the *Wind Star* with a jangling of gold. "This time is ours!"

"What's this all about?" I asked Ardin.

"Sibling rivalry," he answered sardonically. "Welcome to the family."

***

The rivalry played out on Portoferriao's pier. *Wind Star* and *Wind Surf* docked nose-to-tail, white masts rising high over the ancient 'port of iron', as the city was called.

Very close to the embanked shore rose stacks of tall, Italian-style houses, higher and higher, as the land lifted away from the sea. Between the clusters were moments of stone, shaggy with green. The pier itself, however, was merely a hard strip of soiled functionality. The air was hot and fishy, the concrete just hot.

Francois waited at the gangway with orders to gather all staff members. I joined those indicated, perched atop a line of concrete barriers. Being all young women in street clothes, I presumed them to be gift shop or spa employees from Canada, perhaps England, based solely and stereotypically on the fact that all had extra meat on their bones. I had learned size to be a surprisingly accurate gauge of first worlders in my three years plying the seas. And, of course, almost no Americans worked on ships but entertainers, who are held to different standards. Near us waited a group of trim brown-skinned men in boiler suits.

With a rattling of gold on wrist, Francois gestured Star-side to a gangly man with a particularly prominent nose towering over his own gathering of boiler-suits. "That ugly Frenchman over there is the Star's hotel director," Francois explained. "He is a horrible, horrible man. He is also my friend. Last time our ships met, the *Surf* lost. If I have to buy him another bottle of Montrachet after today, I'm firing the lot of you. I'd rather spend my money on celebratory drinks for you."

This announcement perked the ladies right up. I snorted quietly at the edge of the group. Alcohol was the last thing I needed on *Wind Surf*, for a wide variety of reasons.

Francois selected three staff and ordered us to a designated spot between the two ships. I followed a spa girl named Natalie, who was astonishingly long. She stood a whopping six foot two inches tall, even in flip-flops. Long black hair trailed all the way down her back to partially cover her butt in tangles thick with humidity. As if these two rare characteristics were not enough, at the ends of her long arms were two-inch nails painted glossy blue, studded with silver stars. Our third member was a shoppie named Janie, who had obviously been a cheerleader at some point in her life. She pumped her fist into the air enthusiastically, crying, "Let's go *Surf*! Let's show them the stuff we're made of! Whoo whoo!"

We were assigned two yard-long planks fitted with three loops apiece.

Natalie and Janie both bubbled with excitement. I was decidedly less enthusiastic, and remarked sullenly, "Those look like some sort of old school navy tool used to enforce discipline."

"Put your stuff in the loops," Janie explained. "And then the fun stuff happens!"

"Put my stuff in the loops so the fun stuff can happen," I repeated deadpan. "Back in Vegas we have to pay for that."

"Brian first," Francois commanded. "You power through, so the girls are forced to go with it."

"Men always think it works like that," Natalie said sarcastically.

I looked up at Natalie the Oak and observed, "I think I'd like to see a macho guy try that with you."

Seeing that I still didn't understand what was expected of us, Janie explained further. "There are three loops on each plank. That's for six feet. It's a race, silly!"

"My career is languishing and I'm ordered to a footrace?" I complained.

We began sliding our feet into the loops, when short

Janie suddenly stopped and craned her neck to exclaim to Natalie, "Your nails are so beautiful! When did you go blue?"

"This morning," she beamed, showing off her nails. "I got tired of red, and last week was black, so I needed something new."

"Focus, women!" Francois snapped.

"Gets kind of lonely down in the spa," Natalie explained sheepishly, leaning closer and nearly tumbling us all.

"They like to do stuff to each other," Janie added brightly.

"We pay a lot for that in Vegas, too," I quipped.

While waiting for the race to begin, we nearly fell over. Our wobbling bodies pressed together so tightly I doubt even a game of Twister offered more intimacy. Natalie was behind me, and gripped my waist with tremendous strength. Her nails dug into my flesh. Painted pretty or not, they scared the bejesus out of me.

Finally the Star's team was ready, a trio of small brown seamen standing smoothly in unison beside us. Francois' eyes narrowed.

"No fair!" Janie protested. "They're all boys!"

"Philippe!" Francois called sternly to his counterpart. "Don't you play me."

The opposing Frenchman spread his arms in feigned innocence. The grin beneath his gargantuan nose was evident. "But monsieur!" he protested with a muddy accent, "I give you the advantage, do I not? Even your woman is two meters tall!"

Before Francois could answer, Philippe raised his arm, then brought it down with a shout. "GO!"

We surged forward sloppily. I hauled hard, but hadn't

bothered to tell my team which foot to lead with. I led right. They didn't. They didn't go anywhere. I did. I fell forward, nearly crashing to the concrete. Just before I struck, Natalie hauled back on my shirt to save my stuff from a nasty scrape on the ground. Within moments the *Wind Star* team was already halfway to the finish line.

"Get going!" Francois ordered. He shot a glare at Philippe, who was all smiles.

We pushed onward, but Natalie's stride was just too long for me to keep pace with. Poor, short Janie was hopeless in the back. She started going over, and with a wail we all followed. We yelped as soft flesh met hard, hot concrete. Good-natured laughter rose from the audience of both ships, not to mention the locals who had gathered to watch. Despite our second set-back, the race was not yet over, for the Star team also tumbled.

"Get up!" cried Francois. "You can do it!"

Untangling our entwined bodies was not an easy procedure. Suddenly Twister seemed easy in comparison: our strapped feet made bodily extraction most... revealing. Natalie's nails nearly ripped my shorts off. Ardin swooped in to document the carnage for posterity.

Surprisingly, we won the race. How is still a mystery, other than perhaps divine intervention. What followed were a handful of races, each with a different combination and order. The all-Asian races were the most exciting. After witnessing the first loss, they regrouped and created a new strategy. They placed their hands on each others' shoulders to stride in better harmony. Asian-on-Asian races moved at an amazingly rapid pace. But the highlight was yet to come. A long rope was laid across the pier alongside the two vessels, the center marked with a prominent ribbon.

"Tug of war!" Janie exclaimed, clapping her hands.

I found myself reluctantly excited, being just macho enough to enjoy a contest of strength. What amazed me, though, was that this contest included officers. My honorary rank of three-stripes was no doubt unrecognized here, but Francois still ordered me to join the men—and one woman, an ensign named Emily—on the *Surf*-side. I was surprised Natalie hadn't been included, but she was apparently too busy showing off her claws to Janie. Francois looked over his team smugly. We appeared obviously much stronger than the competition. Not surprisingly, Philippe threw his knobby arms into the air and cried foul.

"Our ship has half the crew of the *Wind Surf*!" he protested. "We have smaller crew to choose from. I protest that the contest is unfair."

"I think not," Francois retorted. "My biggest man is stationed on the bridge. Is this not enough?"

But Philippe kept protesting. He was specifically pointing at me. The stalemate lengthened. Heat gathered on our still bodies and beaded up. I just wanted to get on with it, or get out of here. Eventually a trim man in a stained boiler suit approached, the handsome fellow on the bridge who had also listened to Barney's singing. He tapped me on the shoulder and said with a delicate Dutch accent, "Thank you. I'll take it from here."

A monstrous wave of cheering crashed over us like a tsunami of enthusiasm.

"What's with the cheering?" I asked Janie, returning to the concrete barriers.

"Ouch!" I suddenly cried, clapping a hand to my shoulder. Giving it a rub, I glared up at Natalie. She had reached down from behind to pluck at my skin with her sharp nails. "What the hell was that?"

"I saw a pimple," she replied sheepishly, adding, "I couldn't resist." For the first time I noticed a blue gem glued to her front tooth, glinting in the harsh sunlight. It matched the blue of her nails.

"That's the XO!" Janie said proudly, answering my pre-pluck question.

"The first officer?" I replied, shocked. "But... I saw him painting railings!"

As an American, I was used to the idea of 'doers' getting their hands dirty regardless of who they were. Not always, of course, but it appealed to our ideas of equality. As an experienced crew member, however, I knew most officers considered menial chores properly relegated to classes beneath them. This XO either hated being on this ship, with such menial labor, or loved her enough to give her his best. Considering his enthusiastic grip on the rope, I sensed he felt the latter. I liked him already. Obviously Janie did, too, as she was hopping and chanting "X O X O!"

Yet Philippe's unrelenting protestations delayed the contest interminably. By the time he was satisfied to begin, our team had been whittled down to a mere eight bodies competing against their eleven. I wished I could rejoin our team. Funny how I felt that way only after being booted off. I made the conscious decision to bite back my apathy and view the competition for what it was. Joy buzzed through the crowd, and I passed it along rather than try to douse it. It was not necessarily enthusiasm, but it was a start.

Wind Star won. This disgusted Francois so much he refused to reward Philippe after the match, loudly calling him a cheater. Officers rose from hot concrete to dust themselves off with smiles. I just couldn't believe what I was seeing. Officers on the ground in front of their own crew?

No, *Wind Surf* was truly not like other ships.

PORTO VECCHIO
CORSICA

CONTINUING ON a theme, perhaps, the next day *Wind Surf* visited the island of Napoleon's birth. Corsica was an extremely mountainous island. Green-smattered granite peaks reared up thousands of feet behind the town of Porto Vecchio. The origin of the town's name—it meant 'old port'—was self evident. Ancient stone buildings covered a seaside hill, clustered for protection in days of old, rising higher until capped by a church steeple. A parking lot of yachts behind a breakwater tickled the eye with masts bristling like a forest. The city was picturesque in the extreme, even with hazy clouds smothering the far mountains. From the *Surf's* anchorage the view was particularly stunning.

Members of the 'family' invited me to tender into town with them. I declined. No doubt they would be surprised to find I did not reciprocate their idea of family. I was getting a little freaked out over the idea that this crew was bound together in any way beyond momentary proximity. The irony was that I was used to making friends at sea fast. Big ships had many, many dozens of bodies coming and going every week—both literally and in the naughty, figurative sense—so you got to know somebody fast or not at all. This compression of time brought people closer than ever, faster than ever, and apart again, too.

With such overwhelming newness at all times, and so many long hours at work to lengthen a day far longer than labor laws allow, by the end of ten months you feel like you've lived years. Working three shifts a day every day for ten months did not triple life: it compounded exponentially. A contract was less than a lifetime, but far, far more than its composite months. Returning home from my first contract had all the strangeness of that first return after college: my room looked like something a kid would live in, surely not me! A New York minute had nuthin' on ship time.

Now, however, I was counting on that elasticity of time. In the past I had been impatiently waiting for someone, my Bianca, and the ultra-fast flow made my wait even more unbearable. I suffered three real-world years that truly felt like a decade. Now, suddenly, things were different. After a promise to be married, within days we were apart again, and this time for good. I was unused to working a ship without expectation of Bianca joining me.

And here was the weirdest cruise ship in the world, *Wind Surf*, stuck in a sluggish backwater of time. More irony. It was awful.

Indifferent to any emotional pangs, work crowded my attention. Though having been on *Surf* for several days, I was still clueless how to proceed. I spent a long morning going over the previous auctioneer's paperwork. The sales figures were almost all zeroes, and not the good kind stringing along at the end of a number. These were big, fat goose eggs on the bottom line. Jeff's lack of notes, documentation, or even advertising material implied that he had not held any art auctions at all. I concluded that he just 'hung out' at his gallery, hoping for sales to walk in. Trouble is, he had no gallery. Or even a desk. Certainly he had no sales.

But he had hats. Lots of hats. Weird hats. My cabin was a veritable menagerie: a plush lobster sat on the chair, hiding a hole in the seat; a woolly parrot stared down from between bottles of shampoo in the cruddy shower, a giant salmon wallowed beneath my lumpy pillow as if it were a rock in a stream. The hats weren't just in my cabin, either, but crammed between works of art in the locker or hiding behind stacks of folded easels. Nor were they all stuffed animals. Subjects ranged from the mundane, such as the large block of cheese, to the unlikely, like the astrolabe. It took me a minute to identify that one. Its fat, fuzzy tubes formed a round-bottomed triangle with the eye piece containing an actual cartoonish eye, complete with button pupil.

So I sat in my crowded cabin and stared at a puffy pig hat for a while. He was buried up to his snout in a clutter of work-related detritus Jeff had left. Eventually I rose, tucked the pig under my arm, and strode out into the hall. I wandered through the ship, lost in my caressing of this pet. I hardly noticed the surprised glances from guests, or the knowing smiles from 'family'. Eventually I found myself at the hotel director's office, where I paused. Francois immediately noticed the large zombie in his doorway.

"Come in, come in," he said reassuringly. He chuckled when he saw me petting the hat. "What can I do for you?"

"I'm not entirely sure," I admitted, sitting down. "I'm at a loss to explain how my predecessor made any money. Did he even have an auction at all?"

Francois leaned back and thought for a moment. Finally he said, "I do not entirely understand your position here, I must admit. As hotel director I know everything that happens on this ship and money is my business. But I am French, and we have a different way of looking at things than you Americans. Art is an essential part of life, something to be passionate about. I can understand being an art dealer because I believe in art. I would become an art auctioneer for the joy of bringing beauty into peoples' lives. Only then would I mention—and only perhaps—that I hope to make some money doing it.

"When art auctioneers talk, it's only of money. They tell you how much they have sold, or how much they are worth, feeling quite content to have fully identified themselves to you. I have met several from your company over the years, and observed them talking amongst themselves. They do not discourse on the art at all, but merely the value."

Francois paused for a moment, then concluded, "I submit to you that, though our passengers are predominantly American, they sail with us in order to escape it for a while. Jeff was unable to perform because his expectations of selling volume to the lowest common denominator were not met. Windstar Cruises is not Walmart. He was unable to adapt his approach."

There was no rebuke in Francois' explanation, even if it sounded less than complimentary to America. He was just commenting on his observations regarding different cultural ideas on success.

"I understand," I said. "Jeff was very young and no doubt straight out of Sundance training. They aren't big on thinking outside the box, though they claim otherwise. So that explains why he was here for only two months. But what about the previous auctioneer? Paperwork indicates she was here a long, long time. That should imply she was successful, but she didn't sell anything, it seems."

Francois giggled. "No, not much at all. I didn't hold it against her, though. She was blind."

"I beg your pardon?"

His pinched features spread with amusement. "Yes, little old Gertie was legally blind. She could see a bit, of course. She wore bottle-thick glasses and with a large magnifying glass could read large-print books. That's what she spent her days doing. She was too old to really do anything else. She was nearly seventy."

I blinked, not really sure I believed what I was hearing.

"Are... are you serious?" I asked carefully. "Seventy and working at sea? Blind? That defies belief. And yet..."

"I think you will find a different business model on *Wind Surf*," Francois explained. "Sundance at Sea doesn't expect to make any art sales here. As you know, they are on nearly every fleet in the world. I believe they just want to have a presence in order to prevent anyone else from gaining a foothold. Gertie was here over a year, minding her own business and generally staying out of everyone's way. Sundance paid for her cabin, so I didn't mind, and her hats made her entertaining to the passengers. I even think the older guests appreciated all the large-print books she left in the library."

I stared at Francois, numbed with shock. I knew *Wind Surf* was by far the smallest ship in the Sundance fleet. Even her sister ships, *Wind Star* and *Wind Spirit*, were ignored because they were just too tiny. *Surf* was barely big enough to pretend to be interested, but the reality was that she was just a tax write-off for a business bringing in millions elsewhere. To say it was a demoralizing realization was an understatement.

The question for me now was whether I should flee like Jeff and pray for a better ship, or just quit outright. The options were really one and the same. Because I had come to sea for the sole purpose of being with Bianca, and had focused on that so exclusively, I had sacrificed my career. My employer Sundance was not happy with me, for reasons both real and imagined. They put me here so they could forget about me. In my company's estimation, I was equivalent to an elderly blind art dealer in a pig hat.

So this was it. The end of my career at sea.

I returned to my cabin to think. It was not a location conducive to it. In fact, it was the worst cabin I had ever been assigned. That's saying a lot. It was an interior cabin, small and cramped and poorly lit. With all the animals peeking from behind dark recesses it felt oddly menacing, like an underground cave hiding all manner of creepy crawlies. My every movement was observed by dozens of button eyes.

And it was a crew cabin. Art auctioneers should be given guest cabins. Ships were contractually obligated to do so, regardless of cost. On my last ship, the six star *Seven Seas Mariner*, I had even enjoyed my own private balcony and free wet bar. But on minuscule *Wind Surf* space was so limited that auctioneers were denied guest space. Considering the art department had yet to pay for itself this entire fiscal year, such accommodations were not unwarranted.

So I had bunk beds again. Broken, stained and vandalized bunk beds. My nose wrinkled at the thought of laying on that bottom bunk, surrounded by walls scratched and etched in exactly the same manner as a stall in a public toilet. No doubt Gertie hadn't even seen the carved profanity and penises. The top bunk was off limits entirely, being occupied by several hundred unframed works of art and two cow hats. The Moo Sisters, presumably.

And everything was broken. A large, gaily colored print stretched across the wall, peppered with sticky notes, plexiglass shattered. The sink's plastic basin was smashed and leaked through brown-stained cracks spreading out like a cobweb. It was in the shower, of course, pressed against the toilet, above which no longer hung a towel rack. Sharp, rusting screws bristled where they had once held onto the aluminum rod. If I leaned my head back while sitting on the toilet I would be in for a nasty wound. Luckily I had the pig hat as a safety helmet.

I stared at the grimy telephone. Dirty fingerprints were ground into the numbers, obscuring them, and the handset was so gross that the mere thought of pressing it against my ear made me my stomach roil. I didn't want to ever use that phone again, and not for fear of some sort of infestation crawling into my ear. I had only used it once, and that had been on the very first morning aboard *Wind Surf*. That had been the most hated call of my life. The most hated day.

The day I told Bianca to stay away.

***

Frustrated with life, work, and my new home, I wandered out on deck—pig-less—to catch some fresh air and think. Below me swarmed a handful of kayakers, surprisingly close to the ship. I soon realized they had come from the ship. I leaned over the rail and looked aft, nearly falling overboard in surprise. The entire stern of *Wind Surf* had opened up like a great, gaping mouth. A drop-down deck extended out as if lapping the sea, with people swarming over the teak-planked tongue in life vests.

With work ideas at a standstill, I figured I might as well see what that was all about. I wandered down to the lower decks, aft, until I saw stairs labeled 'Marina'. They curved down below a series of windows to reveal a garage-like area open to the sea and sky. I stepped into the salty air and waded through all manner of snorkeling gear and water skis. A stack of kayaks glistened in the corner, resting after an early-morning dip in the sea. Beside them was a dripping mound of lifejackets. Above all hung sailboards from rafters. Despite my gloomy mood, the fascination of the place perked me up.

A tall, solid young woman in a *Surf* polo stood at the edge of the deck, squinting into the sun. She had long, dirty blonde hair and a delicate haze of freckles on her cheeks. I walked up and introduced myself.

"Just a minute!" she said, cutting me off. She ran further down the deck and caught a rope hurled over by the driver of an approaching power boat. As she secured it, she looked up to me and called over the rumbling of the engine,

"I'm Susie! That's my man, Eddie!"

The driver was a trim young man with spiky black hair, loads of freckles, and a generous grin. He cut the engine of the small boat—a four seater Zodiac—and the assault of noise eased. Between occasional squeaks of the rubber-sided boat against the ship's deck came the calming gurgle of the sea. The three of us sat upon the deck, sheltered by the overhanging marina. It was very peaceful. Eddie in particular looked like he needed some relaxation.

"Busy morning," Eddie commented, shaking his head. "I had to rescue Mr. Gleason twice."

"I told you," Susie said smugly. "He didn't look like he could handle that sailboat at all. He hit his head on the boom before he even got ten feet."

"Shop talk on the marina must be a lot more fun than in the art locker," I mused.

"I don't know about that," Eddie said, "But we do have bikinis."

Susie was clearly not as enthusiastic. Her disdain came through via posture, loud and clear. What she said, however, was, "I'm more than ready to drop it for real life. We spent two years on St. Maarten before signing on here. It's been a long time since normal."

Eddie looked up, surprised.

"St. Maarten was awesome!" he protested. "Beer was cheaper than milk!"

"My point exactly," Susie snapped.

"You said you liked living on the island," Eddie said indignantly.

"I did," Susie said with a sigh. "For the first six months."

"What did you guys do for a living there?" I asked. While I was loathe to jump into their spat, I was genuinely curious. I myself had lived outside the box for several years and was keen to learn about further career options.

"Dive instructors," Susie said. "That's how we got here, too. Running the marina is just side work for when we're not leading dive tours."

"Sounds awesome to me," I said.

"Diving is," Susie agreed. "Living in a tin can on the other side of the world is not. I haven't had McDonald's in months!"

"Then what are you guys doing here?" I pressed. "Sounds like you were ready for home before signing onto *Surf*."

"Sure as hell didn't say so," Eddie grumbled before Susie could reply. He quickly added more brightly, "This isn't just a joyride. Each dive gets me closer to my application as diver for the RCMP."

"The what?"

"Royal Canadian Mounted Police," Eddie explained. "You're American, then? They're not just cops on horses, you know. They need divers, but you have to be supremely qualified. Here I'm exposed to a wide variety of situations and places that look good on my resume. We tour reefs and stuff, sure, but I also search the hull for bombs and damage. Whatever they need."

"That's encouraging," I said slowly. "I think."

"And besides," Eddie said with emphasis to Susie, "You were happy yesterday when Cosmina finally promised you your gondola tour."

Susie brightened a bit, but still managed to correct her boyfriend, "Our gondola tour. I've always wanted to see Venice, and now we're going to see it in style. You could learn some romance, Eddie."

"Beer being cheaper than milk is faster than

romance," Eddie retorted. "With better odds of success."

"We're going to Venice?" I asked. "Tomorrow we're in Sicily or something, aren't we? I'm having trouble keeping up. Seven ports in seven countries in seven days, and each cruise different. How the hell am I supposed to plan? Anyway, is Cosmina the tour lady I keep hearing about?"

"She's the port excursions manager," Susie answered, rolling her eyes. "From Romania, wherever the hell that is. Russia, I guess. She organizes the group tours, but not the diving tours, thank God. She's awful."

"She's not that bad," Eddie disagreed.

"Only because you're with me!" Susie retorted. Eddie just shrugged.

Our conversation was cut short. Descending the stairs from the ship's interior came a knock-out blonde in a skimpy bikini.

"Ah, she's here!" Eddie cried. He jumped to his feet —perhaps a bit too enthusiastically. Obviously mollifying Susie's annoyance was not his priority.

Susie shot a glare across his bow and said with particular emphasis, "Yes, they are."

Following the attractive mother were two equally beautiful daughters. There was no question they were family because they looked like small, medium, and large versions of the same person. The youngest, about ten years old, wore her hair in a quivering ponytail like her mother, whereas the daughter of fifteen sported a sassy pixie-cut. All three wore matching bikinis of dark blue, which matched their eyes. My, were they idealized.

"Good morning," the mother said, flashing a pretty smile. "They've drug me here for a banana boat ride. We have a reservation. The Deiters."

"Yay!" the youngest burst out, squirming with excitement. "Banana boat! Banana boat!"

"You bet," Eddie said as he fished through the lifejacket pile for appropriate sizes. "I'll have you out in no time."

"I'll have you out in no time," Susie corrected again. "Eddie will be manning the platform."

Any thoughts that Susie and Eddie were just enjoying good-natured banter were soon squashed. She left with a huff that indicated she was clearly upset with him. Eddie took it all in stride and presented the Deiters with a genuine smile.

"Where's the fourth person?" Eddie asked as he assisted the youngest into her lifejacket.

"Oh, my husband won't be able to join us," the mother said. Her face soured as she added bitterly, "Work, he says. Can you believe that?"

Eddie glanced at his wiggling charge, looking chagrined.

"I'm sorry," he said earnestly, "but we can't go on the banana boat without four people. Ship rules."

"Why not?" the mother asked. Her stance hinted that she was used to men giving her whatever she wanted. And what she wanted right now was to keep the light in her daughters' eyes from dimming.

"Ship rules," Eddie repeated. "Insurance rules insist on maximum safety, which means four bodies. For balance and weight and stuff. I'm sorry, there's no one else here to join in. Usually the deck is packed with people, but they're all out already. I'm sure if you just wait a bit..."

"That won't work," the mother said. She indicated her teenage daughter and explained, "My daughter Lisa and I have spa treatments in an hour. This was for Tina."

"Mom," little Tina asked in a tiny voice. "Why can't we go?"

The mother brushed a soothing hand over the girl's pouting cheek. It was unpleasant being witness to the girl's disappointment.

"Unless..." Eddie said. "Hey, Brian, you wanna go on the banana boat with them?"

I glanced at the athletic bikini-clad woman, suddenly envisioning us thumping together through the crystalline Mediterranean—sans children, of course. I quickly realized how rude that was, so I mentally added in the hot teenager. At that point I wisely dashed all damning visions from my head lest I reveal myself by accidentally making eye contact with Susie.

"Uh, yeah. Of course I can," I said, emptying the pockets of my dress shorts. I paused a moment before removing my shirt, suddenly recognizing I had a protruding gut. Where the hell had that come from? I sucked it in as much as I could.

Mrs. Deiter required Eddie's assistance getting onto the inflatable banana boat. She was all beauty but no balance. She all but clung to the lucky bastard. Despite his appreciation for Mrs. Deiter's overt beauty, Eddie was every bit the professional. Securing his guests properly occupied the whole of his attention. He hauled little Tina into place behind her mother, giving her clear but kind instructions. Before our very eyes Lisa bounded through the air to land expertly on the shifting, wriggling banana. It was a most impressive leap. Obviously she inherited balance from her dad.

Lisa tossed her head back in satisfaction and boasted, "Lead cheerleader!"

Eddie muttered, "No surprise there."

Susie sniffed loudly on the Zodiac.

I was strangely nervous sliding in behind Lisa. My designated handles were nuzzled right up under her pert bottom. She was fifteen going on twenty, and knew exactly what it meant to be a hot blonde cheerleader. She was workin' it, too, arching her lithe body in all the right ways to secure a male's attention. Talk about overkill: to turn on a fifteen year-old boy she need only breathe. Yet here she was, working that giant rubber banana in ways best left to a Vegas VIP club. I should have been secretly enjoying it. I was nothing if not dirty-minded. But I had yet to reach the inevitable mid-life crisis, when twenty year's difference in age was desired. To me she was just a girl. More or less. I was still alive, after all.

Susie aggressively gunned the engine of the Zodiac and we were hauled to sea. Obviously Eddie's joy had piqued her anger. Even more obvious was that she was going to take it out on us. We crashed over and through the waves at break-neck speed, criss-crossing our own path to hit the wake as hard as possible. I began to think Susie's goal was to intentionally dunk the women as punishment for being so beautiful.

Mrs. Deiter and Tina shrieked in good-natured fun. Lisa whooped and leaned in a desperate bid to add more excitement to the ride. I tried not to cry. Keeping my hands on the slippery handles was difficult enough without the powerful distraction of tight, Prime A cheerleader buttocks bouncing and rubbing on them. I was going to get sued. I just knew it.

Five minutes later, it was all but assured.

Eventually we pulled back to the marina. The Deiters were wet, bedraggled, and beaming. I was all those things and nervous. When I saw Yoyo at the marina with his camera, I almost began to panic.

"Have fun?" Eddie asked Tina as he lifted her gently onto the deck. Lisa, of course, leapt up herself, making sure she stuck her butt out at just the right angle to ensure I'd see it. She need not have bothered: it was seared into my memory for life.

"Whoa, Brian!" Eddie said. "You okay? You look pale."

"I'm fine," I said, scampering off to the side. I retreated to the back of the marina, but for some reason Waryo followed me, snapping pictures.

"Jesus, Yo," I complained, holding up a hand. "Get your camera out of my face. Keep it on the banana boat, man."

A frown darkened Yoyo's delicate features. "Banana boat? Ardin just said go here for pictures. He didn't say banana boat."

"Yoyo," I said delicately. "It's your responsibility to take photos that people will want to buy. Hey—stop taking pictures of me, for cryin' out loud. Them! The guests. How on Earth could you not notice them?"

"But I didn't bring zoom lens," Yoyo whined. "You guys were so far out."

"Well, next time you will, right?" I said. I resisted the urge to repeat Ardin's catchphrase 'time to learn'.

Actually, I was thrilled to hear of Yoyo's mistake. I didn't want any photographic evidence of the ride for the prosecution. Even with a trademark Yoyo blur, any good lawyer could prove just about anything—and they wouldn't even be lying. For, on a particularly sharp curve near the end, when the banana hit the wake, I was nearly thrown off. I had reflexively grabbed whatever I could to save us from all going over.

"Mom!" Lisa cried, hauling on Mrs. Deiter's arm. "Did you see that last bump? I thought the fat old guy was a goner—until he grabbed my butt!"

Mrs. Deiter looked at me, brow raising. I smiled wanly, grabbed my clothing, and fled.

***

I stared into the mirror of scuffed plastic and sighed. Somewhere since becoming an art auctioneer I had lost my athletic physique. Before ships I had always taken advantage of my height to hide a few extra pounds, but working as a waiter on Conquest I had been literally starved, so I stopped paying attention to the size of my middle. But then came two years as an art auctioneer, which meant three meals a day in guest buffets. Or, in the case of my last ship, mandatory five-course meals with guests. Passengers always complained of gaining weight on cruise vacations—imagine what it was like to live in a horn of plenty? When I was a 'young and hungry' auctioneer, so to speak, I had exercised my discipline as much as my body. When had that stopped?

And my middle wasn't the only thing larger than it should have been. When did my forehead get so big? My hair looked terrible, and not just because the sea's humidity made it bushy. My head looked like a scrub forest that had been partially deforested, with two clear-cut swathes extending back from the temples to create a pronounced widow's peak. I grabbed the pig hat—for safety always kept on the back of the toilet—and slid it onto my head with a strange intensity. I hoped some silliness would ease my sharp self critique. It didn't.

I had been aboard for less than a week. That time

offered a few mild sprinkles of interest and a deluge of woe. At the peak of my ambitions I would have been hard pressed to make anything out of this mess I had inherited. Correction: I had earned. I wanted to blame Bianca for getting me into this, but that was just me being petty. She had warned me about the sea, spoke cryptically of the toll it took on the body, on the spirit. I had thought my spirit indomitable, my youthful verve eternal. But now there was a thirty-something, chubby man with a receding hairline in the mirror.

My time at sea had been a mistake. I was alone in a way I never felt before. Oh, I had been alone for nearly unendurable tracts while at sea, sometimes fighting for Bianca, other times waiting. But I never felt truly lonely. Bianca was ever just out of reach, but never too far. I refused to let the distance be too far, even if it was just in my mind. I had been sustained by the idea of Bianca, and fought the good fight in the hope that someday we would be together, forever. There had been no tangible proof that my unconditional love was reciprocated, but I felt not only sustained, but emboldened by the giving of it. Is that how people with faith felt about God?

But it was all gone now. Before Bianca I had found inspiring the world at large, the great accomplishments of man in art and architecture, exploration and science. Everything held fascination for me, if it was but new. Then I met a woman who blasted away all other thoughts as mere trifles. I became obsessed, a one-dimensional man. Could I resurrect my love of knowledge, of culture, and return them to my life? I was in the Mediterranean, after all. But I didn't want to tarry on the *Wind Surf*. It was time to admit my mistake and move on with my life. Can't fix a problem until you admit you have one. Well, my issue had resolved itself, more or less, as I was bound to fail on *Surf*. So why let it take any more of my fast-dwindling youth? I had no reason to fear abandoning the sea, for it owed me nothing. Certainly it hadn't owed me Bianca. Certainly it hadn't helped us be together.

I ripped the pig hat from my head and dropped it to the wet shower floor. There was no way I was going to merely exist here, abandoned and forgotten like an old blind woman. A plan came to mind; a plan to make ends meet, a plan to get the most out of this so-called ship life. And step one involved finding the shore excursions manager, this Cosmina. Everybody had warned me about her—Jeff, Ardin, Eddie and Susie—I didn't care. Once again, my hopes lay in a woman. Once again, she was Romanian. At this point I was fairly certain that the translation of 'Romanian' was 'issues'. Would I ever learn?

VENICE
ITALY

I MET COSMINA in her office. She was very proud of her office, despite it being one of those old-style ship rooms the size of a stacked washer & dryer. It was so ridiculously small I doubted she could actually sit at the desk and have the door closed simultaneously. Not that Cosmina would ever want the door closed. How else would passersby see who was worthy of this personal space, such as it was? The fact that only a dozen or so bodies had access to this part of the ship, and already knew and worked with her, was irrelevant. Cosmina held a position of import. Cosmina held sway. Cosmina had an office!

I knocked on the open door. The port excursions manager was bent over a ledger, head buried in her hand. She jumped at the noise, and glanced up with eyes red-rimmed and blinking from too much reading. Her hand instantly moved through her short hair in an effort to hide hint of paperwork frustration. I obliged her gesture by giving her a compliment.

"Nice office," I said.

"You think I don't deserve an office?" Cosmina bristled defensively.

"Of course you do," I replied soothingly. "You have a lot of work to do. Shore excursions are always important, but on this ship they're paramount."

Her expression softened. She wore a standard issue *Surf* polo of turquoise over white shorts. Her face was Romanian-round with big cheeks. Rather than being high-boned and rosy, however, Cosmina's cheeks were those of a chipmunk whose feast was interrupted. Her hair was dark brown and bobbed.

"It's because of all that work I'm here," I continued. "I thought maybe you could use my help."

"What's that mean?" she said, defenses rearing again. "Who says I need help?"

"Nothing, no one," I answered quickly.

This was not exactly true. I had observed her that morning and found her people skills quite lacking. Despite it being the last day of the cruise she did not seem to have built any rapport with any passengers. I had overheard plenty of grumbles about her apparent lack of organization, and I concurred with the several guests who commented that she appeared distracted and harried. Perhaps she had just had a bad morning, but to me she looked overwhelmed. To be fair, organizing several hundred passengers into separate groups, all of whom had to be escorted from the lounge at different times for half a dozen different tours was a big job, and she was more or less alone.

"Let me explain," I hastily added. "I'm experienced in handling large groups and I have nothing to do in the mornings. I thought I could help when your lounge is full. That's all."

She eyed me shrewdly for a moment, then pursed her lips. "You're the new art guy," she said.

"That's right. I've been an auctioneer on the big ships and am used to handling crowds of hundreds. I thought we could work together. I'm having trouble with visibility, and everybody on board goes on your tours. So as long as I can introduce myself and my job, I'll be your assistant all week long and help with the crowds. Really, I'm not doing anything else and you look like you could use the help."

"What does that mean?" she challenged.

I defended weakly, "We're all family."

She pursed her lips again, even as her eyes scanned me up and down. She seemed somehow satisfied with my wardrobe of a silk shirt over khaki slacks, but lingered on my shoes. Worry flushed through me. I well-knew how Europeans judged a man by his footwear—assuming he didn't wear tennis shoes, at which point he was dead in the water. For that very reason I had eschewed my usual Birkenstocks in favor of soft leather loafers from Romania. I sensed she had recognized the brand. Wearing them may have been a mistake, I suddenly realized. Few people are more critical of Romania than Romanians.

"All right," she said reluctantly. "We'll talk tonight. I have a group doing a gondola tour at 7PM. Meet me there to discuss it. Dress nice."

She returned to her work, indicating the audience was over. I thought that the meeting hadn't gone too badly. But like always with ships, like always with Romanian women in particular, I had no idea what I was getting into.

***

We had actually arrived in port the night before. Like everybody else, I had stood huddled upon the open deck as the *Surf* sailed past the huge floating dikes, past the famed Lido island, and towards the city. It was a surprisingly cold night with low, broken-bottomed clouds dropping rain lazily over Venice. The sleepy drizzle made the old palaces drab and tired, scars highlighted with bright new mortar in the cracked backs of the ancients. A gentle rumble of thunder settled over the city as a breathy snore.

We sailed down the Canale della Giudecca, a wide artery that was restless and choppy and imminently forgettable. Far more interesting were the canals that spread through the floating city in lieu of streets. I pondered who would make an entire city without roads. Why? And why here, on this stinky backwater? The canals were flat green opal in color, barely disturbed by the fitful rain that made it past the bunched shoulders of age-old palaces. Such were the capillaries filtering through the living heart of Venice. Imminently ugly, utterly impractical, undeniably romantic.

Originally Venice was anything but romantic. It was interesting, though. Venice, as we know it today, began with a bunch of people running for their lives with nowhere else to go. The good ol' Germanic barbarians had forced the remnants of the Romans—folks from Spina, Adria, Altino, and Padua, among others—off their land. They could either drown or settle on the briny, lagoony, and all-around crappy islands.

Not surprisingly, the refugees chose the latter. Being savvy types, they even turned their plight into advantage: they became salt producers. Back then, in 600 A.D. or so, the distance between the mainland and the Venetian lagoons was not the two miles of today, but twenty-five. The spread was treacherous enough to be nicknamed 'the Seven Seas', in part because of all the sandbars sectionalizing the waters. That is not the origin of the term 'seven seas' because the locals immediately filled it in. This new land, now called Chioggia, was conducive to salt, and this new people, not yet called Venetian, was conducive to business. How else could they survive on such briny, lagoony, and all-around crappy islands?

Venice became a major producer of salt and got involved in all sorts of nasty turf wars with neighbors who also had briny, lagoony, and all-around crappy land. Their biggest competitor in the 'salt wars' were some upstart Benedictine monks, but they proved no match for the Venetians, who utterly trashed their saltworks in 932. Unfortunately, that act only strengthened the position of the third largest salt producer, Cervia, controlled by the archbishop of Ravenna. That's when things got really ugly, because the archbishop invoked the hand of God for their side—standard operating procedure in those days. In this case the invocation had tangible results: despite also being Christians, floods destroyed their saltworks around 1200 or so.

Devastated, the Venetians had to import all their salt or go out of business. Yet they soon discovered something marvelous: it was more profitable to buy and sell salt than make it themselves. The golden age of Venice began. This was the time of Venice monopolizing the spice trade for all of Europe, the time of Marco Polo. The building boom created the islands, canals, and palaces we see even today. Astounding, that. America has changed a zillion times since its creation, yet Venice hasn't really seen a new building in triple the time we've even existed.

Thus, I was excited to see those canals up close and personal. I wished fiercely I could tag along on the tour Cosmina was organizing. Unlike most tours, which departed from the ship, guests taking *Surf's* gondola tour were to make their own way to the launching point. The ship docked perhaps a mile from the site, but a wide stone path hugging the edge of the city made walking easy.

Well, the route was easy to identify, but the walk was anything but easy: it was fraught with danger. There were umpteen tourists to navigate, each and every one of them holding aloft an unfurled umbrella. The mass of wavering vinyl pulsed and flowed over the walkway so densely that I never once saw where I placed my feet. But tripping was not the danger—oh, no. I was absolutely terrified that my eyes were going to be gouged right out by the pointy tips of umbrellas. This was no silly concern, but a very real threat. My cheeks were poked countless times until they were not only sore, but even bleeding.

My jealousy over those taking the gondola tour swelled as I passed each 'parking lot'. Countless wooden trunks, like sunken telephone poles, rose from the ugly water to keep boats from banging into each other in the sluggish current. Before businesses of means were poles more slender, gaily painted in candy cane stripes and capped in gold. Bobbing between all were long, sleek black boats glistening in the dark, their superb varnish reflecting yellows and oranges cast from the windows of restaurants, cafes, and shops. All the waiting gondolas wore neat, tight-fitting hoods over their openings.

I arrived just as Cosmina was finishing up the tour. Her short figure stood out prominently from the crowd. This was in part from her standing on a box and screaming, but more due to her raincoat of DayGlo yellow. Clipboard in hand, she directed the last of the huddling guests in single-use rain gear to their boats in groups of four. The line inched off the pavement and into the gondolas manned by gondoliers hunched in the rain. I stayed at the back of the thinning group and waited for Cosmina to finish. Only then did I notice Eddie and Susie waiting their turn. Susie clung to Eddie's arm and wriggled impatiently.

"The gondola tour!" I called enthusiastically to Susie, hoping to amplify her excitement. Only then did I notice that with them waited tall and burley Barney, the *Surf's* second officer. "Why, good evening, sir!"

"None of that," the husky man said jovially. "I told you before: call me Barney. Have you met our lovely doctor yet? Faye, this is our new art auctioneer."

He introduced a ruggedly pretty woman with dark skin tightly defining her face. Her hair was thickly braided and raven-black. I would have thought her surely Native American but for her arresting, electric blue eyes. Her figure was so trim as to be almost wraithlike, and combined with her eyes she did, indeed, look like the undead. But her smile radiated life and warmth, as did her handshake.

"Whoa," I said, smiling. "I wish I had a doctor like you! My guy is like eighty years old and somehow manages looks like his name, which is Greenblatt."

"You must sell a lot of art with that smooth tongue," she replied.

"Not lately," I groused good-naturedly.

One last gondola eased towards the sidewalk. Susie would surely have leapt across the closing gap but for Eddie's restraining arm. Cosmina scribbled the last of her notes on her clipboard and shoved it into a large black duffel at her feet. As she turned to regard the two eager couples, her eyes locked onto me. Or, rather, what I was wearing. Not having any clothing appropriate for the cold weather, I had chosen a sweatshirt gifted from Romania. The RO logo on the chest seemed of intense interest to her.

"Good evening, Cosmina—," Faye began, but was interrupted.

"What are you wearing?" Cosmina asked me abruptly. Her tone evinced surprise.

"Just a sweatshirt I got when visiting Romania," I said simply. "Sorry I didn't have anything nicer, but I wasn't prepared for the weather."

"Good Canadian weather!" Susie bubbled brightly. With each excited bounce on his arm, Eddie's shoulders sank a bit deeper. Her enthusiasm was obviously wearing on him.

But Cosmina ignored Susie, too. She asked me accusingly, "You said you are from the States."

"Yes," I defended lightly, confused. "I live in Nevada."

"You're American?" Faye asked, surprised. "I'm from Oklahoma!"

"Go to the front," Cosmina ordered the doctor brusquely. Cosmina seemed intent on cutting off any conversation that did not involve herself. "Barney, you go to the other front seat across from her."

While Faye and Barney complied, Susie tried to ask Cosmina a question. She was rebuffed as the tour manager continued ordering us around.

"Now Brian, pick up my bag."

Barney reached out from the gondola to accept the bag from me, but Cosmina remained firmly in control. "Thank you, Barney, Brian can handle it. In the boat with it. Come on."

The contents of the bag clanked and shifted awkwardly as I stepped onto the boat. Though its rocking could have been eased by the bored gondolier leaning upon his pole, he did nothing to help stabilize the craft. Indeed, he sniffed disdainfully at the whole of our group. Cosmina stepped onto the gondola directly behind me, so close as to actually bump into me.

"Andiamo!" she snapped to the gondolier. "Move it!"

I jerked upright, surprised, even as Cosmina hauled me down into the seat beside her. Behind us the gondolier heaved onto his pole and pushed the gondola away from the sidewalk—the sidewalk where Susie stared, dumbfounded. No longer did the Canadian bounce enthusiastically. No longer did she even breathe. Instead she stared, open-mouthed and gaping, as her long-anticipated and promised gondola departed without her. Only after the distance between the boat and shore grew to ten feet did Susie regain her wits and her lungs. She screamed her indignation, but the sound was lost to the murmuring of the crowd, the patter of rain on water, and the grumbling of the gondolier.

I didn't say anything about my abduction as the gondola pushed further and further into the black waters of the night. I was too stunned. Or perhaps too scared. For the gondolier—a short, slender fellow wearing the traditional black and white striped jersey of his profession—did nothing to reassure us we were in safe hands. He struggled mightily to control the craft, which pitched and bucked like

73

an unruly bronco. Barney kept looking back at him, frowning in concern.

"I've spent my life on boats," he muttered, "and never seen such an idiot operating a watercraft."

"I'm sure he's qualified," Faye said lightly. She did not look at all to the floundering gondolier, nor even at Barney. Rather her dazzling eyes stared in wonder at the porticoes and palaces, colonnades and bridges, all stone, all glistening with rain.

I couldn't help but agree with Barney. Though I knew next to nothing about boats, I felt sure I could handle the gondola better than our gondolier. His name was Gianni—information we gathered between puffs of effort at fighting the slumping, sluggish waves of the Canale di San Marco. He was obviously new to his profession.

The seating arrangement in the gondola was surprising, all the more so because it was advertised as a romantic ride. Yet of the four seats, only two were actually side-by-side. The love seat had not been given to the young Canadian couple to whom it had been promised—who no doubt fumed yet back at the sidewalk—nor to the apparent couple of the second officer and doctor, whom Cosmina had placed diagonally from each other and facing different directions. No, the love seat had fallen to Cosmina and I, for reasons that were soon to become abundantly clear.

"Lean right!" Gianni suddenly cried. Cosmina was so surprised that she nearly jumped into my lap. The gondolier thrust his pole deep into the dark, churning water and leaned dangerously out over the side, all while continually shrieking, "Lean right! Lean right! Madre di Dio, lean right!"

We complied, as best we were able, and soon the danger passed by—in dramatic fashion. Roaring past came a long, squat tour boat: two, four, six, finally eight rows of windows flashing in the dark to merge like frames in a motion picture. The pilot's cries were drowned out by the deafening rumble of a fume-belching engine, but through the windows of his enclosed cockpit we saw him shake his fist.

Gianni, for his part, responded in kind. His gestures were far more vulgar, however, and he continued to hurl insults into the darkness long after the tour boat had departed. It didn't matter to him one whit that he was in the wrong traffic lane. But it mattered a great deal to Barney, as he made quite clear.

"You better get one helluva long pole if you're gonna go into the channel," Barney chided with open condescension. "Tour boats stay close because of low draft and flat bottoms, but further out..."

Faye calmingly patted his leg, prompting him to check his tongue. Instead his brow furrowed deeply in agitation. His point was made, however, as Gianni finally seemed to realize his inability to control the gondola had led us far out into the open waters of the wide Canale di San Marco. High-powered boats of all sizes and shapes buzzed and flashed chaotically, like an angry swarm of bees unsure of a target.

Sheepishly—I sensed for probably the first time in his life—Gianni quit his grumbling to focus on the job at hand. He poled us towards a moderately lit, open plaza that ran right up to the water's edge. It was dominated by a fat tower of red bricks topped by a soaring pyramid of green tiles. Mounted upon the very top was a large, well-lit sculpture of some sort, but the rain obscured anything more than the glint of gold.

Once we were safely near the shore, Gianni

remembered that he was supposed to narrate. "The history of the gondola...," he panted and poled, "...a boat traditionally used by dwellers of the lagoon...is one thousand years old."

The subject of his broken speech, which he had no doubt been required to memorize by rote, was obviously of no pride to Gianni, nor even interest. His disdain for all things Venetian was so thorough that living there must surely be a fate worse than death.

"Said to date to the times of the first doge... in 7th century..." he huffed contemptuously on, "the gondola was actually mentioned for the first time... in a public document in the year 1094. The gondolas built by the Venetian master hewers, according to a tradition that was handed down orally... were not always as they are today. Those depicted in paintings of the 15th and 16th centuries were flatter bottomed and the stern and prow not as high. The planking was brightly painted and decorated with costly appliques, and the various noble families vied with each other in showing off their wealth. Since the year 1562 all gondolas have been lacquered black. In the 18th century the gondola was standardized and is now 10.75 meters long and 1.75 meters wide. They are asymmetrical because they are now propelled by only one oar.

"The gondolier, too, was once much more interestingly and elegantly outfitted," he added with evident bitterness. "They did not wear a simple striped jersey and straw hat."

Gianni spat, trying to hide his snide act behind an artificial sneeze. He fooled no one.

"The gondolas now number barely one for every twenty there were in the 18th century. All are built and repaired at the Squero di San Trovaso, where artisans keep the ancient craft alive."

"I'll bet that's something to see," Faye commented enthusiastically.

"Hardly," Gianni retorted. "The buildings are old, some only made of wood instead of brick. The landing is wide, but so slick with algae it stinks."

Cosmina leaned in to whisper directly into my ear. "Considering the entire of Venice is so slick with algae it stinks, I'm scared to imagine the Squero di San Trovaso."

I leaned back from Cosmina's advance, startled. Our hips were pressed against each other in the small bench, but she had leaned into me as if we knew each other intimately —or she wanted us to. She unzipped her raincoat to reveal a low-cut black dress that plunged deep down the front. Her efforts to appear sexy were laughable, with the two of us directly beneath the bitching gondolier and her fumbling through a plastic DayGlo yellow raincoat in a bid to emphasize what was obviously not her best feature. Still, I sensed laughing would have been a very, very bad idea.

Not receiving the response she had hoped for, Cosmina instead bent over and rummaged through her duffel. The gondola pitched just then, and Cosmina's head fell into my lap. I immediately pulled her back up, chagrined. This whole evening was turning out completely unlike the quiet read I had imagined!

"I brought us an extra," she said, smiling up at me.

"An extra what?"

Her hands opened, revealing a bottle of champagne. Her eyes glinted like those of a predator who had spotted prey.

"An extra bottle of champagne?" I asked, surprised. "I didn't expect even one!"

"One per couple," she said sweetly, fluttering her

eyelids. With a loud pop the cork flew into the night. Using the extra light provided by the nearby Piazza San Marco, she poured bubbly into two plastic champagne flutes. I tried to stare at the world famous facade of the Doge's Palace, but Cosmina shoved a glass in my hand and arrested my attention by offering a toast. A polite 'ahem' came from the bow, prompting Cosmina to kick the bag towards Faye and mutter, "Yours is in there."

I tried to protest, but Cosmina would have none of it. Eventually she whispered harshly, "I got you a free gondola tour, so shut up and enjoy it!"

Chastened, I gulped my champagne in silence. The bubbles caught in my throat awkwardly, which actually pleased me.

The gondola moved past the famous pillars and pedigree of the Doge's Palace and into a narrow canal to its right.

"The Bridge of Sighs," Gianni said, referring to an enclosed, arched walkway connecting the Doge's interrogation room to the prisons. The stonework was ornate and arched some fifteen feet across the Rio di Palazzo, boasting two tiny openings of one square foot. "A name given by Lord Byron, who observed that the condemned would sigh at their last glimpse of Venetian beauty before disappearing forever in the dungeons."

Apparently Gianni was impressed enough with the macabre idea to give it a proper narration. Unfortunately the drama was effectively squelched by the huge billboard bolted to the stone directly below the bridge, blindingly lit by three floodlights.

"Oh, and local legend says those who kiss beneath the bridge in a gondola are blessed with eternal love," Gianni added with anything but delicacy.

Cosmina nudged me hard. I happily continued choking on bubbles.

The gondola snaked deeper into the watery labyrinth. We heard rain tapping against tiles overhead and felt fresh dampness pulse down from above. Venice was not a world of water, as I had expected, but a world of walls. A different wall meant a different palace, which meant different colors, materials, weathering, personality. On the left was a wall of white stone blocks and tall, wide windows. Each pane offered a tantalizing vignette of Venetians' daily life, here a bookshelf, there a television. On the right was a smoothly plastered wall painted mustard yellow. Ahead, forcing us to turn yet again, was yet another wall. The rust-red plaster sagged with age, undulations catching the side-cast light of windows in sharp profile.

The ubiquitous presence of iron gates covering all the 'ground' floor doors and windows reminded me that we were far from the security of home. Quietly—secretly, even —slipping through danger heightened the sense of romance, as did the damp moments of intimacy whenever we passed under a low brick pedestrian bridge and plunged into darkness. Not that I was wanting intimacy of any kind with Cosmina. Nuzzled up next to me, she missed no opportunity to present yet another glass of champagne. Had romance been something desired, having been paid for even, it was impossible to find with Gianni hovering above. Our gondolier was an asshole. He was absolutely rude, barking orders the whole time.

"Don't touch that! Lean back! Lean forward! Don't look that way! Turn around!"

At one point our gondola neared a wall and suddenly pitched starboard. Cosmina was nearly thrown into the canal. Only by dropping my champagne into the water was

I able to haul her back safely to the bench. Faye tumbled out of her seat and into Barney, whose strong arms managed to not only catch the waif-like doctor but also thrust a hand to the nearby wall and steady the craft. Gianni, whose inept handling had caused the drama, was not impressed.

"No touch palazzo!" he shrieked at the burly officer. "No touch palazzo!"

This last order, repeated with the volume and emphasis of which Italians are well known, irritated me as much as Gianni's inept seamanship incensed Barney. Gianni constantly used his hands and feet to push off the walls. Indeed, sometimes he leaned his entire bodyweight onto the pole mount in order to kick off the crumbling bricks with both feet. Cascading bits of millennium-old mortar bounced off the soft soles of Italian leather shoes. Through it all he wrestled with his pole, shouting and snapping the history of Venice through gritted teeth.

Gianni's piloting made me uncomfortable. Cosmina's nuzzling made me uncomfortable. But most unnerving of all was Barney. Too polite to stare at us, he instead bored his gaze into our bench, obviously more interested in Cosmina's antics than the tour. His brow furrowed deeper with each of Cosmina's maddening purrs.

To make the situation even more uncomfortable, we turned into a long, narrow canal. The rain could no longer reach us, so narrow was the canal and so tall the walls. Everything was dark and abandoned: no lights graced any of the buildings, on either side of the canal, far into the distance. Gianni poled along sullenly while the ancient, bleached palaces loomed above us, windows dark and ominous, like the empty eye sockets of a line of skulls.

"I hear you like Romanian girls," Cosmina whispered

so close that her breath tickled my neck.

"Where did you hear that?" I asked, surprised.

"Small ship," she said, offering me a sip from her champagne flute.

"Yeah," I said, declining the drink. "Well, I'm done with all that. No more feisty foreign women for me."

"We're not all feisty," she purred.

I tried not to chuckle at the implication that she was anything but feisty. The gondola slipped into nearly total darkness, and all grew quiet. Even Gianni's grumbling ceased as he poled quietly along. The sensory deprivation was nearly complete: no sight, no sound, and feeling only a gentle, floating sway. A hand slid up my thigh and I felt the warmth of lips near my ear. Cosmina asked, "Tell me about living in America."

Four hundred years later—or was it forty minutes?— the gondola slid up to the sidewalk where we began the tour. I almost didn't recognize the area, as it was now more or less deserted. Night had progressed such that locals had begun to dine and tourists had begun to retire. The area was not entirely deserted, however. A very wet and very angry Susie stood ramrod straight and steaming in the rain. Beside her hunched Eddie, arms folded and grumpy, looking more exhausted than ever. He had obviously long since lost any argument over whether or not to remain at the launch.

Gianni remained true to the last, nearly crashing the gondola against the concrete. He hissed with alarm, but fortunately the boat slid sideways to bump instead into a cluster of sunken piles. Even so, I winced in sympathy for the splendid black lacquer. Barney, Faye, and I wasted no time in fleeing the craft, whereas Cosmina seemed in no hurry to leave whatsoever. No doubt Susie's enraged pacing kept her back more than Gianni's spluttering outrage at no gratuity. Just for good measure, Gianni gave me one final harangue at how I exited the craft in a manner not to his liking.

Susie, of course, had not waited for the boat to be secured before hurling her outrage at Cosmina. Fists clenched, she shrieked, "What's wrong with you?!"

I tried to escape along with Barney and Faye, but the sturdy blonde spun on me and let loose another volley. "Don't you run away, you son of a bitch! This is your fault!"

"My fault?" I protested. "How could this be my fault? I got railroaded onto the tour!"

"You promised me that gondola tour!" Susie screeched at Cosmina with a voice curiously similar to nails on a blackboard.

"Well I couldn't exactly boot the second officer, could I?" Cosmina retorted.

With the two hellcats focused on each other, Eddie pulled me back to safety and muttered, "Sorry, dude. She's pretty mad."

"You think?"

"It's not your fault," he consoled. "I'll buy you a beer sometime. Come on, let's head back with Barney and the doctor."

"What, and leave these two arguing?" I asked, incredulous. Susie and Cosmina were literally screaming at each other now. A physical confrontation appeared imminent. The passersby, predominantly Italian at this hour, ignored the fireworks. This was Italy, after all, and Italians were used to creating such scenes themselves. And Eddie, it seemed, was used to leaving them: he was already disappearing around a corner. I hurried after him.

CORFU
GREECE

THE NEXT MORNING I did not talk to Cosmina about the fiasco over the gondola. What was the point?

Now it was a new cruise, and my attitude was improving. This was my eighth day on *Wind Surf*. My head was still spinning from all the different places I'd seen. The list was distinguished, but exhausting: Athens to Santorini to Elba to Corsica to Sicily to Rimini to Venice. Today, Corfu. Tomorrow? How 'bout Malta, just to mix things up? It was just too much to see. Suddenly I envied blind old

Gertie. And none of that newness was taking into account a new home with new people and a new job.

My helping Cosmina with organizing her crowds went well. There were many shore excursions for an island so large as Corfu, and Cosmina had her hands full. She was too stressed to cause any drama—unrelated to work, that is. Cosmina thought she was decisive and bold, but really she was just hyperactive while things spun out of control. To be fair, during her panics she did move particularly fast, but it looked exceedingly unprofessional. Jitters do not equate efficiency.

But we soon found our balance, wherein I kept a necessarily relaxed commentary running on the microphone while she buzzed ever faster behind the scenes. After two hours of this, the final batch of guests had been safely placed onto their tour bus and Cosmina could wind down. This meant she could snack on cocktail onions—a decidedly strange daily ritual of hers—and suck down half a pack of cigarettes.

Smoking on *Surf* was one of the strangest aspects to my new home: crew could smoke in guest areas. *Surf* was a ship with a different attitude—and no space. The crew mess was so tiny that there was simply no room for people, food, and smoke, so the latter was only allowed after hours for the seamen denied guest access. As there was no crew bar, staff wishing to smoke had to mingle with guests. This applied to drinking, as well. Cosmina's preferred smoking location was at a table under the port steps outside the Compass Rose, the stern lounge open to the sea.

"Join me in port?" Cosmina asked after a loving suck of smoke-tainted air. "I know a great restaurant. Overlooks the sea."

"Sounds nice," I said. "But I can't. I'm going out

today with Faye."

"Oh, yes, of course," Cosmina said with obvious contempt. "Ms. America."

"Doctor America," I teasingly corrected. "I know it probably sounds lame, but we're both big James Bond fans. They filmed For Your Eyes Only on Corfu. We thought it would be fun to sightsee with a theme."

"So she claimed," Cosmina said dismissively. She tilted her head to the side to light another cigarette. "She asked if I could arrange a car. Couldn't help her."

"A taxi would probably be better anyway," I said. "A local would know the spots. Faye found a list online."

Cosmina reviewed me and inhaled deeply.

"Uh huh," she finally grunted. "James Bond."

"Yes," I said simply.

"They film in any hotel rooms?" she said, smirking.

"Stop," I implored.

It was obvious Cosmina didn't believe me, but all she said was, "You kids have fun."

***

One of my favorite things about James Bond movies is the alluring beauty contained therein; not just in the particularly exotic and beautiful parts of the world, but more so in the particularly exotic and beautiful parts of the women. It didn't start that way, of course. As a wonder-filled youth I couldn't possibly imagine anything more exciting than a car chase in India, unless it was a boat chase in China. After a few more years I couldn't possibly imagine anything more exciting than a Russian secret agent codenamed XXX, unless it was an airplane pilot named Pussy Galore. Oh, yes, how could any teen not be profoundly struck by Dr. Goodhead, or Ms. Onatopp? In all that suave coolness, my favorite film had always been For Your Eyes Only, even as my favorite Bond girl was its Melina Havelock. A drab name, true, but there was nothing mundane about a French model shooting a crossbow.

Each time I watched it, the film always grew more exciting as it progressed. By the end I was overwhelmed with fantasies of exploring sunken shipwrecks in the Ionian Sea, ski slope assassinations in the Alps, pistachio nut smugglers, babes galore, and finally an impossible assault of an enclave perched atop thousand-foot rocks in Meteora.

Faye had different memories of the decades-long series, of course, but they were no less important to her. How we discovered each others' love of the films was quite by accident. Her favorite Bond film had always been Moonraker—for some unfathomable reason—a fact discovered during our return to the ship after the gondola debacle. She had spent the day searching for St. Mark's Piazetta and the Venini glassworks, both of which were featured in the film. I had excitedly shared that I had just recently toured the monasteries at Meteora, where they had filmed the climax of For Your Eyes Only. Both of us expressed frustration that our companions had simply not been cool enough to appropriately geek out. But with Corfu the very next day, problem solved! Faye procured a list from the internet containing all the filming locations across the island.

Corfu was about forty miles long and shaped like a giant backwards comma. Because it floated in the Ionian Sea, rather than the Aegean with its bare, rocky islands like Santorini, Corfu was quite lush. In fact, the entire Ionian coast of Greece was excessively green. Trees of olive, fig, and pomegranate were everywhere, as were grapevines.

Oodles of kumquats, too. Thus Corfu's beauty nourished more than just the soul.

Faye and I began with a walking tour of the huge Old Fortress that protected Corfu Town from marauders and pirates. To say it was impressive was an understatement: a solid heap of stone, bulky yet lofty, dominating a rocky peninsula that juts into the sea. Over the last dozen centuries the peninsula had lost all semblance of its natural beginning. The first defensive walls and accompanying Byzantine castle came up in about the 8th century. Later the Venetians took over. When the Turks came knocking, the Venetians thought it was time to up their defensive game. This conclusion came rather late, for the Turks had already conquered most of the island—to the tune of whittling Corfu's population of 100,000 down to 10,000.

Thus in the 16th century the Venetian rulers cut a deep chasm into the rock, separating the fortress from the mainland with a deep moat. Centuries later the British— who had by this time pretty much taken over every rock on Earth worth having—shaved the sides of the peninsula and capped them with smooth stone, providing no purchase whatsoever for any would-be ascent from the sea. The Brits abandoned the area in the 1860's, but not before destroying many of the defensive walls, much to the annoyance of the Greeks. But things were peaceful for a while after that, until WWII came and everything was bombed to hell. But even yet the stone monster lives, slumbering, crumbling with age and shaggy with unchecked growth.

Access to the Old Fortress—the nearby New Fortress being an adolescent 400 years old, by the way—was across Europe's second largest square, the Spianada. Faye and I crossed it without recognizing what it was, for it had long since grown into a park riddled with shaded walks and bristling with sculpture. Originally the Spianada had been clear-cut to allow unobstructed access for cannon fire. Ah, the good old days. We crossed the bridge over the long-since dried moat, and entered the complex.

The whole of it was so huge that it took twenty minutes of winding stone steps and walkways just to access the tower at the top. Every step of the way offered breathtaking views of the sparkling Ionian Sea and the mountains of Albania looming across it. Using Faye's list we identified the various locations of the movie filmed there: the harbor house for the Albanian warehouse action sequence, the underground tunnels where the henchman Locque almost ran over Bond in his Mercedes, and finally at the upper stone gate where Bond shot Locque and pushed his car over into the sea. What surprised me was how little movie moments were so easy to spot: both of us recognized a particularly long and distinctive set of stone steps that actor Roger Moore had run up, Walther PPK locked and loaded.

But we had other sights to see, and soon headed off into the countryside. Our joy was shared by our taxi driver —at first. He puffed up over our comments on his home's natural beauty and positively beamed at our eagerness to see so much of it. But circling the island's airport we were stopped up short by a surprise red light. Our road passed right by the runway, so close that approaching planes would actually collide with passing cars. Hence the red light. The wait was interminably long, a blow from which his enthusiasm was unable to recover.

Next stop was the famed palace called Achilleion. All the casino scenes had been filmed there, which evoked in me mixed feelings. Having lived in Las Vegas, I was not overly keen on seeing any more casinos. But I need not have worried about boredom: the palace was a marvel.

Built by Empress Elisabeth of Bavaria, the palace was designed with Achilles as the theme and heavily laden with world-class paintings and sculptures. Overlooking the lush garden's awe-inspiring beauty was the gargantuan bronze presence of Achilles himself, splendid in his hoplite uniform and standing defiantly with a spear easily twenty feet long. The centerpiece of the gardens was even more impressive, however, with the famed 19th century marble Dying Achilles. Here the fallen warrior lay prone, gripping the arrow in his ankle, anguished face upturned to implore aid from his divine mother. After perhaps an hour, which culminated in a drink at the eastern square where Bond met with the villain Kristatos, we headed onward.

Our taxi took us on a tour to the northwest corner of the island to an area called Paleokastritsa. The road rose ever higher and passed through numerous ancient villages of quiet distinction. Then the land dropped away into a dramatic jumble of coves and jagged cliffs; the sea particularly blue, the land particularly green, the villas particularly lucky.

We descended a narrow, winding road with hairpin turns through forests of robust olive trees. The taxi driver boasted that they were initially planted by the Venetians a millennium ago. The road, he continued, was built to keep pirates away from the villages uphill. Indeed, the road was so freakishly curvaceous—with quintuple S-curves switchbacked so tightly that straightaways were directly above each other like giant steps—that the Bond filmmakers used it for an elaborate car chase scene featuring Melina Havelock's poor little yellow Citroen 2CV. That scene was meant to simulate Spain, but the olive-harvesting extras had clearly been Greeks.

The beaches at the bottom, however, were mesmerizing and worth every caught breath of the descent. Not wanting to let the moment end, we decided to extend it by hopping onto a small tour boat. Half a dozen of us tourists buzzed around the picturesque inlets and coves, even sailing into the open mouths of caverns. We mostly ignored our driver, who droned on about various gimmicky touristic nonsense, such as calling an almost-cave St. Nicholas because tossing something into the water brings bubbles so fine they look like a snowstorm. He caught our attention, however, when he paused beside a cliff face.

"Though you can barely see it," he said. "There is a cavern in this rock. See at the water's edge? The entrance is only ten centimeters above the water—about three inches—but plenty deep. You can swim inside if you want."

Faye's electric blue eyes flashed with excitement.

"I'm not missing that for the world!" she exclaimed.

When she unbuttoned her thin white blouse, my eyes flashed. Sparing a glance at the other tourists aboard, I asked her, "Are you serious?"

"Why not?" she replied, grinning, as her shirt dropped to her seat. "Nobody knows us here. Nobody's from the *Surf.*"

"We are," a hesitant voice called from the back of the boat. Two wavering hands rose from an elderly couple.

Faye looked back in surprise, but then smiled wryly. "My bra's staying on anyway."

"More's the pity," I teased. "I suggest you keep the blouse and lose the bra."

Nobody else made any move to join her. The other tourists just reviewed the trim doctor with surprise and, I daresay, not a little envy at her adventurous spirit. My envy was directly solely to her almost criminal lack of body fat.

"Come on," she ordered brusquely. "I'm not missing a chance to swim into an underwater cavern!"

For an instant her waif-like form poised upon the rail; barefoot, black hair swishing over slender shoulders, white bra and white capri pants radiant against Indian skin. Then she disappeared with a splash.

Before I knew it I, too, was shirtless and shoeless and stroking through dazzling blue after her. The warm water was immensely comfortable, even in clothing, and tiny bubbles tingled as we slid along beneath. We broke the surface inside the cliff face with a gasp, followed by a laugh of delight.

A neon blue glow in the shape of an eye emanated from the subsurface entrance, startlingly similar to Faye's own bright eyes. The cavern was perhaps twenty feet deep and ten feet wide, with every nook and cranny highly visible through the crystal-clear waters. White stripes wavered across the uneven cavern roof, reflected from below. I was surprised at the fresh smell in the air, reminding me of laundry still damp after detergent. Just outside the cave the air had been tinged with salt and fish. We splashed around a few minutes playfully, then returned to the boat. The driver hauled us up, dripping and flopping like the morning's catch.

On the way back to Corfu Town that afternoon we paused in one of the little gorgeous villages. After some quiet wandering we stopped at a café nuzzled in where the winding streets finally winnowed into nothing. Across from a warm wall of old mortar that had been patched and repatched, painted and repainted over the centuries, was an opening in the cobblestoned road. It was too small to be a square, but rather a swelling of open space dwarfed by neighbor buildings bristling with rickety balconies of whitewashed wood probably older than the Nina, Pinta and Santa Maria. Three tables were shaded comfortably by a cream-colored awning and a thick habitation of grapevines. One would presume there were more tables inside the stone structure—especially considering each was graced with placards numbered 12, 13, and 14—but one would be wrong. Inside was only a tiny kitchen.

Faye and I chose a table beside a towering fern and eased off our tired feet. Within moments a 50-something man with an unshaven, grey-flecked chin bustled towards us, placing upon our table an ashtray and a dish of olives.

"My kind of place," Faye commented, pushing the ashtray away with a long finger and then snapping a photo of the olives. They were elongated and fat, brownish-purple skin glistening with a fresh pour of olive oil and green with a cascade of oregano. Faye popped one in her mouth and her eyes widened at the intense burst of briny goodness. "I love little quaint places like this. You can't get olives like this at Olive Garden!"

"From my home," boasted the proprietor. "I also recommend the kumquat liqueur: also from my garden."

"You can juice a kumquat?" I asked. "Does it get mad? Bring us a couple while I try to think of a joke using the word kumquat. Might take me awhile, but I know there's one in there somewhere."

The kumquat liqueur came and we enjoyed the experience, if not the drink. It was dense and syrupy, like Coca Cola from a broken fountain that didn't add enough carbonated water. Perhaps inspired by this, we sipped on a bottle of sparkling water.

"I'm so enjoying this, you know," Faye said. "It's so fun to travel with someone like-minded. I hear you never really know somebody until you travel with them. Of course, that really pertains to sharing a hotel room."

"You know..."

"Which we're not doing," Faye quickly added.

"At least I saw you in your bra," I replied, grinning.

"For what that's worth," she said self-mockingly.

But I quite agreed with Faye's sentiment. I was sick of traveling alone. My first overseas traveling had been with Bianca. The experience had been so sublime that I had followed her to ships in the hopes of keeping it going. Through sheer effort we made a go of it, but the initial excitement of wild international travel had succumbed to logistical fatigue, the sizzle to cold steak.

"It's so important to share these experiences with someone," Faye continued, as if reading my thoughts. "Life is about people, after all, not places. But when you're with another, even if you can't make a personal connection with where you're traveling, you still have that connection with the person you're with. You're sure to bring something back."

"Interesting," I said. "I hadn't really thought about travel in regards to a personal connection. I always thought it was about keeping yourself out of it as much as possible, so you can be open to the ways of the others you're visiting."

"How can you keep yourself out of it?" Faye asked. "You are seeing things through your eyes and remembering them with your brain. But it's more than that. As a ship doctor I've volunteered on dozens of ships and seen dozens of countries. Most are nothing at all like Oklahoma. But my family and friends are there. How else can I share with them—they, who've been nowhere and seen nothing—the joys of travel? If I don't make a connection when I'm in that far off place that is so different, how can they? The best way to let my family share the experience is to live it, even if only a moment, through me. Bringing back a T-shirt is a meaningless gesture."

"To play Devil's advocate," I countered lightly. "A T-shirt is proof you're thinking of them while you're away. That's not meaningless."

"I disagree," Faye said, shaking her head. "If I'm in Greece, I don't want to be pining for the plains of Oklahoma. I'm only here for a short time, so why waste it? My family knows I love them. I don't need to prove it with a trinket. If my bringing back a thing is that important to them, they're being selfish. Traveling is my chance to grow and I shouldn't waste such a wonderful and rare opportunity gathering stuff to prove my love. That's not how you prove love anyway."

"Interesting," I said again. "I quite agree that traveling is an opportunity to grow. But here we are, focusing not on Greek culture—other than these orgasmic olives!—but finding the spots where they filmed an English movie twenty-five years ago. The personal connection I understand: I'll think of this every time I see a James Bond movie, past or future. I'll have this joyful memory popping up the rest of my life and, unfortunately for those around me, I'll tell the story again and again, ad nauseum. But I don't see how it has made me grow."

"Self-awareness is an important manner of growth," Faye offered.

I snorted. "Yeah, I'm now more aware than ever that I am not the stuff of James Bond."

"Like I'm a Bond girl?" Faye rebutted. "Maybe we're not, but you have learned that you are a quest taker. You create new and intellectually stimulating challenges for yourself, and aren't afraid to undertake them."

"At least today," I agreed, pleased with Faye's take on things.

***

"How was your date with the Witch Doctor?" Cosmina asked through a cloud of cigarette smoke. She exhaled upwards, billowing it towards the awning above our table.

"Witch Doctor?" I chided lightly.

"Fine," she retorted. "Dr. Faye, Medicine Woman."

"So she's from Oklahoma," I defended with lessening patience. "And has some Native American in her. What's your problem? You're from Romania: should I call you a gypsy?"

That shut her up. There's nothing Romanians hate more than being called a gypsy—unless they were one, that is.

I sighed inwardly and looked away. We sat upon a long terrace on the edge of a thirty-foot seawall. Twilight was soon to pass into night, and numerous points of light popped up in anticipation, some wavering at the tops of masts of ships hidden in the gathering gloom, others steady but blinking across the distance to the Albanian coast opposite. I was surprised at how black and menacing the Ionian Sea looked at night, a total disparity with its inviting tropical blue of day. We were at a restaurant tucked behind the St. George's Gate in Corfu Town, located in a dingy five-story apartment building at a noteworthy bend in the road down to the Old Harbor.

"Anyway," Cosmina said into her glass of white wine. "I asked you all here so I could apologize for last night's... mix-up."

I made an overt motion to point out there were only two of us at the table. "Yet only I am present."

"Barney's on watch," she said simply.

"And Faye?"

"Apparently your Bond girl can't read directions. I'm not waiting for her to get her shit together."

"Yeah, physicians frequently have trouble following directions," I sniped back, intentionally tweaking Cosmina's jealousy over station. "I hope there wasn't a medical emergency or anything."

"Hmm," Cosmina said blandly, stamping out her cigarette butt. I marveled that the neighboring tables didn't mind the stink while they were eating. Then again, most of them had a cigarette burning in the ashtray while they tackled food themselves.

"And what about Susie?" I asked. "She's the one who's upset."

Cosmina answered by tilting her head to light another cigarette.

We waited a bit longer, no doubt so Cosmina could keep up appearances, then ordered dinner. We both had Greek salads, which were utterly unlike salads in America. There was no lettuce of any kind, but rather chunks of meaty tomatoes and snappy cucumber, copious rings of red onions, and plentiful juicy kalamata olives. Atop the large bowl were several thick triangles of feta cheese upon which olive oil was dumped and oregano tossed. The flavors were brilliant and bold.

"So tomorrow," Cosmina said, "I take you to Valletta."

"Who's that?"

"It's the capital of Malta," she said, giving me a look that clearly indicated only idiots didn't know that.

"Okay," I said, feeling more embarrassed than perhaps I should have. "What's in Malta?"

"Damien," she said. "He owns the biggest tour company in Malta. Also ones in Sicily and Libya. He wants to meet you."

"Me?" I said, blinking in confusion. "What do you mean?"

"He wants to create a ghosts of Malta tour."

My jaw dropped and I stared at Cosmina, dumbfounded. "How did...? I never told anyone here I wrote a book about ghosts."

"Real ghost stories of an Old West ghost town," she said with a proud wiggle, like a parent boasting of her child's accomplishment. "With maps and history of each haunted building."

"You... you Googled me!" I suddenly realized.

To her credit, Cosmina did not bother denying it. Instead she just continued, "Damien was excited when I told him about your book. He is extremely important. Trust me, you don't want to miss this. You'll see."

"Sure, sure," I said, anything but sure of being ready to head out into port with Cosmina again. But she did have me intrigued.

Taking a swig of my local beer, Mythos, I gathered the courage to say what I felt needed to be said.

"If we're going into port together again," I began cautiously, "Well, I just want to make it clear that it's all business."

Cosmina looked up at me, face pinched in innocent confusion.

"You know I used to date a Romanian," I explained. "That's over. Not just with Bianca, I mean—and I do not want to talk about it yet—but with foreign women in general. It's too soon and it's too complicated."

Cosmina grunted while reaching across the table to spear the last hunk of feta from my salad.

"I'm serious," I said decisively. "I just broke off a three year relationship with Bianca very suddenly."

"Yoyo said you proposed to her," Cosmina prodded. Then with a gleeful flippancy she asked, "That not work the way you planned?"

"Actually it did," I snapped, suddenly irate. "Coming to *Wind Surf* didn't work the way I planned. It's... whatever. I'm just done with women for a while, leave it at that. Certainly I'm done with Romanian women. D-U-N, done."

"Sure," she said with a slight shrug. I was not at all reassured. Tomorrow, I sensed, was another trap.

VALLETTA
MALTA

THERE ARE OFFICES, and there are offices. The difference between the two can be excellent furniture, extreme views, or excessive spaciousness. Sometimes all three. Damien's office had none of these things, and was a paper-filled mess, to boot. His furniture of solid-colored cloth was new, if not particularly nice. His third-floor view of a Maltese harbor was unique, if not particularly beautiful. Of space his office had but little. Yet those other criteria, arguably commonplace, could be bought. Damien's office walls were loaded with something that could not be so easily put on a credit card: photographs of Damien with U.S. President Carter, Damien with U.S. President Reagan, Damien with U.S. President Reagan and Soviet President Gorbachev. A fourth photograph was of Libyan President Qaddafi, autographed in Arabic with text surely reading, 'to my good friend Damien, love Moamar.' Yes, Damien had an office.

After being chauffeured to the office by one of his drivers, Cosmina and I had only a short wait before Damien himself arrived. I nearly did a double-take upon sight of him. Based upon the pictures of presidents past, I had assumed Damien would look at least middle aged, if not older. He most certainly did not. Yet when he smiled the wrinkles around his eyes contracted to reveal a man who had seen many, many summers. His oily black hair was slicked back in a wet look that at a glance hid the shoots of grey. He was incredibly handsome and groomed, his handshake that of a self-disciplined as well as a self-made man.

"I greatly appreciate you taking the time to see me," he said in English with an ever-so-slight hint of British accent. "Cosmina says you might be able to help me with a project I'm considering."

"I find it hard to believe I have much to offer a man with such esteemed colleagues," I replied, nodding to the wall of awe with an appropriate sense of, well, awe.

"Colleagues?" Damien demurred, "Certainly not. Men for whom I've performed a service, yes. Malta has ever been a bridge, between south and north, west and east."

"A service?"

"As host," he clarified with a smart smile. "For being

a host is everything in my country. Tell me, Brian, have you been to Malta before? No? Then first: a tour of my home."

"Surely you're too busy a man for—."

"Nonsense! Come, I'll show you a place in the world unlike any other."

I hadn't known what to expect of this meeting Cosmina had arranged, but certainly not a personal tour of the island by a man such as Damien! Within minutes we three were in Damien's Mercedes sedan—sleek and black as his hair—cruising through some of the most unique streets I had ever seen.

"Malta is in the very center of the Mediterranean," Damien explained as he barreled down streets so narrow that to poke my head out the window meant decapitation. If that were not nerve-wracking enough, his emphasizing words with both hands was downright terrifying. Apparently being on an island a mere 50 miles from Italy rubbed off. "A land bridge between Africa and Europe for millennia! We have some of the rarest and oldest archeological finds on Earth. Our ancient temples are unrivaled, our collection of Venus figurines unparalleled."

"Really?" I said, impressed. "We studied Venus figurines in college. I remember clearly the Venus of Willendorf, but I've never seen one in person."

"What's a Venus?" Cosmina asked. She did not sound curious so much as annoyed at not being part of the conversation.

"Venus figurines are paleolithic fertility symbols," I explained. "They are always really fat women with big breasts and big bellies. For whatever reason, they never have heads. They are some of the oldest sculptures mankind has ever made, probably for ritual use. Usually they're found in Europe. I understand that they are only inches tall."

"Not all of them," Damien said proudly. "We have an intact Venus of human size. In fact, we have the largest of them all. The entire temple of Ħaġar Qim was built in the rounded curves of a Venus. It's the oldest stone building in the world, built a full one thousand years before the Pyramids of Giza."

"You've got to be kidding!" I exclaimed.

"Would you like to see it?"

"Are you kidding?"

"He's not kidding," Cosmina muttered irritably from the backseat. "That's a horrible expression. He's not a child."

"Please, let me take you there," Damien said, beaming. With a sharp push against the pedal, onward we zoomed through the streets of Valletta.

The capital city of the island nation of Malta was originally built as a fortress at the tip of the great peninsula that split the great harbor in two. Generation after generation of defenders ensured the fortress grew in height, wave after wave of invaders ensured the fortresses grew in number. Over the course of well over a millennium, the forts and bastions and auberges enveloped the entire peninsula.

Reflected in the dazzling waters grew city after city along the irregular coastline, surrounding one of the world's best natural harbors with a jumble of piers, quays, ramps, bastions, and cliffs. Not a single structure was without something stacked upon it, be it house, warehouse, or henhouse. In 2005, Malta boasted 350,000 inhabitants on a cluster of islands only 123 square miles, making it the densest urban environment in all of Europe. And Malta, though at a glance staggeringly non-Western, was indeed of Europe. Their currency was part of the British Commonwealth and valued nearly three times that of the U.S. dollar. Being the perfect crossroads kept the Maltese pound stronger than that of even the British pound sterling.

The contrast of the sea and stone was particularly striking, with the waters a stunningly bright, baby-blue despite being deep enough to harbor the entire British Royal Navy. Pretty as the calm waters were, the stone was what arrested attention: the color a creamy, pale tan, like the wax of a honeycomb. Every single building was made with it through and through: every castle, fortification wall, pier, park, and street. As far as the eye could see, both nature's bedrock and man's infrastructure were of color alike.

"This stone is amazing," I commented. "It's beautiful. It reminds me of a big, important building I saw on Corfu yesterday."

"Yes!" Damien exclaimed. "The Palace of St. Michael and St. George is indeed made of Maltese stone. I'm impressed you observed that. I'm pleased I'm not the only man who gets excited over good stonework."

"Yes, exciting," Cosmina mocked beneath her breath. I was thrilled she had been relegated to the back seat.

"Every building in Malta is made of this limestone," Damien continued. "The whole island is limestone, so in the beginning it was the obvious choice. The ancient temples of Tarxien and Ħaġar Qim are made of it, as are all the fortresses built by the Crusaders. Now it is a law, a way to keep our heritage despite global influence. Some will cover it with plaster and paint, but most people are proud of our stone. Some call it simply Maltese limestone, or perlato maltese, but its real name is globigerina."

Damien continued at length about the limestone and its role in the long, convoluted history of Malta. He seemed to know everything there was to know about the stone, just as he seemed to know everything there was to know about Malta. He was a very charming man, very smart, very rich, and very driven—not to mention very nice and very handsome. Some people have all the luck!

But Cosmina was certainly not feeling lucky. She obviously had no idea what she was getting herself into when she thought up this meeting. No doubt it was a shock to her to discover that normal, everyday people can enjoy not only history, but even paleontology and urban development. If she'd been intent on luring me into a trap, it certainly backfired this time. I was greatly amused by this. Her inability to hide her boredom, while rude, was hilarious. I would have laughed out loud if I wasn't so distraught over presenting ourselves badly to Damien. Yet he seemed to take it all in stride.

"Can I smoke in here?" Cosmina suddenly asked.

"Of course," Damien replied smoothly. "What is mine, is yours."

Before he even finished replying, Cosmina had already tapped open her pack and was lighting a cigarette. She took a long, loving drag, then blew out an even longer, more loving stream of smoke. It billowed across the roof of the car to waft into every corner. Thusly fortified, Cosmina asked, "Let me guess: the Venus things are made of limestone, too?"

"Of course," Damien answered, chuckling.

"How interesting," she huffed, indicating it was anything other than interesting. Under her smoky breath she added, "Fat women and limestone. That's what gets Brian off."

Damien gave me a significant look. A light was gleaming in his eyes, a light that outshone any wrinkles to make him appear downright youthful. He craned his neck back to tease Cosmina, saying, "If you think that is interesting, you'll love Għar Dalam. I'll take you there en route to Ħaġar Qim."

"Great," Cosmina pouted dully.

Half an hour later we pulled up to the entrance of a huge cave hollowed out of the living limestone bedrock of the island.

"Are you kidding me?" Cosmina blurted, staring out the window in horror. I bit my tongue rather than remark about her choice of expression—a real rarity, to be sure. "You want to take us in there?"

"It's quite interesting," Damien explained. "It's nearly one hundred and fifty meters deep and loaded with fossil remains of elephants, deers, bears, and foxes: all animals that haven't been on Malta for 10,000 years. They found two molars from a Neanderthal as well, but they think those washed in later."

"Is it damp?"

"Yes."

"Are there bats?"

"Yes."

"I'll wait in the car, thank you," Cosmina declared. She crossed her arms under her breasts and heaved a great sigh.

Damien, nearly laughing aloud, led me to the cave. Once we were safely out of earshot, he confided, "I enjoy teasing Cosmina. She brings me a lot of money, but she takes things far too seriously. Life is a gift from God and meant to be enjoyed."

We did not spend much time in Għar Dalam

(pronounced ar dàlam), though I always found animal fossils to be fascinating. We agreed that teasing Cosmina was one thing—the cave was on the way to the temple anyway—but unduly dragging our feet would simply be mean-spirited. Likewise we hurried through the Copper Age temple, Ħaġar Qim (pronounced hadzar eem). It was a magnificent archeological site but, when removed of in-depth analysis, evoked none of the mystique of other famous sites, such as Giza or Easter Island.

"Just a pile of rocks," Cosmina sniffed.

"Stonehenge is just a pile of rocks," I pointed out.

"And I don't want to go there, either," she retorted with all the subtlety of Gianni the Gondolier. "Is it time for lunch yet?"

Before returning to Valletta, Damien pulled his Mercedes up to a large structure overlooking the sea. The setting was magnificent, with the brilliant harbor behind pulsing with life. Lazing beyond were countless small fishing dhows, each sporting a painted eye on the prow—an ancient superstition, still very much alive today, designed to ward off evil. The house itself was sprawling and blockish, rearing high with three stories of well-built, well-cut solid stone. The bottom floor was unusually devoid of windows, though the upper stories were pierced by many. The sockets marched across the facade empty, lifeless. Indeed, the entire structure was empty and lifeless. Centuries old, it had outlived its makers and, apparently, everyone else. Nothing grew around its base, which rose stone on stone from the road, bone on bone. It was surprising to find such an impressive structure on such a magnificent overlook sitting unclaimed.

"Of all the haunted houses I've heard of, this is the most unnerving to me," Damien explained. "Interestingly enough, I don't actually know the ghost story itself."

"What does that mean?" I asked, intrigued.

"A little history is necessary..." Damien teased, nodding to the back seat. He smoothly ignored the strangled gurgling that emanated from there. "A little history about World War II. Being the perfect crossroads, Malta has always been in the thick of things. World War II was no exception, and easily the most frightening of all. In short, Malta—a British colony—was crucial to the war in the Mediterranean and North Africa. Hitler showed no mercy. It's been estimated that our little island was one of the most intensely bombed areas in the entire Second World War. The people were hit so hard, in fact, that afterwards King George VI did something never before done in history: he awarded the entire civilian population of the island the George Cross.

"We earned it," he added ruefully. "Hitler ordered more than three thousand air raids on our little island. In the first six months of 1942 there was only one day without air raids. They averaged three major attacks a day, nighttime being no exception. They hit us with every kind of bomb you can think of. The Luftwaffe dropped sea mines into the harbor and used delayed-action bombs over the city. So many bombs...

"The worst were the cracker-bombs, which exploded a hundred meters in the air to shower the city with thousands of pieces of shrapnel. Because of those brutal cracker-bombs, as well as random strafing runs from fighters shooting any sign of movement on the ground, everybody was forced underground. Buildings were systematically reduced to rubble, and soon there was a severe shortage of shelter. People built whatever they could from the debris, moved into caves, even dug into the cliffs.

Many thousands were wounded, and thousands more killed. The children suffered the worst, of course.

"And in the middle of all this hell," Damien narrated with a wide gesture, "was this house right here. Big and solid, it survived the Crusades, survived the Turks."

He glanced up to the thick stone exterior.

"Empty," he said. "It remained empty. Even when typhoid epidemics raged through the Blitz survivors because they were packed into underground rooms like sardines in a can, nobody stayed here."

"Why not?" Cosmina asked, finally interested, cigarette burning alone.

"Nobody knows exactly why," he explained. "In the beginning this building was an obvious choice for safety. Most of the men were off fighting in the war, so it was mostly women and children hiding within. But something else hid within, something more terrible than even the Luftwaffe.

"It happened in the middle of one January night, when the dark flashed brighter than any thunderstorm from firebombs and explosions. Air raid sirens screamed everywhere in the dark. Yet, for some reason, everybody fled not into the building, but out of it: old men, mothers, children. Now what could possibly frighten a mother so badly that she would send her children out into the shrapnel-filled streets during a night raid? It would take far, far more than a poltergeist rapping on walls and throwing stones for me to abandon my boys to the Nazis. Yet that is exactly what the men and women did—men and women who earned the King's Medal for undaunted bravery in the face of unparalleled danger and privation. Think about that. What of this world could so terrify them? Nothing of this world."

A chill prickled the back of my neck. Damien was one hell of a storyteller!

"Nobody knows what they saw," Damien continued. "Nobody would talk about it. But this house, empty for decades before the war, has remained empty for decades after the war. And so it will remain forever. The Maltese do not forget their history."

A moment of silence engulfed us. Three pairs of eyes hesitantly flirted with the forbidden house, as if too shy to make contact. It loomed above, drab and heavy, lifeless.

"Finally we're talking about ghosts!" Cosmina suddenly blurted, no doubt with more exasperation than she intended—certainly more volume. She was getting impatient to get down to business. She set up this meeting and wanted to see it get done. The fact that Damien may be using this time to size me up had obviously not occurred to her. Cosmina was used to being wined and dined by tour owners and operators all across the Mediterranean. Having someone else be the focus—a boring-ass bookworm, no less—was more than she could bear.

Soon enough we were having lunch at a modern restaurant, relaxing on a balcony overlooking yet another yacht-filled harbor, sipping sparkling water and enjoying a sun perfectly softened by an ivy-filled latticework.

"I know tours," Damien explained at long last. "I know how to make them and I know how to sell them. A good businessman finds the right pairing of two things that need each other. But tours are not about supply and demand, they are about anticipating someone's desires. Allow me to give you an example you might find interesting."

"More interesting than fat ladies and rocks?" Cosmina asked.

"Oh yes," Damien said. "Tuna."

"Tuna?"

"Tuna," he repeated. "I had an extremely high-ranking Russian coming and was tasked with providing him and his entourage entertainment. Please understand that when I say high-ranking, I'm talking about a man of incredible resources—and he wanted something nobody else could boast."

"Tuna?"

"Tuna," he repeated with a pearly smile. "Malta is a world leader in tuna farming. A couple kilometers offshore you may have seen large rings on the surface. Those are floating cages. The cages are fifty meters in diameter and ninety meters deep. That may sound large, but I assure you it's not as large as you think. Atlantic bluefin tuna are caught in the wild up to 600 kilograms and fattened up in the cages. They are simply huge.

"I rented a yacht and cruised him out to a cage. We could see them circling in the cage, an entire school of three meter tuna swirling below like a flashing, silver whirlpool. They are predatory fish with rows of serrated fins: very large, very intimidating. They swam deep, but the water is so clear you feel like you can reach out and touch them. There were about a thousand of them in there. I told him to jump in for a swim."

"Did he?" Cosmina curiously asked.

"Would you?" he asked, eyes flashing.

"Hell no."

"Nor I," Damien admitted with a laugh. "I don't think he wanted to, either, but he'd die before looking a coward. Took him plenty of vodka before he had the courage to jump in. But he did."

After hearing that story, I felt even less worthy to be

in the company of Damien. What I could offer this man who lived outside the box was beyond my understanding. I was thrilled to have been given so much of his time—the personal tour of the island was incredible—but I felt utterly unworthy of it all. Being the horrible poker player that I am, I said as much.

"Damien," I said, "I'm really not sure I have anything to offer you for all your time."

"First of all," Damien said smoothly, "It is my pleasure to share my homeland—of which I am immensely proud—with someone who appreciates it. One of the greatest aspects of my people is not our science, however, but our spirituality. St. Paul himself converted the Maltese to Christianity when on his way to Rome and eventual martyrdom, which is well known. I want to show something that is commonly overlooked, but part of everyday life here: our ghosts. What gave me the idea was the house I showed you, and a story my father told me when I was young.

"My father told me of a friend of his who, back during the building boom of the sixties, wanted to sell an old house that had been uninhabited for many years because it was haunted. He didn't own the house himself, to be precise—he was a priest—but it was under his care. He was no businessman, but he knew that the run on property —any property, no questions asked—wouldn't last forever. So when a local contractor offered him £4,000 for the house, the priest gratefully said yes. He thought he'd get far less for it. In fact, he thought he would get so much less for it that he felt guilty over failing to mention it was haunted. He called up the contractor and admitted the house was worth less than paid because of this. The contractor agreed and asked for £1,000 to be refunded. The priest agreed, no doubt figuring £1,000 was a small price to pay for his soul."

Damien leaned back and smiled before finishing his tale.

"The contractor was glad the priest had come clean. He already had a buyer lined up, an Englishman who already agreed to pay £6,000 for the property. The contractor called up the buyer and told him the house came with a ghost and the price would have to be adjusted accordingly. Thus the Englishman paid £7,000."

I chuckled good-naturedly.

"True story!" Damien was quick to clarify. "You see, I understand how British people feel about ghosts. They love them, and are very proud of all their abandoned castles and haunted ruins. I know American business very well, but I don't know American people. You see, in Malta we are saturated with history and forget nothing. Our ghost stories, how we share them and how they affect us, are dependent upon this. We have this in common with the English. But America is so young and always looking for the next new thing.

"I've thought about this for years but never got past the idea stage. Then Cosmina mentioned you wrote a book for American tourists about an Old West ghost town, with an aim at providing them their own walking tour. I thought you could share with me some of your experiences with hauntings and history with Americans."

"Wow," I said. "That's a pretty flattering view, Damien."

Regardless of my feelings of inadequacy, we talked for the better part of an hour. It was an amazing experience, a perfect cap to a surprising day. Nothing of tangible value was exchanged, but that did not mean it was a waste of time. We both learned something. He had a greater understanding of what would be expected of his product, should he choose to create it, and I gained some worldliness. Previously, on land, I had only mild experience in doing business with foreign professionals— not that I could call this business, and not that I could call Australian investors particularly foreign. Still, I had never before had such interaction in a place where business was conducted over tea and sealed with a handshake.

Yes, one lunch with Damien was enough for me to feel I had become a networking guru—not just feel, oh no, I knew. For now I had worked intimately with a European —not just a European, oh no, African too! A good businessman finds the right pairing of two things that need each other, Damien said. The time was ripe to apply this mantra to my situation on *Wind Surf*.

My auctions were relegated to the main lounge during afternoons only. Who in their right mind would skip seeing Venice in favor of a cruise ship art auction? Nobody. I had to pair the droves of art-starved guests with my art supply. And now I had the negotiating chops to do so. Now I was ready to mediate—nay, demand!—a new auction arrangement with Francois. I was ready to handle him. Oh, how I pitied the poor, poor man. I was going to mop the floor with him and his delicate French sensibilities.

I don't actually recall the meeting. After Francois' verbal slap-down, I don't even clearly recall what I had proposed. All words exchanged buzzed in my memory like the teacher's voice in a Charlie Brown cartoon. Francois crushed me—that much I know—with the utmost calm. The only thing I distinctly remember was a single, too-black hair curling around his eye. I desperately wanted him to push it back into place, or brush it aside, or something.

Anything. But no such trifle would ruffle Francois' feathers. He just locked eyes with me and completely dismantled whatever obviously stupid idea I had proposed.

After the excruciating failure I stumbled back to my cabin, intent on crawling into my graffitied bunk and crying into the Moo Sisters. But then a thought occurred to me. Impulsively I spun on my heel and returned to the hotel director's office. He was still in the same place. The stray hair was not.

"What is it, Brian?" he asked, sighing. He obviously considered the matter closed. A hotel director's word was law onboard, after all. But by pure, blind, dumb luck I happened to say the right thing.

"Bar sales suck."

Francois stared at me, though his pinched face opened in mild surprise.

"I beg your pardon?" he said.

"Surely you've noticed that guests are not filling the main lounge every night. It's because of the band."

Francois continued staring at me, only now with his hands folded neatly upon the desk. He was giving me the full posture of disapproval. Quietly he said, "I happen to like the band. They did not come cheap. Did I not make it clear that I will not vacate the lounge for your art auctions during the evening when the band plays?"

"You did," I agreed hurriedly. "But I'm not thinking about the main lounge. I'm thinking about the ship's bar. People need options. Let's give them an evening activity that is something different. I will teach guests how to appreciate art—bring beauty into their lives! And maybe even sell some in the process."

Yes, I was blatantly quoting Francois from earlier.

"One thing's for sure," I continued. "If you give me

one evening per cruise—just one!—I'll fill the back bar with people."

"The Compass Rose?" Francois scoffed. "That's absurd. It's far too small for an art auction."

"Let me try," I pressed. "We'll offer art-themed drink specials, like a Picasso-tini, and I'll display all the Picassos I have for sale. I will dress the bar with only the best works, only high end stuff. Less is more. I can't sell art that's locked in a closet and you can't sell drinks to people not in a bar."

His pinched face frowned again.

"I just don't think it will work," he finally said. "But I do recognize that you're trying. Because you're showing initiative in helping shore excursions, I will give you one chance. Just one."

***

The Compass Rose was a great little bar overlooking the delicate wake left behind the *Surf* as the wind tugged her across the sea. The small room was dominated by a tall bar trimmed with lacquered tiles of blue and white. The navy blue carpet echoed the theme with a sparse diamond pattern. The entire back wall was comprised of folding glass doors that could open to double the floorspace. For the Compass Rose was less a room and more an open deck, with glittering stars above and grainy teak below. With my best art in an arc of easels radiating outward from the bar, everything felt intimate, classy. At least I hoped so, because Francois told me it had to be. He was in attendance.

Things did not begin well. The only assistant I could find onboard was Yoyo, and he proved to be more of a liability to me than he ever was to his mentor, Ardin. At his best, he knocked easels over: squealing like a girl as thousand-dollar artwork smacked flat on its face. At his worst he offered to take photographs of the artwork for people to buy, rather than the artwork itself. Adding to my discomfiture was that Francois spent the entire time closely watching the effeminate photographer rather than watching me strut my stuff. Not that I had much stuff to strut. I barely sold anything before Francois got bored and left.

Then something stupendous happened.

Three Native American brothers, who had been quietly sipping Dalí-tinis all evening, began discoursing over a Salvador Dalí work. As more Dalí-tinis were downed their voices became raised. Before I knew it a shouting match erupted.

"Gentlemen, please!" I soothed. "We need to keep it civil."

One man stepped boldly forward. I presumed he was the eldest simply because his braided ponytail was the longest, being all the way down to his turquoise and silver-studded belt. He gestured to the Dalí and asked curtly, "How much?"

"Fifteen thousand dollars," I answered. "It's part of his famous Collect—."

"I'll take it," he interrupted. Abruptly spinning on his heel, the man regarded his brothers haughtily and declared, "There! It's mine."

A brother, adorned in turquoise, pointedly ignoring his elder, asked me, "Which of this guy's art is worth more?"

To prevent stammering was more than I could manage. "None, sir. This is the most expensive Dalí we have onboard."

"What about those?" he asked, stabbing a finger at a

trio of Dalí woodcuts. "They a set?"

"Yes," I stammered. "They represent—."

"They add up to more than fifteen thousand?"

"Uh, yes, probably a little more."

"Wrap 'em."

Both men looked to their remaining brother. I couldn't help but do the same. He regarded them both for a moment, then grinned and asked, "What else you got?"

***

After I locked up the last of the artwork, I returned to the Compass Rose—site of a downright miracle—for a much-needed drink. I figured Cosmina would be present, as it was time for her routine drink before bed. I, too, found a quiet drink on the open deck to be quite relaxing, Cosmina's reproachful bantering notwithstanding. I was just waiting for her to dish on Indians. With a sigh, I resolved myself to be as civil as possible. As lucky as I'd been, there was no question that my aiding her tour excursions provided the boost that made it all work. It was imperative that I maintained that extra visibility. But staying on Cosmina's good side was like walking a tightrope.

I ordered a Dalí-tini and sat beneath the stars. Actually I sat beneath the stairs, at our usual table. The sky above was not particularly black and the stars not particularly bright, so I instead focused my gaze on the glittering of city lights on the none-too-far horizon. The chalky white limestone of Malta receded like a fading ghost.

"Mind if I join you?"

"Faye!" I called in surprise, looking up at the waif-like physician. "Please do. Celebrating alone is no fun. I thought Cosmina might show up, but apparently not tonight. Maybe they're out of cocktail onions."

"Celebration," Faye agreed, slipping into a chair beside me and gently swirling a bottle of beer. "So I hear. Big sales tonight."

"How did you hear that? It was like an hour ago!"

"Small ship," she answered.

I happened to glance past Faye at that moment to see Cosmina stepping into the Compass Rose. Her eyes locked on me, then narrowed on Faye. With an obviously feigned nonchalance, Cosmina mimed to the bartender that she had forgotten something and promptly departed.

"Speaking of a small ship," I said, suddenly reminded of a previous Cosmina quirk, "I haven't heard that anybody is hurt or anything."

"What do you mean?" Faye asked, frowning.

"When you didn't make it to dinner last night in Corfu with Cosmina and me," I explained. "I thought maybe there was a medical issue or something."

"What dinner?" she asked.

TUNIS
TUNISIA

I WOKE VERY early the next morning. *Wind Surf*
was nearing Tunisia and I wanted to see as much of it as
possible. We were not scheduled to return for the
foreseeable future. While I had bought myself a measure of
future on *Wind Surf* with the previous night's auction, its
duration was far from certain. One auction does not a
career make. Yet hope is the most powerful motivator of
all. Thus I felt good waking for a pre-dawn, coffee-laden
stroll on the open deck before the ship docked.

The Tunisian coastal air was humid and smelled different than the sea, different than the European coasts of Greece or Italy. The immensity of the Sahara was on the wind. *Wind Surf* slid quietly through the choppy gulf towards the fabled desert, towards a sprawl of orange lights hugging its slender green edge. They twinkled unappealingly through a brown haze smothering the sea.

I sipped from my steaming mug, alone and quiet, on the forward bridge deck. Yet I was not alone.

"Good morning," a cheery voice greeted from beside me. I turned and was shocked to see I had been joined by none other than the captain of the *Wind Surf*.

"Why, good morning sir!" I called back enthusiastically.

Noting the energy in my voice, Captain Turner commented upon it. "You seem happy as Larry this morning. No doubt due to all those sales last night."

Though I had no idea what 'happy as Larry' meant, I presumed it was good. "I should be surprised you know about that already," I said, "Yet I am strangely not. But speaking of sales—if you pardon the pun—I've been meaning to ask someone of authority what the names are for *Wind Surf's*. I presume they aren't main-topsil-jibs or whatever."

"They're one through seven," he answered. "Not very romantic, I'll grant you, but imminently practical."

"Nomenclature aside, it's a pleasure to work on an actual sailing vessel."

"It is that," he agreed, smiling again. The poor arrangement of his teeth did nothing to lessen their charm. Captain Turner was a portly man of middle to late years. Beneath his captain's cap sprouted short curls, unruly and besieged with grey. His was a plain face, looking less a dashing captain's and more a pragmatic fisherman's. He placed his hands upon the rail and joined me in regarding the approaching port. The humid air was soft and quiet, the moment ripe for reflection, conversation.

"Have you always captained sailing ships?" I asked. "I'd imagine there aren't so many anymore."

"Oh, not always," he answered. "But when offered an opportunity to work under sail, how could any captain worth his salt refuse? As a lad growing up in Portsmouth, I was struck early by the romance of sail. I used to moon over the HMS Victory—Admiral Lord Nelson's flagship during the Battle of Trafalgar, of course. Oh, how I dreamed of captaining one someday, much to my mother's consternation. She forbade me joining the Royal Navy, but there wasn't a lot of opportunity in Portsmouth that didn't involve the sea. I wanted it so badly I made my way up through the hawsepipe."

"As a lad surrounded by a thousand miles of farmland, I never dreamed I'd be talking to a ship captain someday," I replied. "Or have the gall to ask him what a hawsepipe is."

He smiled again. I could tell this was his usual expression. It was a welcome change from the predominantly Italian and Dutch captains I had heretofore worked with. While the source of their temperament was fundamentally disparate, a chronic lack of smiling was inherent to both.

"A seaman's expression," the captain explained kindly, "to evoke an image of a dripping boy whose ambition is so desperate as to drive him up the anchor chain, through its pipe, and onto a ship's deck for a chance at a job. Yet for me it was quite literal."

"You wanted it that badly?" I asked, impressed. "No

wonder you made it to the top."

"Oh, not compared to Admiral Lord Nelson," he mused. His ruddy cheeks bobbed with fond recollection.

"One can look at a sailing ship as a tool and, if so inclined, reflect that it was the most influential vehicle in human history," Captain Turner explained. His tone was not didactic, but pleasantly open to the sharing. "Sailing ships rediscovered the continents and far flung islands over which men had scattered over millennia. Sailing ships made the human world one again, and they did it—from discovery, to trade, to conquest, to empire—in just a blink at the end of their days. Imagine all that, in just the last five of the fifty centuries during which boats with sails have plied the waves. What poor Portsmouth lad wouldn't want to be a part of all that before it's gone for good?

"In my early days there were only a few fleets of working sailboats left in isolated corners of the world," he continued. "For most of us sailing ships are just a part of history, a part as removed from our experience as the industrial revolution blacking London's streets."

"But not for us stalwart few," I offered, intentionally glib. "Dare I ask if your mother ever joined you on a ship you've captained?"

Captain Turner chuckled. "Certainly not. But I am proud to have my son aboard. I don't know if he'll ever have the chance again to learn a ship of sail."

A smudge of orange to the east slowly rose red. The rugged silhouette of a ship against the bold brown and orange and red caught us both by surprise. Not just any ship, but a fully rigged sailing ship, the very subject of which we spoke.

"I have to say it," I said reluctantly, "That scene looks startlingly like a painting from William Turner."

"Why so it does," Captain Turner agreed with a laugh. "My favorite artist, not surprisingly. At least that was one profession of which my mother more thoroughly disapproved than sailing."

I was pleased to hear I wasn't the only one with a mother distressed over her son's piratical ways. Though small, it was desirable to have a connection to this accomplished man of the sea.

The ship slid closer, revealing three tall masts fully rigged with sails. The hull gleamed a rich, shiny black, the sails a drab off-white straining in the brown wind. It cut an impressive figure against the dramatic sunrise.

"Now those sails are tonsils," I observed.

Captain Turner pointed to each individual sail, enthusiastically identifying each. "The two triangular sails on the front are the jib and the flying jib. On the foremast there is the fore topgallant, the fore topsail or tops'l—not tonsil—and the fore sail. Behind the mast, those triangular sails are the staysails: the main topgallant staysail, the middle staysail, and the main topmast staysail. A fourth, the main staysail, fits below but is furled."

Without a pause Captain Turner proceeded to identify over a dozen sails. His uneven teeth smiled enchantingly, revealing his joy to discourse his knowledge to someone genuinely interested.

"I hope there's not a test," I laughed, admitting defeat.

"All the large, square-rigged sailing ships that parade as tall ships today are purposefully scaled-down versions of the last big sailing ships," Turner continued. "Rigged much shorter than their ancestors for safety's sake. A short rig means the ship has less sail than her hull can carry."

"For safety's sake?"

"Oh, yes. Those wooden clipper ships that figure so

prominently in our imagination were nary one hundred and fifty feet long. Windjammers—their descendants—were of the same idea but, being constructed of iron and steel, grew to monstrous proportions. So monstrous they became sailor killers.

"The Preussen, a five master, was the largest engineless sailing ship ever built, over four hundred feet long with well over an acre of sail. Rumor had it that no deckhand would ship for two successive voyages onboard. She was too hard on her crew. And the Thomas W. Larson, the largest American-built schooner at almost four hundred-foot—made of steel, like the *Surf*—with seven masts, rolled over at anchor while waiting for a fair wind in the Scilly Isles. Killed fifteen of the seventeen men on board."

"Why were the sailors so scared of the Preussen?" I asked. "Scared it would roll over, too?"

"Not Preussen," Turner answered. "But those square-rigged topsails had to be set, reefed, and furled by hand in the old days. Very dangerous when at sea in a storm. Eventually they built rolling yards that turn from the deck. Sails can now be automatically rolled up to furl and unrolled to set, and they can be reefed safely in strong winds by simply rolling in a portion of their area."

"Reef meaning only half open?"

"That's correct."

"So that requires power," I pointed out. "What about all these ships I hear losing power?"

"Modern, sail-less cruise ships, you mean."

"Yeah, I guess that's what I was thinking," I admitted. "But can masts get hit by lightning or anything? I assume it's computer controlled and not some sailors who pull levers or anything."

"You mean assuming the backup generators are not working?" he asked lightly. "Computers begin reefing automatically when power is lost. The sails are furled completely, automatically, when anything of that magnitude goes wrong."

"But no power...?"

"We have tanks filled with oil under pressure," he finished, now smiling broadly. "We store energy, even at sea."

"I had no idea," I mused, impressed.

The captain's lips tugged at a smile, indicating his pleasure at sharing an interesting tidbit usually expressed only in technical terms among knowing colleagues. At least that's how I liked to think of it. No doubt he was just wasting time until we arrived at port. As we did so, Captain Turner turned to me and said, "I know you assist in shore excursions. After the majority of passengers have left, perhaps you would be so kind as to help out the officers, as well?"

"Of course. What can I do for you?"

"We need a dead body," he replied with an amused smirk.

***

"It's hard to find dead Americans," the slender man said from behind a paper-cluttered desk in a desk-cluttered office. His presentation was so deadpan I almost questioned if he had made a joke at all. "Thanks for being a team player."

"My ex-wife frequently described me thus," I quipped. "Unfortunately I think she was referring to the bedroom."

There was no question whatsoever that I had made a joke. Whether it was funny or not... well, the XO's strained courtesy smile answered that question. Alas, my jokes generally prompted such reaction.

The XO, or first officer, was a Dutchman named Emmet. He was the slight, handsome man I first saw in a boiler suit upon the bridge. He had been painting railings. Unlikely as this act was in a man of his rank, his later participation in the ill-fated match of tug-of-war was downright shocking. Emmet was a man who chipped in anywhere and everywhere he was needed. Yet despite such a hard working attitude, he did not chide Barney for playing guitar on the bridge. In short, Emmet was unlike any XO I had ever met. Not that I'd met many—only when I was in trouble—but I was familiar with many.

Of second officers, however, I knew more than a few. And like all things *Surf*, Barney, too, was unlike his big ship counterparts. Besides his proclivity for Bon Jovi, he easily had the physique of a lumberjack. He pounded me on the shoulder and roughed me up as if old friends.

"You've got the easiest job of them all," he boomed. "Stick with me and we'll make sure you're good and dead."

"Exactly what my ex-wife said," I said, taking one last stab at an ex-wife joke. Can't have enough of those, now.

Via the crew stairs, Barney descended down into the forward bowels of the *Wind Surf*. We passed all manner of hallways and storage areas I had not known existed. On a big ship there was always more compartments, but on this tiny vessel it was a surprise. Like living in a small house for months and discovering a new room. Eventually Barney stepped into a chamber so large it was a wonder it fit into *Surf's* narrowing bow. He slapped the wall to ignite the lights, half of which only flickeringly obliged. The still-dark recesses revealed a nondescript metal bar. Behind hid a kitchenette; dark, cold, forgotten. Obviously once a crew bar, the room now hosted a raucous pile of tables, chairs, and rolling desks.

"Find a spot you like," Barney said. "Don't climb into a cupboard or anything, though. That's not realistic. Just lay down and play dead. Easy. Don't freak when the lights go out and things get nasty."

Seeing me raise my eyebrows, Barney explained further. "We're going to simulate a fire as realistically as possible. The fire team won't know if anyone is below decks or not and will systematically search every room for unconscious victims. Our fire team is really good, so it shouldn't take more than twenty minutes. What makes this drill more accurate is that you're our first American."

"Why does that matter?"

"The fire team only has experience hauling out other crew members, and they're all Asian. In a real fire, a guest passed out from smoke inhalation won't be ninety pounds. You're about two hundred, which helps us create a much more accurate scenario. When they come for you, don't make it too easy for them. Be dead weight. Cool?"

I picked my way through the detritus of the dead crew bar to become a dead crew member. Propping my back against a cupboard, I splayed my legs out. From the doorway Barney snapped off the lights.

Darkness swooped in, solid, tangible. This was not the absence of light, but the presence of a thing. Just a few minutes of such absolute black made even an egomaniac feel small. Not scared, but small, insignificant. This was not a place for living men, here, deep below the surface of the sea. I strained to hear a sound, any sound, but there was none. Not even the slap of waves made it into the pit where I lay. I fancied I was in a sensory deprivation tank, but for the sharp tang of back-bar alcohol and solvents stabbing my nose.

After an interminable time, my ears tickled with the muted call of the ship's intercom announcing to passengers the impending fire drill. Don't panic at the alarms, the muffled voice said. Don't panic at the smoke.

Smoke?

A minute later, another sense tickled. The air became chemically dense. The smell was not of smoke, but something equally unpleasant. I mulled over what it could be when I was scared out of my wits by the ship's alarms suddenly blaring. Hearing the ship's horn blasting the fire alarm was nothing new—I'd heard it every cruise for years —but hearing the alarm in my current environment was something else entirely. It was downright unnerving. Red emergency lighting pushed at the black from below rather than above. Though dim, the illumination was sufficient to see the hallway outside. The red opening pulsated in a rapidly thickening haze.

Smoke curled into the chamber, first slow, soon robust. Tendrils of white crawled across the ragged carpet, claiming more and more of the room. Behind the vanguard was a supporting wall of swirling grey, gradually thickening until I could no longer clearly see out into the hallway. The red remained, wavering, undefinable.

Only slowly did time tick, tick away. The simulated smoke became hard to breathe. Not only did the unceasing klaxon urge me to rush into the red, so, too, did instinct. The sensation was so powerful my legs twitched, itching for action, for escape. Yet I remained, having been charged with death. After twenty minutes came a flicker of a different color. A beam of yellow wandered across the reddishness of escape, then left. Eventually it returned with a companion. Then both vanished. Disappointment flashed through me. They had overlooked my room.

From the glow materialized two phantoms of black. Backlit by blazing red, each cut a dramatic figure in full-on fire gear, complete with oxygen tanks and face masks. Thickened by heavy layers of fire retardant gear, they seemed to move in slow motion. Beams from handheld searchlights roamed the smoke-dense room, lighting across old, clustered junk. Revealed in streaks were fallen stacks of chairs and tables upended upon each other, cobwebs flashing. I was living a movie thriller: the heroes had just discovered the killer's creepy lair.

A beam of light fell across my legs. Another zeroed in. Two bulky forms pushed through the thick directly towards me. Heavily gloved hands grabbed me by the shoulders to haul me bodily from the floor. I drooped and flopped as awkwardly as possible, feet dragging uselessly on the floor. Undeterred, they slung my arms over their shoulders and hauled me out. Between the deafening klaxons their respirators labored. Though much taller than my saviors, both men worked as a single unit to compensate. No words were exchanged. None were needed; both knew what the other was supposed to do.

It was a very interesting experience, this playing dead. I left with a much greater understanding and, thusly, a much greater appreciation for how well prepared the crew was to handle a variety of situations. Fires have always been a ship's greatest enemy, more so than rogue waves and certainly more so than pirates. These weren't waiters playing with fire hoses. The ordeal the fire team maintained as routine was most impressive. But then, to be honest, I always wanted to be a fireman. They're totally badass.

***

Tunis exceeded my expectations mightily. It was clean and organized, pretty and prosperous. Despite the local language being Arabic, many spoke English. Everybody spoke French. The tour guide had been given explicit instructions to knock our socks off, as this was *Wind Surf's* first visit and a return depended greatly upon the favorability of the tours. Thus Cosmina got the finest treatment. She strutted like a rooster until I thought she would crow.

The guide began by plying us with treats. We dined on a variety of dips, like hummus and baba ganoush, with huge mounds of brown, yellow, and even red dates. The reds were crisp and tart, like apples. Another local specialty was green tea with pignoli. I like pine nuts just fine, but in my tea? That seemed bizarre and was definitely not to my taste.

"I will show you everything!" the slender man in a dark, Western-style suit boasted.

"Any old rocks will do," Cosmina said sarcastically. "And Brian really gets off on limestone."

The driver's whirlwind tour was all but useless. A full catalogue of sites flashed by in moments, highlights blasted like bullet points, with no time to see if any of what was claimed was true, or even self evident. After hearing about twenty or more fascinating things—and seeing none of them—we arrived at our first destination. The first full stop was a village called Sidi Bou Said. Apparently it was famous for its art scene. I was mildly annoyed I hadn't heard of it, but readily admitted that my knowledge of

African art—North or otherwise—was very poor.

Something about Sidi Bou Said struck me as off. The village was certainly picturesque enough, with a tight cluster of buildings perched atop buildings perched atop a cliff. The whole assemblage—maze-like layout, steep stairs for streets, vibrant bougainvillea—reared over the harbor for phenomenal views of the Mediterranean. The flagstones were swept clean and the walls whitewashed to such a degree that the city seemed somehow fake. Like Disneyland before the gates open, everything had been tidied and polished to a level unlikely had anybody actually lived there. And, indeed, we saw no people at all. No tourists, no locals. Baby blue and closed was every door and every shutter, like a paranoid Santorini. The mimicry would have been complete were it not for the geometric flourishes of an Arabic nation.

We did not spend much time in Sidi Bou Said, however. The guide had been tasked to show Cosmina everything there was to offer, and by God he was going to do so in record time. We flashed past the luxurious Presidential palace—assuming you could really call the Tunisian autocrat a president—the nicely rebuilt Roman theatre, and the only moderately impressive Carthage Museum. Finally we stopped at a roadside curiosity instead of zooming on by. That's when things went bad. The driver pulled over to a curb along a busy street to show us something not everybody has to offer: a graveyard for sacrificed babies. A big graveyard for sacrificed babies. Perhaps the driver should have stuck to his previous method of all talk and no see.

"Are you kidding me?" Cosmina exclaimed, having unconsciously adopted the expression that so annoyed her in Malta. She ogled down at the excavation. Buried and forgotten for millennia were crumbling stones indicating entire crowds of the unfairly slain. Though shadowed from the Saharan sun by gently swaying palm trees, there was little sense of peace when contemplating row upon row of innocence lost, or, rather, taken. The far side was bounded by a wall that held an even larger cemetery.

"It is very sad," the guide agreed solemnly. "This was during Phoenician times, long ago. Barbaric, but a piece of history that must not be forgotten."

"No history should be forgotten," I said. "Barring my first marriage. Oh! Who's killin' it with the ex-wife jokes? I am, I am!"

Strangely, nobody was laughing. I was tempted to add that dead babies always ruin a good joke, but sensed—finally—that would be in bad taste.

"Filthy Muslims love killing," Cosmina muttered, dripping vitriol. Hard eyes locked on the ancient forest of headstones, she cocked her head to light a cigarette. The end flared red hot. After a long drag she finally looked at my surprised expression and said, "What? You like Arabs? I thought you were American."

"I think you're taking it too seriously," I said. "This happened probably close to three thousand years ago."

"So that makes killing babies okay? It's not like they've improved since then."

"Who's 'they'?" I said with as much patience as I could muster. "'They' have been gone for thousands of years. The Carthaginians were not Muslims. They weren't even Arabs."

"What the hell are you talking about?" Cosmina exploded. "We're in North Africa, aren't we? I'm talking about people killing babies and you're talking about... I don't even know what! Fine, they weren't Arabs. Africans.

Happy?"

She ground out her cigarette with a sharp twist of her foot. "Thank God the Romans won."

The guide wisely slipped back to the car. We followed, still locked in combat—er, conversation.

"Don't go lying to yourself that Romans didn't kill babies by the boatload," I pointed out. "We're talking about the Bronze Age, here. It was fairly common. And, I might add, these people weren't Africans. The Phoenicians were Semites."

"Semites," she said flatly, slamming the door. "As in Jews."

She obviously wasn't interested in anything I had to say. I had encountered this before. The truth was that few people were capable of talking about religious human history without getting emotional. They get suspicious of those who do. But even though guilty of making a crude joke at a bad time, I was still right. I said as much. "Yes, they were Semitic."

"How the hell would you know that?" she challenged.

"I have a university degree in history," I explained in a not particularly gentle manner.

"Art history," she clarified. "Not real history."

"Art history is not about painters as much as their influences," I retorted. "Roman art, culture, and ideas came from Phoenicia centuries before they started emulating the Greeks. That's because Phoenicians were in Italy before the Romans were. Nobody pops up in a vacuum. And this land is also very, very old. Successive waves of people came and went. So don't think for a minute any of these groups are the same as today just because they live in the same place... or have the same label."

Now it was Cosmina's turn to stare at me, open-mouthed. Her emotions were running high, very high, probably brought on by visiting such grisly ruins. As usual when anger takes over, strikes have little to do with the subject at hand.

"I brought you here because I thought you liked ruins, and instead you preach to me over a goddamn Phoenix graveyard full of dead African Jew babies and tell me Christians did it. I'm talking about dead babies and you're talking about the influence of pots and shit! Don't you get emotional over anything?"

To concede to her last point, I shrugged. That was definitely the wrong mannerism.

"Don't you blow me off," she screeched. "You preach all high and mighty to your girlfriend, too? I'm sorry, ex-girlfriend? No wonder she left you. Jesus!"

"Moving along!" the guide finally said, gunning the engine and screeching away from the curb.

While Cosmina fumed in the backseat beside me, I tried to just let it all go. Visiting foreign cultures brings us face to face with our own lack of knowledge. That makes many people feel vulnerable, and a cornered animal lashes out. Unfortunately travel also brings us face to face with the closeted ethnocentrism we all have to some degree or other. Cosmina saw something abhorrent in a land of different people and lashed out a target that fit modern stereotypes: Muslims killing innocents. The fact that Muslims weren't to blame didn't matter much.

The simple truth is that most people don't like something different. Most people eat the same thing for breakfast every day for years on end. When you suddenly pluck them out of entrenched routines and drop them into something different, most scramble for what they know. Sometimes it means jumping on McDonald's, sometimes it means jumping on stereotypes. And most stereotypes—especially about 'others'—are shallow, ignorant, and frequently third-hand labels. This particularly applies to the dinner table taboos of religion and politics. Such inaccuracies weren't just in foreign lands, but also close to home. Case in point: Abraham Lincoln stood for a further reaching central government—the very antithesis of his modern-day Republican party. Labels are best left to canned goods, not people. Unfortunately canned goods have just as little chance of shaking off their labels.

Since Cosmina was already demonstrating a remarkable ability to offend people, I chose not to react to her antagonism. I also chose not to educate her about her comment regarding how 'the Romans won'. The truth was that while the Romans did eventually win their struggle against the Carthaginians, it was only after they lost and were shown mercy. Yes, mercy out of North Africa. The Europeans repaid it by utterly massacring almost everybody in sight. Ah, the good old days. It was a bizarre piece of history that few knew, yet had a direct impact on the entire world as we know it.

The Romans and the Carthaginians fought many battles with many armies over many countries. There were heroes on both sides, but perhaps none more interesting than the Carthaginian general Hannibal. He famously led a force over the Alps towards Rome—a feat in itself that none thought possible. Hannibal cleverly used elephants in the front ranks, which scared the bejesus out of the Romans who'd never before seen their like. He attacked the army of Rome and won. He could have, and probably should have, invaded the panic-filled and generally defenseless city. But Hannibal didn't sack Rome. If he had, the entire Western world—and thusly the entire modern world—would not be as we know it. It's staggering to imagine how world history would have played without Rome.

Whereas Hannibal hesitated to strike an endgame, the Romans did not. They regrouped and eventually conquered Carthage. This, the Second Punic War, should have been the end of it. But the rhetoric was so intense in the Roman senate—"Carthage Must Be Destroyed!" being a battle cry uttered ad nauseum—that a third and final conflict occurred even after Carthage surrendered. This time Carthage was utterly razed to the ground and the Romans slaughtered eighty percent of the men, women, and children who lived there. To make sure resurrection would not happen, they plowed vast quantities of salt into the earth to prevent agriculture. Salt from Venice, maybe? Wrong millennium. Anyway, the Romans took over the land and called it Africa. Yes, that's where the name came from. Eventually the Romans rebuilt the area to their taste. And tasteful they were: they constructed bathhouses sky high.

Soon we were walking the fabled streets of once mighty Carthage. Cosmina took pains to avoid me, which suited me fine. Alone I strode through the thick walls of the great public baths complex. Many walls were still intact as bricked mounds capped in wild flowers. The complex was huge in scope and scale, including a wondrous frigidarium —cold chamber—with columns reconstructed to their original sixty foot height. The vaulted ceiling once reared one hundred feet above the tiled floor. Modern man may be used to air conditioned auditoriums, but the Romans were doing it in 150 A.D.! Who says engineering isn't awesome?

Despite being the gateway to the Sahara, Carthage was built overlooking the sea and, thusly, subject to its weather. The sky was locked in drab grey, with several militant thunderheads circling around to systematically strike every inch of ground. Their fuzzy purple bottoms dropped sheet after sheet of rain, polishing everything like the Cleaning Bubbles.

I escaped the rain courtesy of an archway of stone still strong. I was not alone, but kept company by a stray kitten. He peeked out from behind two Corinthian capitals —the caps above pillars—which rested on the ground. Seeing me seeing him, he rubbed his forehead on their elaborate floral edges, smoothed by passing millennia and, apparently, amorous felines.

Surrounded by the ashes of Eden, it was an appropriate time for reflection. Yet I didn't reflect upon what I came here to, what I wanted to. Those colossal hunks of stone wrestled by earlier men into luxurious function reminded me strongly of the first time I had visited North Africa. Three years ago I had spent a heady week in Egypt with Bianca. Since then we had chased each other over half the world, enacting strategies that would have made Hannibal green with envy. In the end Bianca even allowed herself to be caught. That was right about when I told her to stay away. I stewed yet over that turn of events. A reckoning would come soon, I knew.

Ah, but Bianca would have loved this place. She, too, got off on limestone. She should have been with me. Then again, even had she joined me on the *Surf*, she would not have seen Carthage. Her presence would have precluded Cosmina's favors. No, I was here for one reason and one reason alone: Cosmina wanted a green card, and this lonely American was her best shot. The fact that we didn't particularly like each other didn't faze her in the slightest.

I looked past the rain-spattered bougainvillea and saw Bianca's smile in an empty niche. No, I saw the echo of her smile. What I actually saw was the irascible Cosmina glaring at me over heavy puffs of cigarette smoke.

HVAR
CROATIA

THE NEXT TIME I saw Cosmina she was all smiles. Her ability to smoothly move on after throttling someone's day was a marvel. This had much to do with her ability to take credit for everything good that happened around her, whether she was responsible or not. While all of us have mastered self justification for our indulgences, Cosmina took such rationalization to an entirely new level. But she did not just settle for manipulating her own conscience, oh no....

We were once again in Corfu, Greece. Unlike the previous time in port, I had not assisted Cosmina in organizing her unwieldy groups of touring passengers. When I arrived to the crowded main lounge in the morning to do so, she had casually informed me I wouldn't be needed. I thought nothing of it. After all, we had not parted particularly well the night before. She probably still hated me for my role in slaying babies three thousand years ago. Yet when we crossed paths that afternoon she invited me to her cabin for a drink. I accepted.

Thus that evening I strode down to deck one from my cabin on deck two. In fact, I was the only staff not assigned an interior cabin on deck one. As a reluctant add on, the auctioneer had been given a modified storage closet that happened to be on deck two. Cosmina answered the door in her turquoise *Surf* polo and decidedly non-corporate short shorts. Her skin was a naturally dark caucasian, making her look tan. She had attractive legs, if growing a bit thicker as they went up, due to her abhorrence of exercise.

"You're welcome," she said, motioning me in.

"Welcome, or you're welcome?" I asked, mildly confused.

"You're welcome," she clarified. "For everything I've done for you."

"You invited me here," I said, now thoroughly confused.

Cosmina shook her head almost sadly, bobbed hair bouncing, as if this poor child before her was too obtuse to understand adult matters. She strode to a table cluttered with pamphlets, brochures, guidebooks, and bottles of perfume. Dominating the top of the mess was a huge block of rough white cheese. Referring to it with a flourish worthy of Vanna White, she said, "See this? This is two kilos of fresh goat cheese. Just a perk from the grateful tour company yesterday. One of many."

I said nothing, sensing an agenda. I was unsure how to proceed.

"I get a lot of perks," Cosmina continued meaningfully. "People do a lot for me because I do a lot for them."

"Of course," I said carefully.

"Did I mention how Ardin once worked for me?" she said casually, sitting upon the bed with affected nonchalance. By folding her legs beneath her, she revealed a lot of intimate skin. She patted the covers for me to sit next to her. This was not the come-hither one would expect living on land because the bed was the only place to sit. Further, she soon hugged a pillow over her lap. No, this was not leading to the über-common cruise ship 'land a first-world fish' conversation.

"Yes, for a few days," Cosmina continued, lighting a cigarette. While I knew she smoked a lot, I was horrified she would do so where she slept. Despite being a copious cigar smoker, I failed to understand how nicotine could dominate life. For me it was all about the comforting ritual when the time was right. For her it was about the necessary high all the time. "Ardin was awful, though. Not like you and me. He was insubordinate and not pro-active. Certainly he wasn't grateful."

"Why would he be grateful for helping you out?"

"You don't think I improved sales of his photographs?" she asked, sucking in a cloud.

Understanding blossomed. Cosmina was used to being the center of attention. She was verily treated like a queen by those on shore, delighting in the gifts grateful tour owners bestowed upon her. She also received swag from guides themselves, for one cross word from her could send them packing. As shore excursions manager she was also treated with respect by Francois, for *Wind Surf* was all about excursions. Like the monarchies of old and corporate bosses of all ages, she took credit for the work of those beneath her. In short, Cosmina was assuming full credit for my art auction success.

The fact that it was I who volunteered to help her for our mutual benefit was irrelevant. The fact that my auctions were now held in a superior location was irrelevant. The fact that I had thought of the Compass Rose and had to convince Francois to allow it was irrelevant. The fact that it was all blind, dumb luck was irrelevant. Oh no, Cosmina felt my success was entirely because I was her assistant onboard in organizing her clients.

She wanted me to grovel to get my old 'job' back.

"Cosmina," I said sincerely, but carefully, "I am appreciative of the arrangement we have. It helps me, it helps you. But I'm not going to thank you for me doing my job."

"I see," she said, disdaining me with both a sniff and a shrug. A knock sounded at the door. Cosmina bounded up, saying, "He's here!"

"Who's here?"

"The new cruise director," she answered. "The man who will help me with my shore excursions from now on."

***

"*Champagne!*"

A very small, moderately dark skinned man held up two bottles of French champagne. This was no mean feat, for beneath both arms he also held two French baguettes.

The nuance of his speech clearly indicated his origin as the same as what he peddled. His grin flashed brighter even than when his eyeglasses caught the light.

"Come in, Fabrice!" Cosmina invited, reaching around his arsenal of goodies to give him a warm embrace.

"*'Ello!*" he called to me enthusiastically. "*My name eez Fabrice. Like ze fabrique softenair.*"

I was grateful he repeated his name for clarity, for his accent was extremely thick. His English sounded like a foreign language! It had a wonderful lilt to it, emphasizing many syllables that native speakers shorten. He hurriedly set his baggage on the table and approached to shake hands. Fabrice was even shorter than Yoyo, though he was not nearly as petite. His frame was trim, but thick with strength. No doubt he worked his abdomen constantly with all his laughing. He bubbled with unbounded enthusiasm and was, in a word, adorable.

"It's a pleasure to meet you," I replied, shaking his hand vigorously. He added enthusiasm by cupping our shake with his left hand.

"*Yoo like champagne, don't yoo?*" he asked. "*God's greatest geeft to mahnkind.*"

"No," I corrected, pointing to the block of cheese. "That's God's greatest gift to mankind."

"*Ah, oui!*" he cried joyously, rushing over to inspect the goods. His eyes scrutinized the flaking cuts and chalky texture in great detail. Without looking up he asked, "*Zees eez from Tooneeseea? Excellent! Eet will not be pasteurized. Très bon!*"

"A shame Brian won't be able to have any," Cosmina said with a sly smirk.

I gave Cosmina a flat look and a flat question. "Am I not worthy?"

143

"You're American," she answered tartly. "You'll get sick if you eat anything unpasteurized."

"I've lived in Romania for the last three years," I pointed out. "One of the first things I discovered was how incomparable unpasteurized cheese is. Americans have absolutely no idea what they're missing."

"*And wiz enough champagne,*" Fabrice added brightly, "*Yoo cahn eat a dead feesh right off ze beech and not get seeck!*"

Heads swiveled to regard the strange, little man. Under the scrutiny he amended, "*Eef yoo so desire.*"

Bubbly was poured, imbibed, and appreciated. Fabrice had somehow secured bread still fresh from the bakery. Perks of being a cruise director, he said with a smile. He sure knew how to pick it; soft flesh embraced by a superbly crisp crust. Every hand-shorn chunk gently warmed the flesh, the delicate, cloying bakery scent kissed the nose. And the cheese? Pure ambrosia; a subtle blend of chalky and creamy that pasteurized milk is utterly unable to produce. Not that I blame the milk. I wouldn't be at my best after being gamma irradiated with Cobalt-60, either.

Cosmina watched Fabrice and I eagerly working together and enjoying the feast. And a feast it was. Bread and cheese of that magnitude was as satisfying as a five course meal. Yet Cosmina did not join in. Indeed, she looked positively frustrated. Finally, exasperated, she blurted, "Fabrice is French!"

Not missing a beat, Fabrice held up his champagne and said, "*I am!*"

"Let me guess," I said lightly. "Americans and French aren't supposed to get along."

Reading each others' mind, we clinked champagne glasses.

"*You seem un'appy, Cosi,*" Fabrice correctly observed. "*'ave some champagne. It's excellent!*"

"I don't like champagne," Cosmina muttered, turning her back to us and lighting another cigarette.

"*At least dine wiz us!*" Fabrice pushed. "*It eez excellent.*"

"I don't like goat cheese," Cosmina sniffed.

"Would you prefer something American?" I teased over a mouthful of awesomeness.

"I'm European!" she snapped, cutting herself a huge chunk, proverbial nose in the air. She gobbled down the big handful of cheese aggressively, actions straining the credulity of words.

"So where are you from?" I asked Fabrice as we settled into our meal.

"*Sete,*" he said. "*A coastahl villahge. Vairee beautiful.*"

He proceeded to narrate with a strong, deep French accent. His words were muddy and difficult to understand. Despite this, he was an enthralling, animated storyteller.

"*We'll be visiting een a week or so. I can show yoo ze first ship I ever sailed on. Eet's still zere, all nets and feesh guts. Oui, what a mess zat was. I was fourteen years old and one night I asked my mothair to wake me at tree in ze mornang and take me to ze pier. She asked why, so I told 'air I had signed on as a feesherman. Zat was ze first she'd 'aird about it. She was not 'appy. Of course, she was even less 'appy when I came home tree weeks latair. I stank of feesh. Oui, ze smell! I walked een when my family was 'aving deennair and she ordered me back outside. I was made to streep naked right zere at ze front door so she could trow my clothes een ze trash. But I still stank of feesh. It gets eento your 'air and shampoo won't get eet out. Eet*" *gets eento your skin and soap won't wash eet off. I smelled like feesh for weeks—longer zan I was out catching zem!"*

While Fabrice giggled pleasantly at the memory of havoc, I looked to Cosmina. She sat back on her bed, deep in a haze of smoke that looked like it had settled in for the night. Each time Fabrice mentioned the smell of fish, she flinched.

"And not only did I stink of feesh," he continued blithely, *"but even my bedsheets began stinking of feesh. I slept wiz mackerell all suhmmair."*

That did it. His referring to stinking sheets put her over the edge.

"Stop already!" Cosmina cried, hands clutching her belly. Her face looked pained, like somebody had punched her in the stomach. She jumped up and whipped open the door. "Out! Get out."

Recognizing her urgency, we complied.

"I'll see you in the morning, Fabrice," Cosmina said, shooting a meaningful look at me. Though in discomfort, she was still able to make a jab.

"Toomorrow mornang?" Fabrice said, frowning. *"I'm sorry, but I can't help you. I 'ave meetings all mornang."*

Now Cosmina really did look like somebody punched her. She stammered, "Wha...? What meetings?"

"Zee old cruise director eez leaving. I need to see 'im off with a propair 'andovair. Zen I 'ave meetings wiz Francois all mornang. What about you, Brian? Can you help Cosmina in ze mornang? Francois says you are very good wiz crowds, even suggesting we can work togethair on—"

Cosmina cut him off, saying, "I can handle it." She shooed us out, trying to hide her grimace. Her stomach audibly roiled.

After the door slammed shut behind us, Fabrice and I looked at each other in the hallway. A moment passed, then we both burst out laughing. "*I warned 'air,*" he said ruefully, "*She should 'ave drunk ze champagne!*"

Poor Cosmina. Her perfectly planned evening went badly awry. I wasn't entirely sure why she hoped Fabrice and I wouldn't get along. True, in that year of 2005 America and France were still very much at odds over the Iraq invasion. But working on ships, she should have known better than to think international crew would let petulant nonsense like 'Freedom Fries' dictate how we felt about each other. We got along famously.

But her miscalculations went beyond failed hopes for conflict over nationality, failed hopes for jealousy over the cheese, and failed hopes for groveling over the 'job'. Not only was Fabrice unable to assist her the next morning, but Cosmina spent the whole disastrous day working alone with a horribly sick stomach from cheese she didn't even want to eat. For once the joke was entirely on her.

***

The company I worked for, Sundance at Sea, made an aggressive takeover of the gift shops on the majority of the world's cruise ships. This would not surprise anyone who had actually met the highly energetic and enigmatic Sundance owner, Frederick. His appetite was gargantuan, his pockets deep. He was also the world's worst micromanager. In order to keep the new acquisitions under his direct supervision, he gave control of each gift shop to the ship's resident auctioneer. Thus I suddenly became in charge of the *Wind Surf's* gift shop.

Frederick was literally a genius of the highest caliber

—he was consulted by MIT, for cryin' out loud—and assumed his employees were equally capable of mastering any new subject as quickly and as thoroughly as he. I would argue that being able to sell $100,000 Picassos was not qualification for successfully hustling $10,000 worth of ashtrays and T-shirts every week. If anything, it was the other way around! I was not happy about this one whit, and feared a nasty collision with Janie, the gift shop manager. I need not have worried. In her usual cheerleading manner, she expressed unbounded enthusiasm for the change. The fact that her paperwork would get double-checked before being sent up the ladder didn't hurt, either.

I happened to have dinner that night in port with Janie and one of her employees, not to mention a bunch of *Wind Surf's* other usual suspects. While groups of colleagues on the big ships do occasionally meet up during port stops—I'd had many a debauched lunch with various waiter mafias—it is unusual to have a multi-disciplinary dinner off the ship. After the setting sun turned aquamarine waters fitful black, a mixed bag of 'family' tendered to port. While I represented the art department and Janie and Melanie represented the gift shop, attendees also included Yoyo the photog, Eddie the dive instructor, Cosmina of shore excursion fame, Fabrice the cruise director, and spa giantess, Natalie.

And what a mesmerizing port it was! Hvar island in Croatia is simply gorgeous; an ancient place with well worn and well trodden public squares and walks built right up to the sea. This was necessary, since the entire island averaged a measly seven miles wide—which included a mountain range. During the day, Hvar (pronounced 'far' for some bizarre Croat reason) island looked little more than a huge, ungainly line of limestone. Yet nestled into its nooks, crannies, and sea-worn edges were gorgeous structures of stone. Everything was of stone, in fact, whether hewn and hauled by man or risen and eroded by nature.

The limestone of Hvar is dirty white. At a glance it is very similar to creamy Maltese limestone, but upon closer inspection it doesn't have the purity of color or luminosity. That's not to say it isn't beautiful. Records indicate a bunch of Hvar's limestone was exported all the way to Berlin for the parliament and other governmental buildings. That's not surprising, as the Germans at one time controlled Hvar—as did the Greeks, Romans, Byzantines, Venetians, Bosnians, Hungarians, Venetians again, Byzantines again, Germans, French, and who knows who else. Surely the Turks were involved in there somewhere, and probably some Martians as well. All told, over thirty empires have run the thin strip of stone. Though currently under the dominion of Croatia, it was being utterly invaded by Italians. Droves of them filled the streets, looking beautiful, smoking cigarettes, and speaking not only loudly but also with their hands. Hvar boasted the highly dubious claim of being the sunniest spot in all of Europe, and the Italians were intent to find out.

But we saw the island at night, squinting through the tender's scratched plexiglass at forested islets along the way. Incorrectly translated as Hell's Islands, it was frequently raised there. But our destination was the long, cut-stone quay built by the Venetians to hold their fleet long, long ago. The seaside strip was dark, broken only by lights from the abutting windows of venerable apartments. Ancient stone is best when shadowed. The tender pulled up to the dark quay and the few people shuffled out. Between the noisy, gassy revving of the engine thumped the heavy bass of techno music. The alluring call of modern sirens thumped from the far edge of the quay, where silhouettes of slender bodies gyrated against a backdrop of neon and flames.

Cosmina did not lead us towards the ultra clubs, however, but to the other end of the quay, where it opened into the town square. Dominating the corner was the 'new' arsenal. New was relative, of course, as it was built in the late 1500s to fight the Turks. It reminded me of a gargantuan, five-story barn, but instead of doors it offered an archway large enough to bring inside the galleys in case of invasion. Currently it was stoned up and more or less smooth, which summed up the political situation, as well.

Our group reluctantly passed the beastly building and into the yawning silence of the wide square. No music met the ear, no life met the eye. The only movement was wavering gaslight, which kept the square in mystery. The occasional lighted window above peeked down from the darkness warily, as if we were the invading Turks of long ago. The far end was dominated by a stone church and resident belfry rearing into the night.

"This place is creeping me out," Natalie complained, footsteps echoing off empty flagstone. "It's like wandering in a spooky old castle."

"I'll protect you!" Yoyo consoled. Giggling, he jumped into the air in a vain attempt to reach her height.

Yoyo's levity did little to ease our trepidation, which soon heightened as Cosmina led us into a narrow road between two sentry-like stone behemoths. The flagstones angled up sharply, for the city itself began climbing the steep ridges that formed the spine of the island. Looming buildings leaned in menacingly. After a few twists and turns in the near darkness, the alley-like road opened— swelled, really—just enough to allow a few tables before an octagonal, four-story dwelling. A paltry few gas lamps sputtered, stretching shadows from iron clamps hammered into fitted stone. Above the minimally-inviting tables staggered windows, uneven, shuttered tight.

"We dining with Dracula, or what?" Natalie exclaimed in awe. 'I think there's a serial killer here somewhere."

"You're the one with claws like Wolverine," Janie pointed out. "What am I gonna do?"

"Don't cheerleaders know how to kick?" Natalie shot back.

"Natalie's right," Mel the shoppie urged. "I don't want to eat here."

"*Yoo 'aven't even seen ze menu!*" Fabrice teased. "*Peel and eat eyeballs, pair'aps? A good chef can make anyzing delicious. Sauteed wiz a little white wine and garlic, excellent!*"

Cosmina's hands went to her belly and she passed a sour look. After recovering, she quickly slapped Fabrice on the shoulder. He mimed great pain, then continued with a devilish grin, "*Boiled brains wiz geengair to 'elp settle your stohmach.*"

"I was told they have great pizza by those who know," Cosmina explained haughtily—too haughtily. Her tone indicated overcompensation of setting, not stomach. I strongly suspected she was just as freaked out by the haunting atmosphere as the rest of us. Certainly it was the most Medieval pizzeria I had ever seen. When the door to the restaurant creaked open, I expected nothing less than a minion wheeling out an iron maiden. Instead it was the proprietor, who helped us pull tables together. Several bottles of red wine were ordered. Natalie stuck to beer.

Inspired by—or, rather, intimidated by—the setting, the seven of us felt particularly close that night. Certainly we leaned in close. But forced joviality soon became the real thing. After a few glasses of wine we found ourselves having a grand old time. Laughter wafted up over those shuttered windows, all the way to the stars. Multi-disciplinary shop talk swept joyfully back and forth like world-class tennis players in a friendly pick-up match. I shared with Yoyo the basics of artistic composition to help with his photography. Cosmina explained to Natalie the benefits of using Janie and Mel as tour hosts, not to mention her brilliant idea of using Fabrice and I for her onboard organization. Natalie protested that she wanted to be a tour host as well, but Cosmina quickly dashed that by saying she was 'unreliable'. After the rest of us surreptitiously pointed at Yoyo—an occasional tour host himself—Cosmina quickly amended that Natalie was 'uncontrollable'. This new explanation not only mollified, but actually pleased Natalie.

I sat beside Natalie and, on the other side, Cosmina—as always, whether I liked it or not. I secretly wished Faye had been present, just to keep Cosmina good and riled. Turns out that was not necessary. After the pizzas arrived, so, too, did Eddie's girlfriend Susie.

"What the hell, Eddie?" she demanded before even stepping into the light. Even had we not recognized the voice, Eddie's flinch was a dead giveaway.

"I told you I was going out to dinner," Eddie protested, rising from his chair. He snagged another from a neighboring table and squeezed it next to his own. "You said you didn't want to come."

"Not with everybody, you didn't!" she accused.

"You thought I would leave you in the cabin to tender into port alone?"

"I can see how wanted I am," she fumed, plopping

down, arms folded firmly beneath her breasts. Eddie looked appropriately chagrined and said nothing further.

"Eddie was just telling us the funniest story," Cosmina enthusiastically lied to Susie. "He's sooo funny when he's happy."

"I'm sure," Susie replied flatly.

Eddie, not knowing what to do, meekly sipped his wine in silence. Halfway through the action, however, he gave a sigh and rose. "All right," he said to Susie. "Let's go."

"But the pizza just got here!" I protested. "We have plenty for everyone."

Alas, our arguments stood little chance of softening Susie's icy demeanor. But Eddie took it all in stride, generously reassuring us, "It's okay. I'll catch you guys next time."

They strode down the alley, into darkness. We returned our attention to the pizza, but something felt wrong. As if the setting weren't creepy enough, from the darkness emanated a heavy breathing.

"Okay, that's not funny!" Janie shouted to the dark. "Hey, asshole! You can cut it out."

A huffing and puffing sounded just outside the light, directly behind Natalie. With startling suddenness a heavy hand fell upon the back of her chair.

"Jesus, Rick!" Natalie cried, jumping up. "I thought you were a serial killer!"

Into the light slouched a solid man with thick shoulders and slight paunch. His short hair was slicked forward with sweat, and he looked ready to pass out. Yet while still wheezing he gamely pawed at her shoulders. "Up, woman," he growled, "Can't you see I'm dying here?"

Natalie relinquished her chair to the newcomer, this

Rick. He was a sorry sight, with sweat soaking strange patterns into his turquoise *Wind Surf* polo shirt. It was an amusing pairing with the gold hoop he wore in his ear. Rather than a pirate, he was more like the Big Bad Wolf: huffing and puffing. Still, he managed to down Natalie's beer in record time.

"Fine," Natalie harrumphed. "I'll get my own chair. Have you guys met Rick? He's the new spa manager."

"Not for bloody long!" Rick complained. "Nobody told me I'd be running a bloody haunted spa!"

"If you're trying to scare us," Janie chided, "You can stop. This place is scary enough."

Rick glanced around, apparently noticing the macabre surroundings for the first time. With a solemn nod he said, "Fair dinkum. Bloody ghosts should hang here, not at my bloody spa!"

"All right," I told him, "You've got us hooked. I love ghost stories."

Rick shook his head as if to clear it of cobwebs, or perhaps the memory. After a swig of beer and a sigh, he narrated, "I saw it last night, too. I wasn't sure then. I'd heard Camilla's stupid story, but thought she was a couple bangers short of a barbie."

"She's new, so be nice!" Natalie chided. "Besides, I've seen weird things, too."

"And Natalie's seen things, too," Rick repeated.

The spa was down by the waterline of *Wind Surf*, back near the marina. At night it was a very quiet, very lonely place. Strange that such a small ship utilizing every cubic inch of guest space had locations that felt... abandoned. There were cabins nearby and people coming and going from the spa, to be sure, but something about the spa's location did feel somehow different.

"I've noticed things moving behind the desk," Rick said. "But it's hard to tell when bloody staplers move on their own when you have four employees. But you know the melon slices we keep in the urn of drinking water? I heard a gurgle or something and looked up in their direction. In the blink of an eye—in the blink of a bloody eye—they vanished! Then—splat! Right in front of me, right in the middle of the desk, the melons reappeared. All the bloody things. Soaked my ledger and all my paperwork and everything."

"Oh my God!" Natalie gasped, clapping her hands over her mouth. Nails clicked. "What did you do?"

"What'd I do? I cleaned it up, you cow. What'd you think I'd do? Bloody weird, if you ask me, but—I don't know—somehow not real enough to worry over. That was yesterday. I'd only been aboard two days, so I thought it was just a ragging or some other prank on the new guy. Don't ask me how they'd bloody pull it off. But tonight was different. I was doing paperwork after we closed. A guest walked right past me."

"A ghost?" Janie gasped, enrapt.

"A guest, mate," Rick clarified, looking slightly miffed that she had stolen his thunder. "A bloody guest. I saw her clearly as she passed. Middle-aged, long brown hair, and a T-shirt that made her look chunky. I told her we're closed for the night, but she just walked through the spa and into Natalie's massage room. I followed right behind her, calling out. I was cranky, actually, because I've had a bad time with stupid passengers complaining all bloody day. I was going to give this lady a piece of my mind. When I got to Natalie's room I flipped the light switch on... and nobody was there!"

"I'm switching rooms with Camilla," Natalie firmly

declared.

"I don't believe it!" Mel declared firmly. "You're just trying to scare us."

"Yeah, Rick," Natalie said, giving her manager an accusing slug on the arm.

"We live with many spirits in my culture," Yoyo added. "They are everywhere."

"*Oh, yes,*" Fabrice agreed. "*On Wind Surf, too. Zere ees more zan one ghost aboard.*"

All eyes swiveled to the petite Frenchman. He smiled gamely.

"*I 'aven't seen eet zis contract,*" he explained cheerfully in his muddled accent. "*But my last contract I saw eet two or tree times, just outside my office.*"

"Your office is next to my office!" Cosmina blurted, shocked.

"*Oui,*" Fabrice agreed cheerily. I leaned in, anticipating his thick accent. I focused heavily on his words, because I wasn't about to miss any of this story!

"*In ze allway. Actually right outside ze door to ze pursair's offeece, dead-centair of ze ship. Ah ha—dead-centair—I just got that! I saw ze shadowy outline of a man... but only from ze waist up! I could not see 'iz face, but only a meest. I'm not sure why I even say he was a man, but eet felt like eet. Each time I looked up at 'im, 'ee just faded eento ze dark. Divina—you know ze Filipina pursair? —she saw 'im, too. She was on an errand for more papier. She was een an hurree and ran out of 'air office carrying a load and ran into ze phantom. She screamed, thinking she 'ad run eento an offisair. She saw 'ee was caucasian and of average 'ight, but no more. She couldn't even remember if she saw 'iz legs or not.*

"*But she saw 'iz face clearly,*" Fabrice narrated.

"Because eet was daylight, and Divina's office 'as a window. Eet was bright. Ee looked as solid as yoo and me, and she met 'iz gaze. 'Ee looked as surprised as her! But zere was somezing else as well. A sense of 'opelessness. Very gloomy, very sad. Zees I understand. Though I 'aven't seen ze phantom zees contract yet, I 'ave felt 'iz presence. Sometimes when I'm working late I will feel someone approaching. I'll look up, but no one ees zere. Even zough I don't see anyone, I can feel 'im watching. Just like I do 'ere."

"Stop it!" Janie snapped. She was definitely getting into the spirit of the conversation. Telling ghost stories over red wine in Dracula's castle was sure to evoke some powerful impressions.

"Bloody hell," Rick concluded. "The lady I saw looked just like another fat housewife. But seeing only half a man...? I'd get the hell out of there. In fact, I did get the hell out of there. Had to run to catch the last tender. Guess I'm out of shape. After ten bloody years in the British Army, I didn't plan to ever run again!"

"The British Army? Your accent is Australian," Cosmina said, suddenly intrigued. She had been distinctly ignoring the ghost stories, but now heard something pertaining to her interests. She sidled seductively closer—elbowing me out of the way—and huskily asked, "Tell me about... England."

Rick gave her a scrutinizing look, then leaned in. His demeanor shifted from panting and goofy to smooth. "What would you like to know?"

Cosmina leaned across even further, stabbing an elbow in my gut to do so. The pain was a small price to pay for her switching targets.

"I want it all," she breathed seductively, as if they

weren't surrounded by half a dozen others with raised brows. Yoyo, in particular, watched with open fascination. "Everything you've got. I want—."

An awkward rumble rose from beneath the table, followed by a liquid churning and bubbling, then finally a caustic odor. Cosmina's eyes widened in horror. In a flash she was gone from the table. It happened so fast we were all left as wide-eyed as Yoyo.

Natalie finally broke the silence. Clicking her claw-like nails together, she observed, "Rick, you sure got a way with women."

***

I had never before had such a night on ships, with so much interdisciplinary support, even reliance. While success usually involved relationships, such were very hard to come by at sea; people came and went on the big ships by the dozens every single cruise. Once again I was struck by how not big this ship was. For the first time, this did not bother me. In fact, for the first time I was downright pleased by it. I was struck by the sudden desire to make *Wind Surf* a home as long as I could. I had never felt that way about a ship before, beyond the fundamental fact that longer tenure meant more job security. Yes, for the first time I 'got it'. I was, indeed, a member of the family.

Oh, sailors were all a member of an extended family. We were part of a club that the outside didn't understand and never could. Our experiences connected us and we supported each other, even when we hated each other. The life gets in your blood, kind of like being in the military or the police force—minus the danger, of course. But this was different. This wasn't a small town vibe, where everybody knew everybody's secrets simply because of proximity. This was intimacy, this was family.

The cast was nearly complete, the family—which made my time on *Wind Surf* the best of all my career— nearly whole. Over the ensuing months I would get to know these players and their machinations intimately, officers and crew alike. Before my eyes some would grow not just professionally, but emotionally, dependent upon each other. Others would soon grow to loathe each other. Such chiaroscuro of light and dark defined my role as well. For on *Wind Surf* I made friends for life, loyal even after ships. I also made enemies—one in particular—whose duplicity would hound me even after returning to land life.

You can choose your friends, but you can't choose your family.

POMPEII
ITALY

THE TRAIN, NOT yet moving, shimmied on its track, shuddering from a close call by a passing neighbor. The offender was on a separate track, of course, but with Italian driving you just never know. Fog left over from a passing shower steamed the windows, obscuring the view out across the Bay of Naples. A shame, that, for the cliff-top city of Sorrento offered an unparalleled overlook at one of the world's most celebrated World Heritage Sites.

Tickets in hand, the four of us found seats facing each

other and sat down; Natalie beside Rick, Janie by me. Literally the very second her bottom touched the bench, Natalie piped, "Okay, I'm bored."

"That makes two of us, Natalie," Rick groused, saying her name with a mocking emphasis: 'NATlee'. "I wanted to go to a bar. You've really let me down here."

"You're really not curious to see this?" I asked Rick, surprised.

"Rather see the inside of a bar, mate," he answered, absently tugging on the small gold hoop in his ear.

"That makes two of us," Natalie agreed.

Such support did not please Rick, but rather incensed him. He snapped, "You're the one who suggested this stupid field trip! You're supposed to be my drinking partner."

"That's because nobody told me it takes an hour twenty to get there," Natalie whined.

"Good!" Janie said with obvious relief. "I need to get away for awhile. Francois' all up in my shit about goals. He called me into his office twice last cruise! Sometimes I think he forgets the shops are closed while in port, and we're always in port."

Natalie snorted. "You're lucky! You get to see the ports. The spa's open all the time, so I have to work most ports."

"I don't want to think about it," Janie said. She patted Natalie on the knees and said, "Come on. Let's make a cheer."

"Do I look like a cheerleader to you?" the massive brunette grumbled. "I was bigger than half the team."

Brushing aside Natalie's smart replies, Janie clapped her hands in the air and began chanting.

"Explosive! Dynamic! Sure to pass the test—
We explode with spirit, and eliminate the rest!"

In unison, the entire train turned to stare at Janie. Rick moaned, "Does this train have a bar?"

We were on our way to visit the fabled city of Pompeii, doomed by the most famous volcanic eruption of them all. In the year 79 A.D., Mt. Vesuvius erupted and buried the thriving city of Pompeii in a flood of ash. Though sheer hell and searing death for the inhabitants, the fine ash proved most gentle to the city itself. Smothered beneath the protective blanket of volcanic debris, Pompeii remained safely preserved through the rise and fall of the Roman Empire, through the Dark Ages, through the Renaissance. Only when the Industrial Revolution approached did the ash give up its prize.

Now the city stands open and inviting, as if ready to once again house all 20,000 ghosts of the fallen. Street after street after street, all there. The houses, the markets, arenas, brothels, all there. The ash made a particularly effective preservative, leaving bodies where slain and household goods where abandoned. Archeologists even found unbroken jars of fruit preserves and loaves of bread! That an explosion one hundred thousand times more powerful than the nuclear bomb dropped on Hiroshima could leave so much for posterity was incredible. So, too, were the numbers of tourists. Two and a half million people from all over the planet flocked to the site every year, hoping for a glimpse, a taste, of what the Roman world was like. They flew from hundreds of nations across thousands of miles.

Natalie couldn't make it an hour.

"Hey, sandwich lady!" she cried, flagging down an elderly woman offering snacks. Natalie rose to her full six foot two-inch height and jumped around, meter-long hair whirling in a black arc. As if that weren't enough to arrest attention, she wore a cut off pink top over lime green bra. Her long nails were bright blue, as was the heavy ring of liner around her eyes and, for that matter, her plastic sandals. Decorating her front tooth was a diamond. Though archeology bound, Indiana Jones she looked not.

Soon Natalie was unwrapping a baguette piled with cold cuts. And complaining.

"This looks awful," she muttered, pulling the poor, wretched sandwich apart. She used the top half of bread to scrape off as much mayonnaise as possible, which she then discarded. She downed the sliced cheese in wolfish fashion, then proceeded to do... something... to the salami. Holding in her open palm the slices of meat, she began excising the little chunks of fat with surgical precision. A two-inch fingernail removed the fat like a scalpel, but was unable to smear it onto the waxed paper. Instead she had to use her palm, which soon mushroomed with smudges of white grease. The operation was both mesmerizing and revolting.

"You are so bizarre," Rick marveled.

"Biglietti," a small, foreign voice called from the aisle. We looked up to see the train's conductor holding out his hand. The Italian wore a crisp blue uniform and snappy hat, but his posture was wrinkled with boredom. That changed when he laid eyes upon Janie. She was a cute and solid woman, despite a year of beer having taken its toll on her once athletic body. Thickly muscled thighs had softened considerably along their way into post-high school reality. An extra layer around her middle indicated beer as surely as it would on any man. But ever enthusiastic Janie didn't mind because now her boobs were bigger. The conductor obviously concurred, for despite four arms flapping with tickets, he saw only Janie's breast-bulging T-shirt.

But duty soon took precedence. He frowned at our tickets and launched into a long and irate narrative. Recognizing that none of us understood him, he switched from Italian to English.

"You no validate ticket," he said sternly. "You must validate ticket or be fined."

"Fined?" Rick roared. "We bought your bloody tickets, didn't we? Who cares if we validated them? You can see the time stamp right on it."

"Yes," Janie added, trying to sway the man. "You can see we paid the right amount. Please forgive us if we didn't know the right procedure."

"How I know you buy ticket? Somebody else give them to you!" the conductor accused.

"You mean somebody else who didn't validate them?" Rick challenged. "I already told you the time stamp is right there. We bought them five minutes ago. Use your eyes, man!"

"Stolen ticket," the conductor said, shaking his head with feigned sadness. "Is fine much larger than no to validate ticket. The Carabinieri will be at our arrival in Pompeii. You want to deal with them?"

Rick was angry. Extortion does bring that out in people. "That's a great idea! Why don't you bugger off until we get there?"

"Rick," Janie soothed. "You're not helping. Sir? What's the fine for not validating our tickets?"

"Twenty-five euros," he replied to her breasts. After a pause, he swiveled his gaze back to Rick and added haughtily. "Each."

"You bloody wanker!" Rick cried, rising to his feet.

He leaned over the slender Italian. As they faced off, however, somebody else rose to tower over them both. Both men stared, awestruck, at six-feet-two-inches of irate Natalie. One hand thrust to her hip—still holding the mangled, drooping sandwich that bobbed with her anger— she waggled the other in the conductor's face. His eyes widened further and further at each globule of fat dripping from the two-inch blue talon flashing before his eyes.

"This ends right now!" Natalie declared fiercely, light flashing from the diamond set into her tooth. "This is bullshit. No fines!"

The man forced himself to gulp, nodded, then stammered, "D-do you have a-a pen?"

"Who has a pen?" Natalie snapped. Rick—also suddenly meek—handed the conductor his pen. The Italian scribbled his initials on each ticket with a wavering hand, then returned each ticket to its owner. Without a further word, he retreated in search of easier prey.

We finished the ride to Pompeii with better spirits. Natalie was happier, anyway, because she'd had some action. But the setting was not one for gaiety. The sky drizzled a sad drizzle, the ruins wept. Uncounted thousands had died here most horrifically. The fear was tangible once beyond the gates. The crowds murmured anonymously to drone a low, morose hum. Hugging each other as couples beneath cheap umbrellas, we wandered through the untrammeled streets of a doomed city. The disparity was fascinating.

"So tell me about Pompeii," Natalie said from beneath the umbrella she shared with Rick. "But don't give me an answer that's boring."

After a glance at the map, I decided on a proper course of study. We entered a large, grassy yard ringed by neatly preserved columns. Most were a full twelve feet in height, though the east wall had a row of incomplete and thusly shorter columns. Behind those east columns were uneven brick walls forming a series of small rooms, now roofless and lumpy. The other three sides surrounding the yard had walls mostly intact, indicating the yard was once ringed on all four sides by covered porticoes. One roof still remained, slanting tiles shrugging off the rain. We moved under its protection.

"See these columns lining the yard?" I began.

"They special?" Natalie asked eagerly.

"Oh, yes. You can tell a lot about the purpose of this place by the columns. There are three main types of Roman capitals, you see. See how the caps are all simply just a flat rock?"

"You mean their hats?"

"Yes, their hats," I replied. Stifling a smile, I continued with an intentionally droning quality, "To understand Roman architecture, it's important to understand the differences between Doric, Ionic, and Corinthian columns. The first were Doric, which evolved from a simple post and lintel system used by man for millennia— think of Stonehenge, which is merely a large-scale post and lintel system. Posts and lintels of stone have a terrible tensile strength and it took centuries of innovation to come up with brick archways—used on Roman aqueducts still in use to this day—and, eventually, arched vaults reinforced with concrete—the Romans invented concrete, of course— and—"

"Oh my God," Natalie interrupted with a groan. "Shoot me now."

"I'm just messing with you," I laughed. "This was the gladiator's training yard."

"How do they know that?" Natalie asked, peering around.

"Lots of reasons. One is because behind us are barracks that don't have any of the usual trademarks of being military. Another reason is this yard and its columns. Since Pompeii was during an evolved era of the Roman empire, the use of Doric capitals—a simple, early style—means they were made on the cheap. Gladiators were slaves, remember. These columns weren't meant to look pretty, but simply served to keep the roof up."

"Jesus, Brian," Rick groused. "We could be talking about gladiators fighting each other with fireballs falling from the sky and you're talking about bloody boring columns."

At least Janie came to my defense. To the tune of the ubiquitous high school cheer about bananas, Janie jumped, waved, and sang:

"Go, Vesuvius, go go Vesuvius.
"Steam to the left and steam to the right,
"Feel that rumble and BOOM!- Take flight!"

"This is going to be a long day," Rick grumbled. I was starting to agree.

"I'm serious," Natalie pressed. "How do they know any of this crap? Everybody died."

"Not everybody," I replied. "Pliny saw the whole thing and wrote about it. Pliny the Younger, I think. Yeah, because it was Pliny the Elder who was killed by Vesuvius. You'd like him. Do you have freckles on your butt or anything?"

Natalie stared at me as if I'd gone completely mental. This was not by any means an unwarranted thought. She stammered, "What the hell are you talking about?"

"In Pliny the Elder's book Natural History, he wrote that ghosts were scared of freckled people. Thought they were impure. You don't have freckles, but maybe if you've got a bunch hidden somewhere the ghost of *Wind Surf* won't show up in your massage room. Anything you'd care to show us?"

Natalie just stared at me, open mouthed.

"I'm great at parties," I defended sweetly.

The sun eventually burned through the clouds, making the dead city a hot one. Humidity rolled off rock, sweat rolled off skin. We wandered the silent stone streets and compared them to other streets of other eras. Like today, via concrete, or the Old West, via boardwalks, we walked on raised sidewalks. But everything in Pompeii was solid stone. Many side streets were narrow and deep—sidewalks raised a full two feet!—making the street more a wide gutter than anything else. It was just wide enough for a single cart to be hauled through behind a donkey. This kept the prosperous Pompeiians from getting dirty, but still allowed the lesser folks to go about their business throughout the entire city. If a citizen wished to cross the street, bridges were provided as stone steps, neatly spaced to allow wagon wheels through. Pompeii was a showcase for the best of Roman engineering: simple, efficient, strong.

It was the little things of Pompeii that made an impact, such as a public fountain placed at a crossroads. Via ancient hydraulics, water had poured into a wide basin for people to wash their hands in. The edges of the large bowl were fairly crisp, but for one spot. There people had placed their hands to lean in and drink the flowing water. Thousands of hands after hundreds of years had worn that spot smooth; a reminder of how incorrectly humans comprehend time. We think that because Pompeii was preserved so perfectly, so long ago, it must have been young when buried. Not so. Pompeii was quadruple the age of the United States—nearly 900 years old—when Vesuvius slaughtered its citizenry so long ago.

Then things turned ghastly. Seeing the preserved buildings and streets was one thing. Seeing the birds and flowers painted on intimate bedroom walls was even more enchanting. Seeing the preserved owners was devastating.

The pyroclastic blast of angry Vesuvius did not kill the men, women, and children of Pompeii; they did not mercifully liquify in a split second of scalding heat. Oh, no. Hot ash fell and fell, turning day into night, and kept on falling. Screaming in the darkness, lost, bewildered, the people struggled to survive an event utterly beyond their comprehension. Hordes of victims mobbed the docks, intent on escaping what had once been their home. Dozens died in a writhing mass waiting for boats that would never come. There was no escape for so very, very many. Some dropped alone in the street, others cowered in basements before supporting roofs—unable to bear tons of ash— collapsed upon them. Still others clung to each other as they succumbed to suffocation, hugging each other with their last, dying breaths.

Yet still fell the terror, burying the bodies in powder-fine ash. The ash enveloped every nook and cranny of their bodies, rippling within folds of cloth, filling gaping mouths. When the corpses finally succumbed to time and disintegrated, the ash that housed them had long since solidified. What remained were cavities of exquisite detail. Archeologists discovered countless such hollowed out moments and decided to fill them with plaster. The result was a shocking, city-wide panorama depicting the terrifying moment of death.

I had been excited to see the infamous plaster casts since discovering their existence in a contraband National Geographic magazine. The photos were far too graphic for a child of my tender years. Maybe that's what set me off into the realm of horror fiction and film. But vampire and zombie fandom is merely imagination at play. These were people. Worse, they were people in pain. I was not prepared to feel their pain. But how could I not? The details were staggering: visible were belt buckles, purses, boots. You could see expressions still on their faces. One screaming, plaster mouth lay open to reveal very real teeth, preserved after all this time.

More powerful than expressions were positions. Many hugged each other. One man gently cradled the head of a woman as they together waited for the end. Perhaps the most heart-wrenching was the lone man huddled on the street, knees to his chin, sobbing into his hands. His form conveyed all the animus of Rodin's Thinker.

Astonishingly, Janie was not at all effected by so many human remains preserved in eternal agony. She bounced from displayed body to displayed body. She wasn't just fascinated, she was downright enthusiastic. She even repeated her previous 'Go bananas' chant:

"Go, Vesuvius, go go Vesuvius.
"Steam to the left and steam to the right,
"Feel that rumble and BOOM!- Take flight!"

Caught up in her own moment—for none of us shared it—she added with a jump:

"Ashes to ashes!

"Dust to dust—
"Feel that steam—
"Escape is a must!"

Rick looked like Janie was singing about him rather than Vesuvius. His face swelled a blotchy red and looked about to blow. He snapped at Janie with sharp bitterness. "Will you shut up? Shut up! Shut up! Shut the fuck up!"

Janie's arms dropped to her sides, chastened, stunned.

Rick stormed off. We watched him go, shocked at his sudden, violent outburst. From afar we could see him pacing, extremely upset, muttering with vehemence about 'steam pits'. His thick shoulders bulged with anger and he looked utterly unconsolable. None of us dared try. Needless to say, the tour was over. We slowly made our way towards the exit, taking our time. Eventually Rick caught up to us. Though once again composed, he offered no explanation. We did not pry. I was just glad Cosmina wasn't there to blame me for killing all these guys, too.

It was time to return to our home, our *Wind Surf*. I bought a book about Pompeii—in English, of course—and we made our way to the gates. A register beckoned, and Janie skipped over to sign it.

"The pen's dry," she said. With a hint of hesitation, she asked, "Rick, can I borrow your pen, please?"

Recognizing an opportunity for an olive branch, Rick nodded and reached for his pocket. He suddenly paused, then began wildly patting his person. "Son of a bitch!" he swore, face darkening anew. "My Mont Blanc cost me fifty bloody pounds sterling—and that bloody wanker conductor stole it!"

***

You have to learn how to be rich, they say. While I certainly wasn't rich, I did understand the axiom. Being an art auctioneer necessitated rubbing shoulders with the rich, in order to convince them you were one of them and thusly could be trusted with monetary decisions. That sort of thing. Learning how to be rich also meant accepting certain privileges you felt warranted. I still couldn't bear to have a valet handle my luggage, but I sure did know how to dine with the best of 'em.

Dining on *Wind Surf*, like all cruise ships, was segregated by rank. Officers dined in the Veranda—one of two guest dining rooms—because there was not room below decks for both a crew mess and an officer's mess. During breakfast and lunch the privileged few were allowed to dine with the guests, which was an enjoyable prospect on such a small, familiar ship. At dinner time passengers congregated to the larger, Main Deck Restaurant for their repast, leaving the Veranda for the officers and certain staff.

Only a few dozen were allowed to dine in the sun. The rest of the crew shared a tiny room on a lower deck. Numbering well over a hundred, they were almost criminally crammed into a box around eighteen feet squared. The food offered in the little hot bar was not particularly bad, but it was not particularly good, either. Nobody in his right mind would choose that over the Veranda Restaurant. Yet Yoyo did. Then again, Yoyo was hardly of right mind. His predecessor, Ardin, had dined in the Veranda. He had learned how to be rich, as it were. Most likely Yoyo just felt more comfortable dining with fellow Asians, of which he was alone among officers and privileged staff. Unfortunately, Cosmina was also one of the worthy few allowed to dine in the Veranda—more's the pity.

"I just want to get drunk," she groused into her plate opposite me.

With only a handful of people present, the restaurant felt very empty. It always did, for an interior that sat eighty for lunch served only a few dozen for dinner. What occupied most of the space was sunlight, slanting in through the floor-to-ceiling windows lining the Veranda. It was unbearably hot, but the view of the cliffs of Sorrento rising just off the starboard bow more than made up for it. So, too, did the roast pork loin. Food in the Veranda was actually pretty good. Like the U-shaped room lined with glass, the gleaming metal counters were also mostly empty, but for a few buffet decorations. Hot wells gently steamed two meat entrees and three side dishes, all of which rotated nightly. The salad bar, of moderate quality, did not.

"Dead drunk. Muerta. Kaput."

"I heard you," I offered hesitantly. On a good day I didn't really want to engage Cosmina in conversation. But when she opened a dialogue with 'I just want to get drunk'? Hell no. Thus it was wonderful when the chief officer, Emmet, sat down beside me with a plate full of peas and carrots. This was not a particularly unusual step, this joining of senior officer and mere mortal. Emmet was an exceptionally down-to-Earth kind of guy; always cheerful, he enjoyed being around others of the same mien. Needless to say, it was not to Cosmina that he first spoke.

"Oh, my," he said, looking down at my plate. He shook his head ruefully at my rather large helping of pork, pork, and pork. "Where are your vegetables?"

"Coming," I answered. "I tend to eat in phases, for some reason. After the meat I'll get a plate full of veggies. I promise."

"You're doing it completely wrong," Emmet said. Gamely smoothing his white uniform in a professorial manner, he explained, "Always eat your vegetables first. That way you don't forget to eat them. I can't imagine you'll still be hungry after all that meat."

"Don't bet on it," I said with a smile. "I'm from the pork capital of the U.S. In fact, my grandfather was a hog buyer. How you can make a living buying and selling pigs is beyond me, but I hear he was quite good at it. I have pork in my blood."

"Gross," Cosmina chided, idly pushing peas around her plate.

Emmet chuckled. Pulling from his pocket two plastic wrapped cigars, he handed them to me.

"Here," he said. "I thought you'd like these. The port authority gave them to me and wouldn't take no for an answer. He seems to think the trading of tobacco is some sort of sacred bond or something. You're the only cigar smoker I know on board, so I thought you'd enjoy them."

"Thank you, Emmet. Why don't we smoke them together after dinner?" I gave a slight nod to our sullen companion and added, "I sense our usual table in the Compass Rose will be occupied before too long. Some pleasant conversation would be most welcome."

"Yeah," Cosmina murmured. "We can all plan Yoyo's murder."

Emmet's lips compressed into a wry smile and he said, "Ah, no thank you. I see Eddie has just entered, and we need to schedule a dive."

Emmet rose, gathered his plate, and gave me a wink. "Eat your vegetables."

And so I was alone with Cosmina. Joy. She was

arrogant and manipulative and fiercely opinionated about things that were, quite simply, ignorant stereotypes. She was also one of the few people aboard with a schedule matching my own. We were thrust upon each other at every turn, even when we weren't helping each other out. On the big ships I was used to non-ideal companions—namely the dancers—but of those *Surf* had none. No, I was stuck with Cosmina or Yoyo or the TV. I was seriously considering the latter. But booze held a very powerful draw to me, and the Compass Rose was the preferred place to get it. And really, Cosmina could bitch all she wanted if I could sit on the open deck and watch night descend over the Bay of Naples.

After dinner we moved to our usual table—under the port steps leading up to the Star Deck—and proceeded to drink and smoke. Rather, Cosmina did the former while I did the latter. She wasted no time downing record quantities of gin and tonic. She said nothing.

So she was angry. Or sad, hiding it behind anger. You can tell a woman is angry when she's silent. You can also tell a woman is angry when she's yelling. There's also the heavy clue that they're angry when they act different. Then again, a sure sign of anger is when they don't act differently. Interpreting women's emotional cues was hard enough when sharing their culture, but guessing a Romanian woman's game was like fencing blindfolded. Strange it was, indeed, that I was a shoulder to cry on for this woman I didn't even like. Bianca surely had just as many troubles, but had been far too stubborn to let me help. Even after years together, I had to pry out what ailed her, her hopes, her fears. And what did I get for it all? A greater ability to be 'in tune' with another selfish Romanian.

Cosmina downed another drink—hard and fast—

started to sniffle, then immediately hid it behind a snap at the waitress to bring her another.

"So you're mad at Yoyo," I finally said after several minutes of utterly failing to figure out what the hell was going on. "Just get it out. What'd he do?"

"You mean other than losing eight passengers in the ruins of Pompeii?"

"Are... are you serious?" I asked, flabbergasted. Her glare was answer enough.

"He wasn't supposed to be responsible for any passengers at all," she spat. "Thank God Fabrice was in charge of the bus or I'd have lost everyone! The idiot was only supposed to take photos. Oh, and you know what he did? He took a photo of each person as they entered the main gate. Not inside by the ruins and pillars and whatever. He took photos of them outside the stupid gate by a bunch of cars of the Carabinieri! What an idiot. The local guides split up the passengers into two groups. The buildings they go into are small, so they don't want more than a dozen at a time. Fabrice took a dozen and the idiot was responsible for the rest."

"So how did he get lost if he had a local guide?"

"The guide gave them a tour for two hours then dropped them off by the gate. His job was done. Everybody was supposed to have half an hour to do their own thing. Stupid Yoyo forgot what time the bus left, so he told everybody to meet back at the gate at three o'clock. The bus was supposed to leave at two! Not that the idiot would know: he didn't even have a watch. Can you believe that? Who the hell goes that far from the ship without a watch? Idiot. Luckily Fabrice did a head count or we would have left without them. He had to hire guides on the spot to go find the passengers, who had wandered all over the damn place. That's why people aren't given a lot of time to themselves: they wander off. The very expensive guides found everybody and Yoyo was all giggly and shit. He had no idea how much trouble he'd have been in if he lost eight passengers in a foreign country, an hour and a half from the ship."

"At least it all worked out."

"Not for my budget," Cosmina growled, downing another drink. "Those Italians knew exactly what happened and charged an arm and a leg to go find them all. My budget is screwed for the whole goddamn cruise. I just want to get drunk."

Cosmina lent actions to her words. She downed drinks so fast I truly began to worry about her. Worse, her chant no longer was just to get drunk, but 'to get drunk and forget'. I didn't know what that last tag meant, but growled repetition made it ominous. She was obviously burdened by something greater than Yoyo's mishap. After Rick's sudden outburst that day, and now Cosmina's ambiguous self-torture, I was beginning to wonder what kind of dysfunctional family I had been adopted into. But nobody goes to sea unless they're running—either to something or, more likely, from something.

I did the usual tricks to slow Cosmina's drinking: swapping alcohol with water, ordering food, asking the waitress to avoid our table, that sort of thing. None of it worked, and I knew I had a potential mess on my hands. Cosmina got absolutely plowed. She was a big girl and if she wanted to make an ass of herself, fine by me. Yet it was painful to sit next to someone you know and work with and see her going under. How could I in good conscience not involve myself?

What saved me was the arrival of a group of others:

Fabrice, Barney, and Faye. They were intent on a quality night of social drinking. That meant gaiety, it meant laughs. They dispersed the swelling gloom. Everybody was in a fine fettle. Everybody but Cosmina, of course. But now outnumbered, she merely stewed over her drinks. She didn't even attempt to condescend to Faye—a truly rare thing, even if unattainable.

Eventually the time came to disperse and we rose from the table. Cosmina wavered dangerously, but Barney placed a sturdy hand on her shoulder for support. He offered his large frame for her to ease into.

"Whoa... how about I escort you back to your cabin?"

"I'm fine!" Cosmina snapped. "I need Brian."

The curt dismissal obviously hurt Barney, but he said nothing. I looked at him in a lame attempt at apologizing for her behavior. He shrugged.

"We need to talk... business," Cosmina continued, eyelids fluttering past bleary eyes. Then she blurted, "Tours!"

"Whatever," Barney replied. He eased the noodle-like Cosmina my way and asked kindly, "You good?"

"She'll be all right," I replied quietly. He watched us depart with mild concern, then went on his way.

Getting Cosmina back to her cabin was a chore. She could barely walk. Her key dropped from useless, alcohol-soaked fingers. When I bent down to pick it up, she all but collapsed onto my back. Very awkwardly we managed to get her into the cabin. She flopped onto the bed with a curious mix of giggle and groan.

"Just lay back and fall asleep," I soothed. "I'll set your alarm."

I did so, then began pulling off her shoes. Before I was even through, her eyes flew wide open and she hollered, "No, not the socks! Not the socks!"

My hands shot back defensively. "I wasn't going to. Just your shoes."

Already succumbing again to the alcohol she had so heavily plied, Cosmina still managed to paw at me. "I just want to feel good," she mumbled pathetically. "I need a man to make me feel good. My socks are on."

I didn't know what she was talking about, but she was drunk enough where it didn't matter. I placed her hands at her sides and kindly said, "You don't need a man. The trick is to make yourself happy first, then find someone to share it with."

Her response was snoring. I tip-toed the hell out of there.

MONTE CARLO
MONACO

MONTE CARLO was exciting for several reasons, the least of which was its reputation for glamor. I had a chance to sample such wares in a fully and even unexpected manner. Of more import than all the fun was the easing of tensions with Cosmina. Not all of them, of course. Cosmina was far too insidious for full resolution; agenda would yet rear its ugly head.

Wind Surf had called upon Monaco before. That day had started with a wonderful treat, one of the earliest salvos in Cosmina's shock and awe campaign. Having been granted a free helicopter flight over the French Riviera, Cosmina passed it on to me. When asked why, she had spoken effusively for several minutes before finally concluding that 'she can do things for me.'

I had never been on a helicopter ride, and it was quite an experience. It's one thing to walk up to the small, bubble-shaped craft and another to actually be allowed to buckle up. The lady beside me, a middle-aged and rather portly passenger from *Surf*, joked sourly, "Seat belts aren't going to help us when we go down." Rather, I assumed she was joking. The future would prove otherwise. The voice of the pilot cut her off, reverberated snugly within my headphones. If only they had been trained on him alone.

Before I knew it, we were rising. The ascent from the pad was straight up, if not particularly smooth. The lady beside me grappled my hand the very second we left ground. Up we rose, higher and higher, until we topped every high rise condominium, every cliff, and every high rise condominium on a cliff. The ride became extremely smooth. It was unlike any of my previous flying experiences, whether in a jetliner or an ultralight, for we were not propelled through the air: we just hung there. The impression of hanging was distinct, as if the rotors above weren't moving at all, but actually tethered to the very sky. Below us stretched the city, one of the richest cultural communities on the planet, as well as simply just one of the richest. The splendor of education and wealth shone brilliantly in the soft Mediterranean sun as nothing less than a clean-cut bar of platinum. The sea filled in the rest of the view, splendid and blue.

We quickly passed above all the towns of Monaco, which merged together into one giant bowl of culture tumbling into the sea. First we flew east for a quick jaunt over the Italian border to play with the mountains of San Remo. Then back westward we flew, over the Cote d'Azur past Nice, Cannes, even as far as St. Tropez. I thought it was all simply mesmerizing.

My neighbor most definitely did not. As the pilot narrated points of interest, her voice awkwardly cut him off by declaring, "I don't want any heroics."

The pilot wisely ignored her, then banked the helicopter in a dramatic spin. Below us yawned the stunning aquamarine of the sea. The hooklike, rocky spur upon which rested the Museum of Oceanography was fully visible and most enchanting. Unfortunately I couldn't admire it for, somehow, despite her seatbelt, the lady beside me managed to throw her entire body onto me.

"We're going down!" she cried, "Oh Lord, Jesus Christ protect me! We're going down!"

"We're not going down," I said, rather irritably. She was ruining the moment. The helicopter leveled and continued back towards Monte Carlo. Not a moment too soon, it seems, for the lady was about to have a heart attack.

"When we go down," she said in huff, "I don't want any heroics."

I watched her, marveling as she verily fanned herself to avoid over-heating with emotion.

"No heroics?"

"Save yourself," she panted. "Honestly, you're younger and have a full life in front of you. Don't try to save me."

No worries there, I thought to myself. Why the hell did she take this very expensive tour if she was afraid of heights?

"Really," she continued. "I've made peace with this life."

Maybe you should start making peace with everybody else around you, I thought acidly.

"I'm prepared to meet my maker."

She wouldn't shut up. Is this how everybody felt when I wouldn't let a bad joke die? I resolved to work on that. Then she hurled her camera at me and cried, "I can't do it! Please, please, take photos! I need pictures. Oh, please take photos of the view. Just don't take a picture of me dying. I don't want anyone to see my last, horrible moments in this world."

"I'm sure we'll be just fine," I said with more kindness than I felt.

"Take a picture of that there—that pretty boat—hurry before it's gone! Oh, this is so horrible. No, not from there, young man, there's too much glare on the window. Wait, what are you doing? Don't you dare take my picture! You want my children to see me like this? Don't you care about my children? Oh! Oh!"

Though the helicopter's rise had been uneven, the landing was smooth and instant—and not a moment too soon. One more minute and I was going to beat the woman with her own camera.

***

Crazy helicopter lady's overreaction, though annoying, was harmless. One must expect unreasonable behavior from passengers because they are people. People are dumb. The next passenger to create havoc over Monte Carlo was not unreasonable. Nor was he prone to overreaction, though he caused plenty of it. For crew, too, are people. That Cosmina was involved in an epic overreaction was not surprising. For Francois to get involved was.

The drama began a full week before Monte Carlo was again a port of call. Francois personally asked both Fabrice and I to work with Cosmina regarding some 'special' passenger. When we arrived to her tiny office, Cosmina was so stressed that she hadn't time for her usual preening. Her plumage was already plucked.

"They call him Crazy Al," Cosmina explained, nervously tapping a photograph on her desk. Her feet also rapped a tune on her chair. I'd never seen anyone so in need of a cigarette in my life.

"Sounds like a used car salesman," I replied.

In Cosmina's tiny office, space was tight. While leaning over her for a better look, I accidentally pushed into Fabrice. He pantomimed being thrown aside, then 'came at me' with exaggerated elbows. I smiled. Cosmina hissed.

"Looks like a used car salesman," I continued after seeing the photo. Crazy Al wore an over-the-top suit of bold pink, including a matching fedora. It was difficult to ascertain where the photo was taken, other than in a crowd. Trying to lighten her mood, I joked, "For the best deals, call Crazy Al on the duck phone!"

She was not amused.

"*I 'ave nevair sold automobiles*," Fabrice agreed, shrugging.

"He's not a damn car salesman!" Cosmina snarled. "He's a high roller."

Seeing us both staring at her expectantly, she ruffled her feathers angrily and squawked, "A high roller! Don't you guys know what a high roller is? What the hell?"

"Whoa, chill," I soothed, holding up my hands. "I

lived in Las Vegas. Of course I know what a high roller is. But I don't understand what that has to do with the *Surf*."

"You lived in Las Vegas?" Cosmina blurted, eyes widening. Squealing with delight, she lunged from her seat to plant a big kiss right on my lips. Fabrice clapped his hands in celebration. Now it was my turn to be unamused.

"What was that all about?" I gently pushed her back into her seat, trying to act like I was used to women throwing themselves at me.

Though not gone, Cosmina's nerves had been soothed enough to answer with a wriggle of hope louder than the rhythm of stress. She explained, "Crazy Al is a high roller from Las Vegas. He doesn't look like it, but he's rich."

"Oh, he looks like it all right," I said. "Flamboyance is part of the game. So why are you so stressed? What's up?"

"As part of some big jackpot, a Las Vegas casino gave him a free cruise to Monte Carlo. If he raves about it, the casino will do it again, maybe a lot. It's on me to make sure his Casino experience is perfect, or I'm in big trouble. Francois specifically ordered me to do whatever it takes to show him a good time."

"*Ooh la la*," Fabrice breathed lasciviously.

Cosmina glared at him. "So I need your help making sure he'll like it."

"*Both of us? Ooh la la!*" Fabrice repeated more energetically, this time erupting in laughter. Before Cosmina utterly destroyed him, he pantomimed surrender.

In fact, Crazy Al caused consternation throughout much of the ship. The ship's casino, in particular, was all up in arms. The manager, Dimitar, was a young Bulgarian who had just moved into his management position. He felt utterly unqualified to entertain a man of Crazy Al's magnitude. The night before the cruise was to even begin, Dimitar kept me up until midnight poring over every little detail. 'Are the stakes high enough? Too high? Should we only have men dealers? Or do they have women dealers in Vegas, dressed sexy?'

Inevitably the fateful cruise began. During the days, when the casino was closed, Dimitar fretted. During the nights, when the casino remained empty, Dimitar freaked. For the small casino did, indeed, remain empty. Gambling had never been a big draw for the *Wind Surf*, necessitating only a handful of gambling tables and a roulette wheel. Dimitar kept them all open, all night—much to the consternation of the dealers. But dealers were cruise ship employees, so they had little say about being forced to work an extra forty hours that week, unpaid. The nights were very long and very boring, for Crazy Al did not make an appearance.

The night before *Wind Surf* reached Monte Carlo, Cosmina and I were sitting at our usual table at the Compass Rose. I sipped an adult beverage, whereas she chain-smoked cigarettes. To our surprise, Francois approached.

"May I join you?" he asked, toting a snifter of cognac.

"Of course!" I said, gesturing to a chair. Cosmina, lost in a cloud of smoke, appeared equally lost in a cloud of thought. She hadn't even noticed the hotel director's arrival. Francois set his drink upon the table, rattled his golden bracelets to set them straight, and leaned back. He watched Cosmina ignoring him for a long moment. Finally he took his glasses off and, with a great deal of poise, lightly asked if she would grant us a moment alone.

"Cosmina?" he repeated gently.

"What?" she snapped irritably. Only then did she realize who she was speaking to. Her cigarette dropped from slack lips, flaring as it struck the table. Reflexively trying to hide her faux-pas, she scooped the hot ashes into her palm. She hid her grimace as poorly as her surprise. But Francois, always unflappable, merely raised an eyebrow. Cosmina hastily excused herself, nearly tripping in her rush to escape. Watching her go, Francois finally cracked a smile.

"She's had a rough week," he said. "As has Dimitar."

"He has," I agreed. "I heard that last night Crazy Al made an appearance sometime after midnight. He played a few hands and left. Poor Dimitar actually woke me up to take a look at the casino, wondering if he'd overlooked something obvious."

"So he informed me," Francois agreed. "Thank you for obliging him. It's not your responsibility to help in this, and it's appreciated. I was informed by Cosi that you have lived in Las Vegas. May I, too, ask your opinion? Do you think we're doing something wrong?"

"Not at all," I replied. After a moment of thought, I suggested, "I suspect it's because he's alone. High rollers in Vegas come in two types. There are the serious gamblers who are quiet and focused. Many of them work private salons and high limit areas secured from the crowds. But Crazy Al wouldn't be called Crazy Al if he was one of those. He wouldn't wear a pink suit and pink fedora. No, he's the other type. He's a showman. He's used to being in the thick of things. He wants the action from a crowd: the admiration, the noise, the excitement. But I don't know what you can do about that. Our casino is pretty quiet."

Francois nodded thoughtfully.

"We can make that happen," he finally said. "After

Monte Carlo tomorrow there's only one more night. I'll arrange a casino-themed party. I'll get him a crowd."

"Preferably drunk," I suggested. "Babes will no doubt help."

Francois smiled, "The former will not be a problem. I'm in control of the drink prices, after all. The PR value of this cruise will more than make up for slashing the price of drinks. His word of mouth can be a big boon for us."

Francois leaned towards me. His eyeglasses flashed. "This Crazy Al was given this cruise specifically because *Wind Surf* is the only cruise ship that overnights in Monte Carlo. We must impress him. Cosmina is capable, but in this she's out of her depth. She's prone to panic. Further, she has no experience wooing elite clientele. You do. I need your help. I want the two of you to scout out the Casino during the day. A dry run. I don't want any surprises."

Oh, but there were surprises. Big, nasty surprises.

***

Monte Carlo was extremely dense. It had that 'houses stacked on houses' vibe one expected from the Mediterranean, but everything was shockingly modern: all clean lines of steel and glass and chrome. The rocky escarpment upon which the small city clung seemed jarringly out of place. Also appearing out of place was the prince's Palace. It sprawled over a huge escarpment overlooking the harbor, looking like it was built in the 13th century—which it was, in part. Of course, not modern does not imply not awesome.

The monarchy itself, however, was completely modern. His Serene Highness Albert II, Prince of Grimaldi

—as well as a laundry list of titles numbering over two dozen—was not merely a figurehead, but actually involved in daily politics. Monaco was one of just three places so. Being American, I was curious about if, and how, they established checks and balances. Turns out the prince proposes the laws and the National Council votes them in. No autocratic dictator, here.

The royalty of Monaco were interesting folks. Prince Reinier III, who just stepped down in 2005, had famously married the American actress Grace Kelly. Their son, Prince Albert, was equally a celebrity. For years he eschewed marriage in favor of a slew of gorgeous, accomplished women. Rumors of his actually being homosexual were not denied, and the people of Monaco loved him even more for it. Whether gay or not, he was the last in one of the world's longest reigning monarchies, so he needed an heir. Sometimes you gotta do what you gotta do. So he married and did his duty. Ultimately it was revealed that he even fathered children out of wedlock. Gay and not gay, through it all, Prince Albert II remained one of the world's most beloved leaders.

In the late morning, Cosmina and I departed *Wind Surf*, intent on our reconnaissance. On the gangway, Yoyo was taking photographs of passengers. That was a good idea. His choice of a backdrop was a bad idea. He chose mooring lines and a dumpster. Ardin would have pulled his hair out. I spun the lad around 180 degrees to reveal a splendid view of the harbor and Casino rising above. With a pat on the head, I said, "Time to learn."

We walked up the ramped street that circled the harbor. It did not seem far, but that was an optical illusion. By the time we reached the top of the cliffs upon which the luxury rested, we were anything but. It was not a hard climb, but not one you wish to undertake in pressed finery and expensive shoes. Cosmina reaffirmed her intention to arrange a limousine.

Eventually we crossed through a tunnel beneath a high-rise hotel. This street was more than just a daily thoroughfare for the locals: it was also the route of the famed Monaco Formula 1 Grand Prix. The race was utterly unlike the Indianapolis 500—the only equally famous auto race—wherein the vehicles raced in an enclosed track. Once a year the regular streets of Monte Carlo became one of the most challenging auto race courses on Earth. Over 100,000 guests from all over the world gathered to watch. Monaco was all sorts of cool.

Then we ascended up to the fabled Casino Square. Around a magnificent series of fountains rose three grand structures, each marvelous and Baroque: the Casino, Hôtel de Paris, and Hôtel Hermitage. All seemed somehow disdainful of each other, as if offended to be constructed with another in mind. All had been built with a purpose to keep Monaco in the tourist race against Cannes and Nice. It worked. The Casino, though originally merely a mansion beside the two lofty hotels, had since been enlarged five times.

Alas, Cosmina and I were not allowed into the Casino. With a sniff at our street clothes, the doorman informed us that entry was black tie only. He snobbishly commented that the other casino—spoken with another sniff—would be more appropriate for us. With a mix of amusement and annoyance, we walked to the nearby American Casino, so named because it featured slot machines. The consolation prize was not impressive. Vegas had easily a hundred small casinos with more machines.

We visited the famed Café de Paris to ruminate. Our

bums settled into chairs of molded semi-translucent white plastic and our elbows leaned upon glass tables supported by neon blue glowing columns. It was an ultramodern contrast to the Baroque canopy overhead. We paid a premium for such grandeur, however. The drinks were hideously expensive. The Montecristo cigar I bought at the nearby tobacco shop cost less than my martini!

"There's a ton of awesomeness in Monte Carlo," I said, blowing a puff of smoke up to the bronze beams above. "But gaming is his priority, so there's really only the Casino."

"Gaming?"

"Gambling," I explained. "It's a silly euphemism casinos adopted in America a long time ago to make them seem less sinful."

"That's stupid," she said. "Gambling is gambling. If you don't like it, don't do it."

"I quite agree. But America's a very conservative nation. The religious types frown upon it. Still, money talks, and now there are casinos in almost all fifty states."

"There are fifty-one states," she corrected. I let it slide. As we smoked, my face assumed an unsettled look. Cosmina picked up on it. "What?"

"Just a concern. I don't want to worry you."

"What?" she demanded, now irritated.

"It has to do with James Bond."

"Oh, God," Cosmina moaned. "Will you shut the hell up about James Bond? You're such a child!"

"I have a point to make, if you want to hear it."

"Will you promise to never, ever bring up James Bond again?"

"All right," I said with a pretend sigh. "Look, my concern is this. You've seen how James Bond gambles in the movies, right? He's being all suave, while spectators quietly watch and admire. Vegas is nothing like that. I'm a little worried this Crazy Al guy might not be interested in what Monte Carlo has to offer. It's impressive in so many ways: museums, art, gardens, sports, culture. But when it comes to the gaming scene and flaunting wealth, Monte Carlo pales in comparison to Las Vegas."

"Oh, please!" she said, rolling her eyes at the absurdity of the idea. "Less money in Monaco?"

"All I'm saying is that more money is flaunted in Vegas. The casinos are just as fine as this one, but also much bigger. And there's dozens of them in a row, all trying to out-do each other. And, I mean, look at that!"

I pointed to the parking lot before the Casino. Numerous tourists were taking photos. I had initially thought they were after the fountains stoically streaming everywhere, but they were intent on the cars.

"A couple dozen high-end BMWs and Mercedes," I said. "Two Porsches and two Ferraris. That's it."

"Oh, Vegas is so rich," Cosmina mocked. "With a new Ferrari in every garage?"

My lips quivered. I couldn't help saying it: "You just quoted Pierce Brosnan in Goldeneye."

Her face turned dark and splotchy. I immediately threw my hands up as apology.

"Sorry. Look, Ferraris may cost a quarter of a million dollars, but the Wynn Casino sells them inside the casino. They also have a classic Ferrari museum, by the way. The Palazzo sells Lamborghinis. I used to park next to one every day at an average coffee shop in an average part of town. Call us nouveau riche, whatever you want, but in Vegas it takes more than just being in a famous place. If Monte Carlo is going to dazzle Crazy Al, the inside of the

Casino better be awesome."

"It will be," Cosmina promised. But the seed of doubt already sprouted upon her brow. I should have kept my mouth shut.

***

Cosmina asked me to join her for the send off of Crazy Al. In fact, she even asked me to tail him throughout the night. When I commented sarcastically that I'm not into spy stuff, she nearly hit me. But the hour was nigh, and so was Al. This was it. Cosmina was nervous as a tick.

We waited on the pier outside *Wind Surf* in our black best. I wore a black double-breasted suit over a black shirt with a silver tie. For being so distraught, Cosmina certainly dressed daringly: a black halter top above a black skirt barely clinging very, very low on her hips. She exposed more middle than if she'd been in a bikini. Her black hair was slicked back, her lips red. Apparently my speech about flaunting had taken root. Waiting with us was a black limousine.

Then he arrived. The man of the hour, the high roller. Crazy Al.

He didn't look so crazy. Al was a middle-aged man with receding hairline and oval glasses, chin gently cleft, bearing gently swaggered. His dress was appropriately sedate for the night: a black jacket of crushed velvet over a blue shirt. A yellow tie dropped from his neck to pool upon his thick middle. In short, he really did look like a used car salesman.

But he strode off the gangway with nothing short of aplomb. Though he seemed a big man overall, he was not: Al stood only as tall as Cosmina. But his voice seemed big, too. He boomed, "Ready to go?"

"Everything is ready, Mr. Wilson," Cosmina said, snapping haughtily for the driver to get the door.

"None of that," Al said, opening the door himself. He thumbed towards the interior and said, "Come on."

Cosmina looked like a deer caught in headlights. "I beg your pardon?"

"You're going to show me what Monte Carlo's Casino has to offer."

Cosmina's eyes darted from side to side, focusing on everything and nothing. Methinks Cosmina finally found a First World fish too big to try hauling in. Al casually added, "Bring as many as you want."

"P-people?" Cosmina stammered. She hurled herself onto my arm and asked, "My boyfriend? He lived in Vegas, too!"

"Sure, sure. Any more women? How 'bout that redhead from the gift shop?"

"Nina is working tonight," Cosmina lied, quickly regaining her usual self.

"No gaggle of spa girls? Nuthin? At least get me a midget or sumthin'! No? It's all right. I'm on vacation, anyway. I'm here to relax. You two, let's see what there is to see."

The drive up the pier to the Casino was not a long one, but rich with view. Upon the harbor gently bobbed billions of dollars worth of yachts, each gleaming silver with moonlight. Embracing the circle of harbor we looked up in awe: above the dark, fuzzy shadows of palm gardens rose the tops of condominiums; above their modern roofs rose rugged cliffs; above 'the Rock' rustled a literal forest of garden and, finally, above all loomed the crenelated House of Grimaldi. The ancient fortifications were lit to great effect, outlining individual archways and towers.

"Nice," Al commented, nodding in approval. But mostly he made small talk with me about living in Vegas.

We topped the rise and the view expanded. Moonlight hummed the sea a subtle, electric hue. The cliffs were splotches of black shot through with green veins of road. Too soon the limo stopped beneath the illuminated façade of the Casino, all elegant brass appointments and sculpture-laden niches beneath the softly feminine curves of the Belle Époque-style roof.

Exiting the limousine, we took in the surroundings. The gardens embracing Casino Square were minimally lit. Most light emanated from the many fountains. Each clean stream of water was cleverly under lit with blue to create sharply geometric patterns of arcing lasers. Silhouettes of young, smoking couples sat upon stone balustrades.

"Very nice," Al said, impressed. But before Cosmina could relax, he continued, "Beautiful, but quite minimal, isn't it? Brian, you ever take Cosi to the Strip? No? Oh, you gotta see it! Neon everywhere, enough to light up the desert for a hundred miles! The beam atop Luxor even shoots into space."

"Surely not as classy as this...?" Cosmina prompted.

"Oh, this is classy all right," Al agreed. "The gardens remind me of Wynn. Smaller, of course. These fountains are nice, but man you should see the fountains of Bellagio at night. Unlike any other in the world, you know." After another glance around, he added, "This reminds me of Paris."

"You've been to Paris?" Cosmina asked admiringly. Then, "Oh, of course you have."

"No, I meant Paris casino," Al corrected. "In Vegas. This looks a bit like it. This is a lot smaller, of course. Less statues, too."

"Modeled after this," Cosmina said, taking a stab in the dark. A worthy effort, if untrue.

"At least the skyline isn't dominated by a fake Eiffel Tower," I said, attempting to aid the reeling Cosmina. "Everything here is the real deal... at least in that regard. I love how Vegas casinos are inspired by the great places of Europe. They do a great job evoking Paris, Venice, Luxor. But it's even better to see the original."

Al gave up a nod, but no more. Glanced at the parking lot, he asked, "Nobody rich here tonight? Too bad, I was hoping to make some money."

Noting the two Ferraris and a Bentley, Cosmina gurgled a bit. Seeing her wilt before our very eyes, Al smiled broadly and cheerfully offered his arm to her. "Come on. I'm not really the ignoramus you think but are trying to hide. Let's see what this place's got."

"You... you mean go in with you?" she blurted, shocked. "Oh, no. I couldn't! It wouldn't be appropriate at all."

"Of course it is," he said easily, wagging his extended elbow. "Come on."

Highly dubious, Cosmina took his arm with the utmost reluctance, prompting Al to comment, "Jeez, I'm not a leper or anything."

"You, too," he said to me. Glancing me over, he added, "Big guy in black on black. I love it! You can play my bodyguard. I'll pretend to be the villain in a James Bond movie. Wish you had a hat. You know, something that could cut somebody's head off."

Cosmina nearly swooned.

We worked our way into the Monte Carlo Casino's gaming room. One cannot help but be struck numb by the elegant decor. Every wall hosted a gargantuan masterpiece of art framed in gold, every flowing archway gilded and filigreed in gold, every column with capital of gold. Crystal chandeliers dripped from the ceiling with the perfect symmetry of a drop of water. Cosmina sighed deeply at the majesty, finally relaxing. Her fears were eased, for this was an undeniably gorgeous and awe-inspiring chamber.

If only it were so.

I immediately spied several locations where the proverbial curtain was pulled aside to expose the truth. Tucked into otherwise ornate corners were cornices broken and battered, revealing they were merely molded chicken wire coated in plaster. Two or more columns were similarly denuded, showing they weren't actually marble, but painted to look so. It was all impressive but, ultimately, even less real than the Eiffel Tower in Las Vegas. Crazy Al didn't make a living gambling by being unobservant. He, too, saw the flaws. Disappointedly he noted, "Less marble in this whole building than in just a lobby back home. Like, an average lobby."

Cosmina winced at the words. She slumped, lost in visions of her career's imminent demise.

"But we're here to gamble!" Crazy Al boomed enthusiastically. His demeanor immediately changed. He hunched slightly to evoke a sinister bearing and began glowering at everyone. He had become the villain. Offering his arm again to Cosmina, he sneered, "Time to take over the world, my pretty."

There were only half a dozen tables in the wide, open space: all roulette. Despite this being a Friday night, only three were open. Following Al's example, I stepped forward as tall and imposingly as I could. Overtly checking the corners, I gave him a surly nod that all was clear.

Al smoothly entered the game that seemed the most interesting. This was a distinction I was unable to make. Nobody made a sound, not the handful of players and certainly not the dealer. The skinny lad just stood there in his tuxedo, stiff as a board. Occasionally he glanced around smugly.

The energy in the Casino wasn't low, it was absent. There was no joy of winning, no frustration of loss. Nothing. Certainly there was no gaming. Perhaps Vegas casinos were onto something with the label after all. Al played perhaps twenty minutes, immersed in his role of James Bond villain. I stood behind him, arms folded in a pose of defiance. Cosmina nailed her role as the disposable girlfriend: silent and brooding, seductively working her cigarettes. But then, that came naturally to her. I found Al's exaggerated mannerisms of ultra suave indifference amusing, but seeing the very same on every other player's face made the whole thing moot.

"I can hear a pin drop in here," Al finally groused. He scooped up his winnings and turned away, though not before flipping a hundred Euro chip at the dealer and saying, "Here, boy, buy yourself a smile."

He cashed his chips, revealing that during the silent play he had won over a thousand dollars. Pocketing his winnings, he turned to me, grinned, and said lamely, "Well, that didn't work. We gave it a shot. But it'll sound better when I tell my friends about it. Thanks for playing along."

Alas, though the limousine was waiting for us, it was blocked behind a tour bus. Cosmina stared at the oh-so-slowly disembarking passengers, horror growing upon her features by the moment. We weren't going anywhere for awhile. Turning her back on both Al and myself, Cosmina staggered towards a fountain. She was freaking out and unable to hide it any longer. She stared into the shooting waters longingly.

Al elbowed me and said, "I don't think your girlfriend is having a good time."

"She rarely does," I quipped.

"Gosh, I hope she doesn't try to drown herself in the fountain."

WIND SURF
MEDITERRANEAN

"RELAX," CRAZY Al said to the obviously panicked Cosmina. "Just not my scene, that's all. I pretty much knew it wouldn't be. I gamble for a living, baby. I'm just here for fun. Relax."

But Cosmina was anything but relaxed. She sucked down three cigarettes and dropped the butts into the fountain. I grimaced deeper and deeper as each sizzled into the gorgeous waters. Cosmina certainly didn't care: she looked certain that Francois was going to put her head on a pike.

"I think a good restaurant is in order," I suggested. "Personally, I find nothing more pleasant than a good meal, a good drink, and a good view."

"Le Grill!" Cosmina shrieked in her urgency to supply an answer. She was so hurried that she gave herself the hiccups. Between gulps of air, she explained, "Top of... awp!... the Hôtel... awp!... de Paris."

"Sure, let's go," Al said. "Please calm down. You're supposed to hyperventilate after you see me naked."

I was really beginning to like this guy. Cosmina, as ever, was unsure of him. She stammered in reply, "W-hat? Do you have any idea how expensive it is? Royalty goes there!"

"Don't worry, I'm buying," Al soothed. "Who wants to dine alone? Brian's right, but he forgot the importance of good company."

Upon entering the hotel, one is greeted with the rotunda. The elegance of the foyer was somehow far richer than anything we saw in the Casino. Perhaps it was the decor of cream and buff, rather than painted gold. Perhaps it was that amazing, circular sky light. Up, up above the mezzanine and its bronze filigreed railings, up above the cascading and intertwining arches of rich cream, up higher still, was a huge polychromatic window. We passed beneath the marble and ascended to the eighth floor.

The views from Le Grill were magnificent in the extreme. Outside, balcony diners looked down at all the grandeur of Casino Square. We did, too, for the walls were more window than not. The ceiling was entirely not: it had retracted over the whole restaurant to allow unfettered access to the stars. Row upon row of tables hosted tuxedoed patrons basking in the moonlight. We hoped dinner would equal the atmosphere.

Dinner began well. We ordered an appetizer of sea scallops pan-seared and sliced thin. Each hearty disk was topped with a mound of paper-thin sliced black truffles. Al skipped the appetizer, commenting, "I don't like truffles. They smell kinda like panties."

"Precisely why I find them so endearing," I said. Cosmina made a little choking sound, but found solace in her plate.

Afterwards we were all given an egg. Yes, an egg. Hardboiled, the top had been exactingly sliced off and replaced with a mound of chilled scrambled eggs and shaved truffles. We had no idea what it was, but it exceeded the sum of its parts. It was strangely delicious.

Suitably emboldened by the beginning, Al ordered some wine. He liked Montrachet and encouraged us to partake liberally. We did so, and soon a second bottle followed. The second offering was brighter and sharper. Cosmina and I enjoyed it, though Al rebuked it for being unrounded. While waiting interminably for the entrees, Cosmina and Al shared cigarettes. We all continued to drink and, far more importantly, shared laughter. Things were improving mightily—until the entrees arrived. Three waiters strode forward, immaculate in their black-tie attire, wearing all the arrogance of mankind on their faces. Each carried a small wooden platter, above which hung our meat, gouged by meathooks and swinging from metal chains. The presentation was strangely barbaric for such a refined place. They delivered the items in unison, then backed off with all the flair of ballet.

My duck breast was deliciously spiced, but slightly overcooked. Cosmina and Al both ordered the rack of lamb, which was unpleasantly and deeply charred. In suitably French manner, the small amount of bold sauces, both sweet and savory, obscured any remaining subtleties of the meat's inherent flavor. Everything was good, but nothing was great... barring the odd presentation, I guess.

The dessert, however, was a travesty. The soufflés were awful. Rather than being a light and airy poof of baked egg and sugar, they were just a mound of ooze. Cosmina and Al had both ordered the Grand Marnier soufflé, but the magic ingredient was not integrated into the dish in any way. Rather, it was dumped upon it. We all stared, shocked, as the bland-faced waiter glugged more and more liqueur over the top, effectively washing the pile of ooze into a puddle. My pistachio soufflé was better in flavor, though similarly lacking in the delicate texture that made soufflés so divine. The accompanying sauce of stewed cherries was so delicious, however, that Cosmina skipped her dessert in favor of slurping it all up.

Ultimately, Le Grill was akin to Monte Carlo's Casino: much more reputation than production. Luckily it only cost $1,400.

Al wanted to walk back to the ship, so staggering home we went. Cosmina carried her shoes and trod barefoot all the way down to the dark harbor. The waves rippled softly against the concrete pier, soothing and delicate. Al began obsessing over the boats. Not the million dollar yachts, but rather the small wooden tenders. With a drunken howl, he staggered off the path and thumped up against a rowboat resting on blocks. With great, comical effort Crazy Al humped himself into the boat—and immediately began roaring that the squall was coming and it was time to batten down the hatches. Suddenly, somehow, all three of us were in the boat, high and dry, yet screaming for our lives.

Who knows how long we romped in the various beached and moored boats. At one point Pirate Al and Cosmina faced off against me in separate boats, hurling work gloves, rags, and even ropes at each other. At another point Al stood tall and bold as Washington crossing the Delaware, while Cosmina and I rowed imaginary oars and shivered in fantastic winds. Perhaps most special of all was Crazy Al's dramatic death scene. While Cosmina stretched a hand out to him from a rowboat, he splayed across the concrete to reenact Leonardo DiCaprio's romantic end in Titanic.

By far, we enjoyed that walk back more than anything else of the night. Fun is where you make it!

**

The casino party that Francois threw for Crazy Al was a huge success. There was a reason casinos gave free booze to the players, after all. Dozens of guests packed the *Surf's* tiny casino, each laughing louder than the other. I attended only long enough to ensure Al was having fun. I was intent on an equally big party; one of a different kind, one in the strangest locale I'd ever debauched at sea. We've all seen the docking ropes rise up from the pier to disappear into those dark, mysterious holes cut into the hull. What lay beyond? The mooring deck, of course, and the night's real party.

This was an area packed tightly with big machinery, smoothed in motion by copious lubings of grease and smoothed in contour by copious layers of paint. Most equipment was covered with tarps. One corner was sectioned off with hanging sheets, billowing like the sails so high above, for we were running under sail this night.

I'd been on mooring decks of the big ships several times and knew they rumbled fiercely. Even half a dozen decks up, the shuddering of engines skipped silverware and even crockery right off tables. But under sail, *Wind Surf* purred through the water. Though mere feet above the propellors, not a shimmy was felt.

All crew were invited, but most were unavailable during the selected hours of night. This party was thrown for the able seamen; the stalwart few who did so much for so many, yet remained unseen and unappreciated. Thusly small, the party was nonetheless lively. I'd never before seen a crew party so narrowly targeted. It was a most welcome sign of gratitude.

From the bar I watched people cut loose. There was no dance floor, per se, but only moderately open areas punctuated by winches, capstans, and the like decorated with party lights. Though nearly all danced, few had a partner because everyone was male. Despite this painful lack of women, Hawaiian shirts flashed in the disco light, bodies spun in strobe. Eventually I spied a lone female, Janie, being fairly worshipped by an admiring throng of Asian men. The entirety of the crew was Asian, in fact.

The song changed from Michael Jackson's 'Thriller' to House of Pain's party classic 'Jump Around'. The crowd thinned to reveal none other than the chief officer, Emmet. Dancing alone, he most definitely moved like a white guy. But oh, was he having a ball! With every shout of 'Jump! Jump! Jump!' in the song, he leapt into the air goofily, pulling his knees up high as they would go.

"It's good to see him having fun," a voice called. I turned to see Barney beside me, also watching.

The song came to an end, replaced by one slower. Most of the men began congregating over beers, to catch their breath and grumble over Janie's choice of partner. She had dismissed her cult with a grateful laugh and wave, and was now grooving with a particularly robust-looking Filipino. Though she didn't know it at the time, that dance sealed her fate.

As Emmet approached, Barney excused himself and stalked past the lone, dancing couple.

"Care to join me, Emmet?" I asked, gesturing towards the windows in the stern.

We hopped up onto a mooring winch; a giant spool of thread, really, with a thick tarp covering the reel. We stared out to sea. Few passengers ever experience the sea so close to the propellors. From this vantage at this hour, the wake was all: a vast, churning and chalky white extending into darkness. It was a strange dichotomy seeing such reaching turbulence so very close, yet feeling nothing. We stared into the chaos, mesmerized, silent.

I really liked Emmet. He was a handsome and genial man. But more than that, I was impressed with his dedication and his enthusiasm through all the hard work that entailed. Though chief officer and second in command of *Wind Surf*, he spent more time in a boiler suit than in whites. Emmet only differentiated the days by whether he was covered in grease or in paint.

Patting the tarp beneath our bums, I asked, "So we're sitting on... halyards?"

"These are mooring lines."

"What's the difference?"

"Halyards are used for rigging a ship: raising a flag, things like that. The term is specific to sailing vessels like *Wind Surf*. It means 'hauling yards', as in yards of canvas. Ever see pirates in the movies pulling ropes? Those are halyards."

"I only see pirates ripping sails by using a knife to slow their descent from the masts. That's on my bucket list to do before I die."

"I wouldn't try it here if I were you," Emmet said with a smile. He pointed to various giant winches and reels of rope, through which the dancing resumed. "Every ship has mooring lines. They're very heavy, so seamen throw out little ropes to people ashore. The dockers haul on those little ropes, which are attached to the mooring lines in this and other winches."

"Those little ropes called painter lines?"

"No, painters are specific to smaller boats like a tender or life raft. Painter lines are no longer than the boat itself to avoid fouling the propeller. The ropes seamen throw to shore have different names, depending upon the order in which they are used. The first rope, the head line, warps the bow to the pier."

"You already lost me," I admitted.

"It's very simple when you don't use nautical terms," Emmet explained with remarkable patience. "They have different names only so we know which step of the process we're in. The first rope hauls the bow of the ship—the head—towards the pier. The head of the ship gets the head line. Simple. The second rope is called the spring line, which secures the stern to the pier. It goes on from there."

"So warping isn't just a playful Star Trek term?"

"Warping is the act of hauling on ropes to move the vessel, usually against the wind or in a dead calm."

"I see. So if I was docking a small boat I would attach a line at the front—the head line—and pull on it to bring the boat snug with the dock—warping. Then I would attach a line at the back—the spring line—to keep the boat firmly alongside the dock."

"Exactly. With ships the warping is done by machinery, of course," he said. Then, with a devilish smile, he added, "Those mooring winches have a first counter pressure medium exerted by each fender. A second pressure medium is relieved when the pressure thereof exceeds the pressure of the first medium by discharging the second pressure medium to a pressure relief tank, all without effecting a recoil action on the fender."

"Well duh," I said, quickly hiding behind my beer. Acknowledging my painful lack of understanding, I switched tactics. "This is the area so prone to fires, isn't it? As I recall, the big fire way back on *Carnival Ecstasy* started here."

"Not exactly," Emmet corrected. "It started in the laundry room with an unsupervised welding operation. They accidentally ignited all the lint lying around. Then the fire moved to the mooring deck and lit up the ropes. Once that happens, you're in big trouble. Polypropylene burns incredibly hot and fast; far more than hemp. So, yes, this area is particularly prone to fire. Notice that though this is a party, nobody is smoking."

"Why do they use such flammable ropes, then?"

"These Dyneema ropes look like any plain old rope," Emmet explained, "but are strong as steel cable. Same diameter, but only one-seventh the weight."

"Wow," I said, blinking in surprise. "So Dyneema ropes go through the hawsepipes and into the ship?"

Emmet's face pinched to indicate surprise and, of course, that I was wrong. This prompted me to admit, "Hey, I'm throwing out every nautical term I've ever heard until one sticks. At least I didn't say 'shiver me timbers'."

"You are close," Emmet admitted. "The hawsepipe is specific to the anchor because it is a steel pipe reinforced to handle the wear of the anchor chain. But yes, conceptually there are similarities between the hawsepipe and the rollers here on the mooring deck."

"I only know it because Captain Turner said he 'came up through the hawsepipe'."

Emmet laughed. "He said that, did he? It's true. He's had a wonderful career."

"How about you?"

"My beginning was also as a seaman," he said. Sipping beer and smiling with the memory, he continued, "I volunteered one summer on a windjammer—out of Holland, of course. It was hard work. All day long, sails going up, sails going down.

"Wow," I said, astounded. "Sounds surprisingly like jobs in my hometown, too. At General Mills people drop toys in cereal boxes as they go by on the assembly line, all day long."

"Nothing like that," Emmet rebuked. "There's no sense of futility at all. Even if there was, I would gladly do it for the rush of climbing the ratlines fifty meters up under a wind strong enough to topple a man."

"You weren't worried about being blown out to sea?"

"Of course not. All sailors know to climb on the windward side of the ladder in a gale. That way the wind blows you into the ladder and not away from it, likely into the sea. But it does take a lot of strength to climb a wriggling rope ladder that far, that fast, in wind that strong."

"Captain Turner mentioned how dangerous the old sailing ships were," I agreed. "I guess that alone might be a draw for some men."

"Ships are temperamental, yes," Emmet said. "But it is more than that. A sailing ship is no more dangerous than any other mode of transportation: a car can be dangerous, or a train, or a plane. But a ship is more than a machine. She is a kindred spirit."

"But what about now? Now ships are just floating hotels."

"Not *Wind Surf*," he said crisply. "Maybe your big barge-like cruise ships too fat for ports and too weak for the high sea, but not *Wind Surf*. Big cruise ships are not of the sea. *Wind Surf* was made for the sea."

He looked at me, searching, then asked, "You do understand that, don't you?"

A squeal from the dance floor drew our attention. Barely visible in the crush of bodies, Janie was held up by the waist by her dance partner. The Asian man was surprisingly strong for his small stature. Another squeal, a giggle, a kiss. Emmet, carefully noting the distraction, took the opportunity to excuse himself. He set his half-empty beer on the winch and, like Barney before him, abruptly left the party.

I stared at the sea, neatly plowed aside afore, tumbling broadly abaft. How many of these sermons had I heard since signing onto this, the world's largest sailing vessel? Four? First Ardin the photographer, then Captain Turner, Fabrice, and now Emmet: all had expressed great admiration for *Wind Surf*. Not just the lady herself, but the family and tradition she represented. Each held disdain for modern mega ships. Nor could I really reproach. Big ships were growing so large that many didn't fit into the majority of ports in any given sea. No longer were cruise ships about visiting far off shores, but rather floating resorts of Vegas-like magnitude. They were awesome to behold and a joy to embark. But they were not of the sea.

Was I?

***

Three years ago I was a waiter on Carnival Cruise Lines. I worked a minimum of 80 hours a week—that is, seven days a week for many months at a time. On *Carnival Legend* I slaved 100 hours a week for 15 weeks before I stopped counting. I was so tired that rising in the morning was physically painful. I 'fondly' remember lying in my bunk, head and feet pressed against the bulkheads and curling my body around my luggage, muscles screaming at the thought of rising. Being a 'rip the Band-Aid off fast' kind of guy, I learned to grit my teeth and make that one, horrid, leap out of bed. Then, if my foreign, stranger roommate was not already standing, I could dress for work. The cabin, of course, was too small for two grown men to dress simultaneously.

But then I became an art auctioneer. Two years of hard work in that role had not led to alcoholism and back pain—well maybe a bit of the former—but to a luxurious guest cabin. It had it all: a couch, a bathtub, a desk with the little green lamp shade, and even a private balcony! Best of all was the fully-stocked and free mini bar. So much for beating the alcoholism rap. But then, we were all sailors. Everybody knows that sailors party harder than everybody else.

Ah, the sailor's life. Now that was something else. On a normal cruise ship, a big cruise ship, thousands of new faces rotate in and out every week. Not only do several dozen crew members depart ship life weekly, so do friends. Sailors continually endure the jolt of nerves that comes with total change. Most people on land experience that but rarely. Finishing high school and/or leaving for college is

212

total change and can be scary, but there's usually friends or parents to blunt the new. A sudden firing or divorce will bring total change. Worst is the loss of a loved one. These are not positive experiences and—hopefully—rare occurrences. But on ships your home literally travels the globe. Total change is constant.

Continual, total change creates an environment that skews time radically. One month on a ship may not equate one year of land life, but it comes close. There is no routine to make the days disappear, no 'same old same old', unless you're at the bottom of the food chain. Time is intense with the constant alertness of adaptation. Plus, of course, everyone is working seven days a week and you are required to find 'living' time outside of eighty hour work weeks. You focus so much on every second that you lose sight of the minute, the hour, the day; you lose the ocean for the waves. Knowing the day of the week goes first, followed soon by not even knowing the month. The first time I realized I couldn't honestly answer what month it was really freaked me out. Eventually you even stop knowing—or even caring—whether you wake up in Bermuda or the Bahamas.

But *Wind Surf* was not a 'normal' cruise ship. The passenger list was small and frequently did not even rotate out at the end of a week-long cruise. Many guests remained aboard for two or more cruises, so as to better maximize their Mediterranean experience. The crew list was downright tiny, so much that wearing multiple hats was a necessity. Replacing bodies was a more involved process which, thusly, occurred less frequently. It was small town compared to metropolis. Wouldn't routine take over, then? Wouldn't life resume a sense of normalcy?

Hardly.

To keep the total change a molten, pulpy mass of slag in which we were hammered, *Wind Surf* boasted something most unusual in the cruise world: not just ports seven days a week, but an ever rotating, randomized list of them. Pirates and even whalers had routine ports of call, but not *Wind Surf*. In the course of a seven day cruise it was not uncommon to hit five or more different nations. My job required liaising with port authorities using different languages and different currencies every day. I learned how to navigate foreign backwaters, when to lie, when to bribe, and when to do neither. By the end of the first month my head was so used to spinning I could have given a Dervish a whirl for his money.

Yet while cast adrift in total change, something was different. My employer didn't follow my performance on *Wind Surf*. There was no chance of getting fired whatsoever because they simply didn't care. And now, bereft of my original goal of Bianca, neither did I. No longer would I miss ports while struggling for something greater, no longer would I pine for something just out of reach. It was time to enjoy the playground right in front of me. After all my years at sea, I finally began to experience what landlubbers imagined working on ships was like.

In Greece alone I dined on minutes-fresh octopus at Cephalonia—not chewy at all, but delectably soft enough to cut with a fork; gazed upon the fabled home of Odysseus, the hard-sought island of Ithaca; ate kalamata olives in Kalamata itself, on the cliff-hugging streets of Monemvasia. Best of all was touring ancient Olympia. I paid homage to Zeus at the remains of his greatest temple, checking off another of the Seven Wonders of the World. More importantly, I got to run on the original playing field of the Olympics. I imagined myself kicking the ass of every competitor back in the day. Such delusions are easy when you stand nearly two feet taller than the average man of 2,800 years ago.

And Italy? I had tasted fresh cannoli on the Aeolian island of Lipari, then after dark watched lava bubble and spew sky-high from the ever fitful volcanic island of Stromboli. I climbed the steps of Taormina's fully intact Roman amphitheater, drank espresso where the compass was invented in Amalfi, gazed upon the frescoes of Rimini, and sighed over the beauty of Positano. Speaking of sighing, what prompted more than world-famous Miracle Square in Pisa? Unless Portofino, of course; there I sipped chianti just twenty feet from George Clooney's yacht. And seeing Michelangelo's David in Florence? Botticelli's Birth of Venus in nearby Uffizi Gardens would weep from jealousy. Those Florentine visits were heady stuff: on short days I only got to visit the tombs of Machiavelli, Galileo, and Dante.

Those were just the highlights from my first few months on *Wind Surf*. And—staggering to contemplate—it was only going to get better. We hadn't yet touched on France, Spain, Portugal, or Morocco. I squeezed entire days into those hours, months into those weeks, years into those months. With such overwhelming stimuli came a swelling of consciousness and, thusly, awareness. For the first time in my ship career, I was content with where I was and where I was going.

And that's when something happened. It happened in Malta, courtesy of St. Paul.

St. Paul was a Christian Apostle who brought Christianity to Malta nearly 2,000 years ago. It was kind of an accident. He was en route to Rome to be tried as a political rebel, but the ship carrying him was wrecked on the coast. As told by St. Luke in The Acts of the Apostles, the people of Malta graciously welcomed the survivors. But while a warming fire was lit, Paul was bitten by a poisonous snake. He suffered no ill effects, which the islanders took as a sign of his importance. This indirectly led to his invitation into the home of Publius, the Roman's chief man of the island, who was suffering a serious fever. Paul cured the man, who was so thrilled he converted to Christianity and became the first Bishop of Malta. That was all fine and dandy, but poor Paul continued on his not-so-merry way to Rome and a beheading.

Malta has many sites dedicated to Paul across the islands, from the rocks upon which he escaped the sea to the site of Publius' house, now home to the Cathedral of Mdina. In the capital of Valletta is the Collegiate Parish Church of St. Paul—more commonly known as St. Paul's Shipwreck Cathedral. I had been lured to the site because it was noteworthy to so very many people. By the time I left, it was noteworthy to me, too—only not for the usual reason.

I did not pay much attention to the reliquary that contained St. Paul's wrist bone or the section of marble column upon which he was beheaded. I didn't even pay much attention to the awe inspiring altar piece depicting the shipwreck, created by Paladini. Despite more noble intentions, I found myself helplessly following a blonde.

She was a dainty, pretty thing. Very fragile, but not like a porcelain doll. Definitely not that: she was no toy to be dressed and coifed and placed upon a shelf. This woman was a wildflower; slender and pleasing to the eye, but one gust away from being lost. She was alone, wandering the cathedral for all the right reasons.

Room to room I followed her. I didn't try to talk to

her, but just enjoyed the enchantment of a pretty lady who caught my eye. It was nice to enjoy the warm sensation of liking somebody without the throb of guilt ruining the moment like a migraine at a party. It was the first time I looked at a woman other than Bianca and realized there were possibilities. Maybe the ships' elasticity of time finally did me some good, after all! Eventually she left, gone forever like a pleasant scent on a passing breeze.

Alas, even if I felt no guilt, there was regret. So much for my sense of personal freedom. I was nothing if not pathetic. But we all shackle ourselves. I knew in my mind it was time to move on and enjoy the sights—I really was starting to—but I just couldn't switch off my regret that it didn't work with Bianca. My last ship, the stunning six star Seven Seas Mariner, would have been the perfect place for us to be together. I went through hell and hot water to get that ship for us. So many sights, so many opportunities, squandered because she said 'no'.

Bianca had said 'no' before because the time wasn't right. I dealt with it and tried to move forward. When I finally had to say 'no' because the time wasn't right, I was left wondering how she dealt with it. She didn't mention it at all. Not one phone call, nary an email.

My first 'no': because of the cabin, because of the ship. I couldn't provide her the better ship life I had promised, despite all my striving. I couldn't provide her the money she needed to take care of her family. That was all justified, for a man was only as good as his word. I had failed.

But the moment I said 'no', something inside me changed. Why? Because it felt like crap to say 'no'. When she said 'no,' didn't she feel like crap? Wasn't I worth it, despite all those bad jokes?

But she had said 'yes' when I gave her the ultimatum in Greece, 'yes' even to marriage. Surely she was just saying that to make me happy... but how did I really know that? I'd been so preoccupied with what I'd done, perhaps I forgot her side of things. I never actually gave her the chance to see *Wind Surf* for herself. Perhaps I wronged her.

I had learned our ships were to meet in port. Bianca was scheduled to visit Cannes while I was in Monte Carlo. Those may be in two separate nations, but they're only a hop, skip, and a jump from each other. I'd never let international borders stop us from rendezvous past. Maybe it wasn't over just yet. Once more unto the breach, dear friend, once more; or close the wall up with passion's death!

NORMAL

is an illusion.
What's normal for the spider
is chaos for the fly.

— Morticia Addams

PART 2
WHODUNIT

TRAVEL

**is to discover
that everyone is wrong
about other countries.**

— Aldous Huxley

CANNES
FRANCE

BARNEY'S RELATIVES HUGGED tightly to their small town in the Canadian Rockies. Despite invitations to his ships for years, they'd never had the temerity to try. That all changed when his mother discovered *Under the Tuscan Sun*. For the first time ever, something other than Canada had merit. She wanted to see everywhere they filmed the movie—a woman after my own cinephile heart. This included Positano, which was an hour-plus boat ride beyond our port of call, Sorrento. That was too far for unworldly folks such as Ma & Pa Barney, but not for me. Thus he asked if I would escort his family to Positano.

Cosmina was not happy at being skipped over for such an important personal favor. Barney explained that he wanted someone they would feel comfortable with—meaning if not Canadian, at least American. Like him, his parents and sister were raw-boned, folksy folks. Indeed, Barney's sister looked even more like a lumberjack than he! The weather in Positano was perfect: warm and sunny along the palm-shrouded cliffs, rainy and blotchy atop the mountain high above. We had a grand time walking upon the steep streets and sighing upon the sweet sights. As ever, I found the Amalfi Coast to be the most enchanting place on Earth.

I wanted to share with Barney's family something distinctly Italian that they could take home with them. I decided to take them to a local pizzeria—one of Italy's Top 100—to teach them the differences between something Pizza Hut and something Italian.

Though snobs may try, one cannot declare that Italian pizza is better than American pizza—or vice versa—any more than toast beats a bagel. The trunk of the pizza family tree split into two different animals. Of those parental branches—Italian and American—the latter further evolved into regional styles: New York, Detroit, Chicago, and California being the most common. Each has its own goals and merits, none being superior to another. So it is when comparing the parental branch. Though, to be fair, superiority does skew towards Italy because of America's chronic lack of quality control.

The first lesson regarded toppings. American pizza has a whole pile of them. One could spin that it is an effort to focus upon complimentary combinations of flavors, but that's bunk: it's because more is better. Thusly, American pizza can be extremely dense, whereas Italian pizzas never are. They have only one topping, and aim to perfect it. The only way in Italy to experience multiple toppings is to order the 'quattro stagioni', or 'four seasons' pizza. But four toppings does not a supreme make, for each is given its own quadrant so that flavors need not compete.

The second lesson was habits in the care and feeding of pizza, so to speak. Using a knife and fork on a slice is common, as is drizzling olive oil over it. Not just any olive oil, of course, but quality stuff. The dried red peppers familiar to American pizzerias are much to Italian taste, frequently used in the form of pepper-infused olive oil. Nobody in Italy shares the American habit of dumping powdered parmesan onto a pizza. That would horrify Italians, and rightly so, for Pizza Hut's parmesan cheese contains undisclosed amounts of ground up wood. In fact, the FDA has *no limits* on the amount of wood pulp allowed in American food—hence the superiority skewing towards Italy.

The wonderful afternoon stretched into a gorgeous night. The return boat ride watching the sun set past the cliffs of Capri was inspiring. They all had a grand time, as did I—not to mention the gratitude of the ship's second officer. Turns out, that's something important to have.

***

Wind Surf's arrival to Monaco was scheduled for noon. This steep cut in port availability was offset by something truly precious: an overnight in Monte Carlo. Thus the hours prior to arrival were not at all buzzing with excitement, but rather leisurely. Taking advantage of the rare hours at sea, Janie organized a fashion show.

"I don't just want any dumb ol' fashion show," Janie informed me. "I want to really blow them away. The theme is 'dress your fantasy life'. Look, I'm really nervous, but think I've got it all worked out. I pitched it to Francois and of course he liked it—he's gay! They love fashion stuff."

"It's in the rulebook and everything," I agreed sarcastically. "What can I do to help?"

"We need an ultra cool guy."

"I am your man."

"We have the athlete, the surfer dude, the golfer guy, and the bikini babe. Now we need Mr. Cool."

"I am nothing if not Mr. Cool."

"You'll wear a Tommy Bahama shirt, Tommy Bahama shorts, Tommy sandals, and a Tommy watch. You'll have a martini and a cigar."

I raised an eyebrow. "So how does this vary from everyday?"

She frowned, then handed me some baby blue sweatpants. So much for my moment of fashion glory.

Before the appointed hour, we participants milled about in the gift shop. Janie's assistant, Melanie, gently moaned in a corner. She drooped as heavily as her natural red curls. Melanie's role in the show was to model a dress or two: a mercifully simple assignment considering the magnitude of her hangover. Janie, by contrast, buzzed around everywhere. She was ever the cheerleader, pumping everybody up with words of enthusiasm: 'Hang ten!' to surfer dude, 'Hole in one!' to golfer guy, and an awe-struck, 'You look hot!' to bikini babe. I perked up at that, but wasn't rewarded with sight of her because she was changing in the office. Luckily for us all, bikini babe was to be played by the gift shop's latest addition: the undeniably buxom Nina.

"Okay, people!" Janie said, clapping her hands. "It's time! We've got a packed house, so let's go out there and strut our stuff! Whoo hoo! Let's DO IT!"

Kicking open the doors, Janie ran out, arms waving. Her demeanor was nothing less than that of a champion quarterback running out into a packed stadium. But instead of a raging crowd there was nothing but silence of the patiently waiting. Her team dribbled out after her.

The main lounge had been cleared to create a runway, the tables and chairs rearranged accordingly. A hundred curious guests sipped coffee or mimosas, waiting. Janie bounded up to the stage and took up the microphone. Beside her was the keyboard player from the new band, Nigel. He brushed back his long, blond hair and smiled charmingly, unfazed by his own crooked teeth. Nigel had the leathery countenance of an aged rock star, which suited him well.

"Good morning, everybody!" Janie squealed. Though the speaker projected her voice, she needed no such amplification. Her enthusiasm easily reached into every corner. It was not exactly reciprocated by the audience, however. Half the audience were hen-pecked husbands who looked downright bored. This did not deter Janie in the slightest. She was experienced at getting crowds going, and going is indeed how she got the crowd. Somehow—I still don't know how, though I watched the entire process— Janie revved up a hundred middle-to-late-aged, upper class men and women. She whipped them into a downright froth. Monte Carlo be damned, they were here to see a fashion show, a fashion show for the ages!

Nigel had prepared perfect music accompaniment. He began with Madonna's *'Vogue'*, wherein the sexy Nina sauntered out in large sunglasses, an even larger floppy hat and—Hallelujah—a dental floss-thin bikini. If the husbands had been secretly harboring any doubts about a fashion show as entertainment, Nina completely blasted them out of the water. Even Francois stared, impressed.

A series of dresses were displayed by both Nina and Melanie in turns. Eddie took his turn as golfer guy, wherein Nigel played the theme to *Caddyshack*. The applause was honest, and people were having a good time. Janie beamed and bounced. Her show was already a genuine success, but the real coup was about to come. For somehow, amazingly, Janie had procured the strutting services of none other than a senior officer.

To the tune of Rod Steward's *'Do You Think I'm Sexy,'* out came none other than the Second Officer himself, the strapping Barney. He played Tommy Bahama, suavely posing upon an imaginary beach. He checked his watch, then delightfully realized it was happy hour. Handed a martini and a cigar, he worked them both like a natural.

The crowd went absolutely crazy for Barney, amazed a senior officer could be so playfully self-effacing. He was an undeniably handsome fellow, but my sour grapes insisted he was too rugged for a convincing beach jet-setter. The audience obviously did not agree. He tried departing, but they noisily demanded an encore. When he obliged, Nigel smoothly moved into the James Bond theme. I grudgingly admitted Barney was indeed the Sean Connery of James Bond. But I was the Pierce Brosnan, dammit.

The perfect foil for Barney's lumberjack manliness followed. Yoyo came strutting out in a little sailor outfit surely meant for children. He was so petite it almost fit him —almost. The shirt revealed his belly and the shorts became short shorts, or should I say hot pants? He could not have been more feminine if he'd been wearing roller skates and seductively washing a car. Nigel appropriately began keying the Village People's *'In the Navy'* to a roar of approval.

I was last. Though not entirely enthusiastic about my role, I was a team player and consummate ham. Donned in baby blue sweat pants and matching *Wind Surf* hoodie, and sporting a fuzzy white headband, I jogged out onto the runway. I toted my gym bag as dynamically as one can tote a gym bag. Not knowing what else to do, I pranced around like an idiot. Audience applause plummeted. Nothing emanated from the throng except, perhaps, the chirping of a lonely cricket. Janie urged me into action from on high. But what to do? How does one rock sweat pants and a hoodie? Did she want me to play with the zipper on my jacket, or what? As if I didn't already recognize my failure, the synthesizer moved into Right Said Fred's catwalk mocking *'I'm Too Sexy.'*

All told, the show was a big hit. Everybody had a grand, silly time. It reminded me of the old sailor days of long voyages, far from land. The crew would perform plays for the officers, Shakespeare and whatnot. The ladies' roles would be portrayed by men in drag, using mops for wigs and sewing extra sailcloth into dresses. While our show featured no such cross dressers, the good-natured goofiness was equally evident. After the show, Janie basked in the congratulations offered by audience and officers alike. She was particularly keen to hear what Francois had to say, but he had disappeared... Yoyo in tow.

***

Walking up the incline towards the train depot in

Monte Carlo, I turned back to look down at the *Wind Surf.* She was a half circle of harbor away. Compared to the luxury yachts filling the smooth waters row upon row upon row, the world's largest sailing vessel looked huge. But she wasn't. My stomach roiled at the recollection of first setting foot upon her. It had roiled then, too.

'Where's the handover documentation?' I had asked the departing—nay, fleeing—auctioneer. He had replied, *'I didn't do any. Doesn't matter. No employees. No auctions. No sales. Ever. Wait'll you hear about the auctioneer before me'*—meaning blind old Gertie—*'It'll blow your god damn mind.'*

Thus, the call telling Bianca 'no.' We'd hardly spoken since. Yet we did see each other once. Making it happen had been a chore of the highest calibre. *Wind Surf* had been docked in Taormina. Bianca's ship had also been docked on the same, eastern shore of Sicily. The distance between the two cities was not so great from an American perspective— just over fifty kilometers—but Sicilian highways were not the stuff of the Eisenhower Interstate System. Unfortunately I had to request Cosmina's assistance to make it happen.

"So you want me to book a hotel in Messina," Cosmina said with a wry smile.

"Just transportation," I had said. This left Cosmina utterly confused.

"Don't you want her back?"

"Things are a little more complicated than that," I said. "We didn't really end it, per se."

"So I'll get you a room."

"I'm not going for a quick romp in the sack," I said. "We need to talk."

"Talk," she repeated flatly. "About limestone? You

talk afterwards!"

When *Surf* passed by Messina that morning—at 8 o'clock sharp, I remember—*Carnival Liberty* was already easing into port. I wanted to run to the bridge and scream, 'Stop the ship!' I couldn't help it. Whenever Bianca was near, I completely lost my head. Fortunately, the taxi Cosmina procured got me there in record time. That was not entirely a good thing, though. He drove over 150 kilometers an hour the entire way, swinging in and out of traffic, invariably on the wrong side of the cliff-hugging so-called highway. I thought I was going to die. But to Messina I asked, and at Messina I was. The crew of *Liberty* was just beginning to tackle the mooring lines. They moved like snails. Apparently Italians take their sweet time on everything but driving. After waiting for an eternity, I had to wait even longer: the passengers disembarked first. The ship disgorged thousands upon thousands of leisurely, vacationing passengers.

After nearly an hour—an hour that chewed deeply into the five we had available—Bianca finally crossed the gangway. As always, she exuded a sexy self-confidence. Just the sight of her made me tingle with expectation—it was ever chemical between us. She wore a body hugging purple outfit with a criminally short skirt. She was well aware that her legs were her best feature and flaunted them accordingly. As she descended the gangway, it was impossible not to ogle at those legs so radiantly exposed— nor was it possible to not ogle at the American flag panties equally revealed. I'd never wanted to salute the flag so much in my life. Maybe Cosmina had been right. Bianca threw herself into my arms and we hugged, hugged, and hugged some more.

We walked the crowded, noisy streets of Messina for

awhile, looking for a place to sit and talk. There were no restaurants, cafés, or any such recreational facilities anywhere. When I expressed frustration at this, she explained she had known that all along. Rather, she had been hoping for an open-topped tour bus so we could see the sights together.

Eventually we found a pizzeria. Three metal tables sat crookedly upon an uneven sidewalk. Traffic buzzed and belched by. The time was short, the weather was hot, and the city was loud. We sat between a squabbling family from California and an incessant car alarm. Still, I had my four hours with her, for what they were worth. Not much, actually. She seemed more interested in Messina than me, which was more than a little annoying. This was a new side to her, an added complication to a relationship that I had already decided was too complicated. We hadn't seen each other in a couple weeks, but noisy, stinky Messina seemed to dominate our discussion.

Now it was closer to six weeks. We had exchanged only a few emails in that time—on ships sending an email was quite an ordeal—but the most recent had been abrupt on a level that infuriated me. Rather, the tone set me off.

My vacation begins Feb. 4. Well?

Another of her vexing 'not now, but come back to me' emails. Only this time, for the first time, she was downright rude about it. No doubt she sensed a change in tone on my end since that fateful phone call on *Surf.* That didn't excuse rudeness. I had been very angry. I didn't feel my efforts were being reciprocated or, for that matter, even appreciated. Yet through it all, I wallowed in wondering if I betrayed her. In my gut I knew she wouldn't be happy on

Surf, but it just wasn't my call to make. I had to give her the chance to prove me right or wrong. A chance—a last chance—to put it all on the table: which is more important, money or me?

And so I stepped on the train, bound for Cannes.

The best way to experience the Cote D'Azur, or French Riviera, is by train. The trip may only be an hour or so, but the ride sears itself forever into your skull through sheer beauty. The experience surpasses all of man's paltry purview, for from the rails one views the coast from on high, as if one of the gods themselves admiring upon the fruits of man. The train snakes atop cliffs tufted with palms and sprouting billion dollar villas; the playground of royalty past and super-rich today. Beyond glitters the sea, painfully brilliant and impossibly blue. But as the train wends its way along, you spy new wonders with each curve: snuggled into natural harbors, protected by cliffs dripping with stately excess, hide quaint villages of intense character: Cap d'Ail, Beaulieu-sur-Mer, Villefranche-sur-Mer. But these are not for you, mere mortal. You are not, and cannot be, worthy. For you is to but gape, to wonder, to dream.

Alas, the experience had to end. But did it? For I alit upon the platform of Cannes. Though crushed by the humidity and heat, I was nevertheless exhilarated. The walk to the pier, outside of which incongruously loomed *Carnival Liberty*, was a long one. I reveled in every step. I passed the famed Grand Théâtre Lumière, where the Cannes film festival debuts its feature films. It was so beautiful it was a wonder anybody wanted to go inside at all. Presumably it was just as impressive inside, though I couldn't fathom how. But, sappy as it sounded, I was more keen to see Bianca. Though no doubt marred by fatigued eyes and bent back after months slaving in the restaurants, her beauty was always my greatest joy to behold. I simply couldn't deny it.

When I finally got to the long, stretching pier, I was exhausted. Though wondrous, the train ride had been quite stressful. Though Cannes was not far from Monte Carlo, it was of another nation. I was blatantly breaking international rules by leaving the country. If I was caught doing so I would be arrested. If I failed to make it back to the *Surf*, I would also be fired. But were it not for Bianca, I would not have embarked upon the sea those three and a half years ago. Were it not for Bianca—who literally begged, bribed, and stole for me—I would not have even been hired. I felt this last effort on my part, for us, was warranted.

The appointed hour came. *Liberty* began to tender in her passengers. Wave after wave of small craft disgorged bodies, but none were Bianca. As my stress grew—we were running out of time—so, too, did the heat. The wait became more and more intolerable on multiple levels. After the long walk, I waited an entire hour in the noonday sun. Sounds all melodramatic until you actually do it. I glanced yet again at my watch. We had only an hour left before I had to return.

Finally a tender loosed a different round of bodies: predominantly Asians. This, then, was the signal that *Liberty* had unloaded all her passengers. And there she was: my exhilarating, vexing Bianca. She bounded lively from the tender then, when the afternoon struck her, closed her eyes and stretched like a cat. Her magnificent legs flashed, revealed high from a boldly slit, body-hugging dress of fiery red. She dropped her head to the side, hair tied high to open a long, sumptuous neck to the caress of the sun. She looked gorgeous. When she opened her eyes, they met mine.

But this moment of connection was different. We had more intent than time. She took my hand and skipped towards the village. We strode along a street lined with cafés, bistros, and boutiques. I pushed for a coffee so we could talk. She pushed for a boutique so she could shop.

"Just one!" she said, even as she flit inside. Grudgingly I followed.

She danced in the shop, gleefully whirling around the shoe racks. Bianca passed from partner to partner, teasing each before spinning off to another suitor. She passed me only long enough to hand off her purse.

"Come on," I said roughly in Romanian, hoping to catch her attention with her native tongue. "Let's go to the coffee shop. We need to talk."

"Soon!" she replied in equal tongue.

"*Acum*," I growled, meaning 'now'.

But she didn't hear me. She was already flirting with another rack of shoes. A middle-aged black couple watched her dance with open admiration. They confided aloud in English—they were American by their speech—and apparently presumed I and Bianca were not. The man said to his wife, "Now *that* is a sexy woman. Will you look at her? I'd go shopping with her any day." He got an elbow in the ribs, but didn't care one whit. Nor was he the only one to openly admire Bianca's playful romp. In fact, I was the only one present who didn't enjoy the show. And boy, did I not.

"This is why I love ships!" Bianca finally said to me —in English—caressing the leather belts on a wall rack.

"Shoe shopping?" I snapped.

"Shopping," she agreed lightly. "I love the constant

change. I'll never get tired of all new, all the time. I've wanted to come to Cannes for months, but could never get off the ship. But now that you've come...! These amazing ports are even more amazing when they're shared."

"The only sharing going on right now is that I'm holding your goddamn purse."

The constant change she spoke of I understood, but I seriously questioned if she got the subtle irony of what she was saying. Love of change, my ass!

Then she said it. She said what I knew she was thinking, what I feared she was thinking. "I wish Regatta was here to see this store!"

"Who's Regatta?"

"My best friend on *Liberty*. She's my assistant waiter and wonderful! She'd like Cannes, even if you apparently don't."

So I was now on par with her new assistant waitress. She would have preferred to share this amazing port with her new friend, not the man she had enjoyed a torrid love affair across continents with. That wasn't real enough. I had come here to put our relationship all out on the table, once and for all. She had come here to shop for shoes.

Everything I had tried to do for us no longer mattered to her. Rather, it didn't matter enough. And at that moment the disrespect I felt, real or not, deserved or not, led me to the conclusion that it no longer mattered that much to me.

"I've got to go," I said, thrusting her purse back.

"Da," she agreed. "Me, too. The tender to Cannes is really bad. I'm so glad I came this time, because I don't think I'll be able to again."

She skipped back to the pier, humming happily. I can only presume that the entire forty minutes she waited for the tender—a wait I used to share with her but this time chose not to—Bianca was still humming, buzzing about her amazing time in Cannes. I'll never know. That was the last time I ever saw Bianca.

CASABLANCA
MOROCCO

THE BAY OF Naples was certainly world class, but I hated working there. I was getting used to handling many different nations' customs officers, but not the Italians. They were hideously corrupt. Bribes were so high for offloading artwork in Sorrento—not to mention the price to prevent the artwork from 'disappearing'—that it became cheaper to pay Sundance its exorbitant late fees and offload later. The nearby Isle of Capri was even worse. This wasn't just the usual bribery of petty individuals. This was the

Mafia—with a capital 'M'.

"The Mafia is oppression, arrogance, greed, self-enrichment, power, and hegemony above and against all others." So described the Italian magistrate Cesare Terranova. Yeah, he was murdered by the Mafia. For the Mafia did, indeed, still murder judges, priests, and children. It is not a monster of Hollywood fiction, but in reality one of the world's most enduring criminal organizations. Though the term Mafia is specific to Sicily, the label is liberally applied to organized crime the world over. So, technically, I never dealt with the Mafia in Sorrento. Those assholes were the Camorra.

They were worse in Capri. Courtesy of a rather convenient law—whether edified or merely understood, I never found out—only a certain union of tenders were allowed to dock on the island. If you tried tendering in with your own boat, you would have to pay through the nose, or be denied access by the port authority. They did not bandy words, and nobody in their right mind would argue. The Camorra controlled all the tenders, of course, in a kind of crooked union set up worthy of Tony Soprano. Because the tenders were so incredibly beautiful—their cover story was maintaining Italy's proper prestige—getting fleeced was almost worth it for the ride. Almost.

But worst of all was Sicily itself. Ground Zero. Palermo.

Adaptability has ever been the key strength of the Mafia. While the mainstay of protection rackets, known in Sicily as 'the pizzo', never went out of style, trafficking in drugs came and went. In vogue now is defrauding the national government through legitimate economy. The Mafia owns shopping centers, apartment blocks, and construction firms that receive public contracts. Bribes, kickbacks, and outright theft by politicians allow widespread theft of European Commission funding destined for Sicilian economic development. In this manner, hundreds of millions of euros are funneled to the Mafia each year.

Walking the streets of Palermo, the Mafia's power was clearly seen. I was shocked at all the old, war-torn buildings left as slums since the 1940's, while noble structures were razed and replaced with modern crap. This was the result of the Mafia's post-WWII rise in dominance. They began by infiltrating the building trades—carpentry, plumbing, and the like—and then bought their way into most government-run agencies. Thus all urban planning is undertaken by criminals for their own gain. The Mafia, indirectly, rebuilt nearly half of post-war Palermo.

Monkey business was not confined to the city. When *Wind Surf* docked in Palermo the first time, the Mafia had been ready. They boarded, prepared to fleece us for all they could. They had experience, they had a plan, and they had the audacity to enact it.

Venerable, yet smiling, Captain Turner had gone on vacation. His temporary replacement was the playboy Captain Bixby. Like George Clooney, he was grey-haired handsome. Also like George, upon his arm was a world-class babe of the highest magnitude. Mrs. Bixby was a tall, curvaceous woman with naturally blonde hair and blue eyes. She was our secret weapon.

The day came, the port approached. Most of us quaked in our boots at the thought of a proverbial assault from the Mafia. How would they come at us? Who would they target for extortion? How could we deny them? Even before we docked, a pilot craft pulled up alongside *Wind Surf.* Two men boarded, one claiming to represent the port authority and the other a customs officer. Both men were slender and olive skinned, with oily black hair. Their shoes were as sharply pointed as the lapels on their uniforms. There was no question they were Mafiosi: pre-boarding was unnecessary, as was sending two men, as was demanding free espresso. They swaggered onto the ship like they owned it.

Francois escorted them to the lounge, looking surprisingly deferential. While browsing for the best spot, the two men pointed to a table by the windows. Rather, they were intent on the table beside the knock-out blonde.

"Oh, of course," Francois said with a meek giggle, only then noticing the passenger reading a magazine.

"Not surprised you wouldn't notice," one said, referring to Francois' flamboyant mannerisms.

Trying too hard to appear macho, Francois snapped his fingers and shouted for expresso. The display was a weak one, a fact that did not go unobserved by the Mafiosi. Flustered at his failure to impress, Francois shook out two cigarettes and offered them. He glanced around surreptitiously, eyeglasses flashing in the sun. He looked almost frightened. Quickly producing two fresh packs of cigarettes, he slid them across the table and said, "With my compliments. I have a personal... connection... for cigarettes."

The men accepted, of course. They lit up. Soon an officer came by, informing the hotel director that the captain required his presence. Francois all but leapt from the table. Once alone, the two men smoked comfortably in the sun and relaxed. After several minutes elapsed, they grew bored. They shared a vulgar fantasy about the beautiful woman who sat nearby. She was oblivious to what they said, for they spoke in their native tongue—not even Italian, but Sicilian. Secure from eavesdropping, the Mafiosi freely expressed themselves.

"This hotel director is like putty in our hands. You see how scared he was?"

"Yes. A 'personal connection' for cigarettes? That will be our target."

The lady at the table next to them quietly set aside her magazine and departed—for the bridge.

On the bridge, Francois and all the department heads anxiously awaited the return of Mrs. Bixby. For though appearing a natural for the Swedish Bikini Team, she was in fact Italian. And she spoke Sicilian. So while pretending to be reading, blithely unaware, she had understood every lewd word they said. Francois had planted her in the lounge, anticipating their adversary's macho behavior. He had intentionally played an effeminate, cowardly fool, and thusly outmaneuvered them.

"Tobacco, then," Francois said to those assembled. "Last time they went after alcohol. Janie, that's you. Make sure all your cigarette inventories match the hard count you did last night. I don't care if your numbers are right or wrong, as long as the hard count matches the paper inventory. Even one extra pack of cigarettes and the customs officer can claim you're smuggling tobacco."

Resuming his usual, unflappable self, Francois began giving orders. Dimitar was to double check that all chips were locked in the casino office. Rick was to triple check that cash equated the number of treatments in the spa. I was to lie through my teeth. "If they target you, be prepared to lie convincingly about the value of everything," Francois said.

The customs officer did take a stab at my department, but one look in the chaotic art locker was enough for him to move on to easier prey. And that prey was Janie. Because my name was also on the gift shop paperwork, Francois ordered me to help Janie in the gift shop. I arrived in the nick of time. For after verifying that the hard count was accurate, the two Mafiosi had resorted to baser tactics. They threatened to hurt Janie.

The gift shop was closed, dark, and silent. But not empty. Through the glass doors, I watched the Mafiosi back Janie into a corner. Like hungry wolves, they inched in, ever closer, ever closer. Their manner was openly hostile. Hurting a woman to gain a false admission of guilt was simply all in a day's work. Janie retreated as far as she could go, then shuffled right back into the wall. Seeing her trapped and frightened, they toyed with her. They carried on a casual conversation with each other, while Janie succumbed to panic.

I kicked open the door loudly and shouted into the dark, "Janie! You in here?"

Though making noises of innocence, I strode directly towards the back corner. It was one thing to push paperwork around, but quite another to push a lady around. I didn't know what would happen, but I was ready to rumble. Rumble with the Mafia? Hard to believe, but the moment felt lightyears away from a casino basement with Joe Pesci flaunting a hammer. And one look at Janie's terrified face would bring out the game in any man.

As soon as the Mafiosi saw me, they backed down. They said nothing more to her, said nothing at all to me. They just walked away. Bullying a lone woman was easy enough for the macho bastards, but the approach of just a single man was enough to send them scurrying like roaches. These were not impressive men, but merely cowards hiding behind organized crime. The Mafia had been outmaneuvered by Francois from the start, and in a last gambit had been unable to break Janie. They departed with nothing to show for their efforts.

But it was not a happy ending. Janie got fired.

**

I sat in my broken cabin. The cracked plexiglass of the gaudy parrot print loomed large. Threatened by the ghastly bright colors as much as the shattered glass, I had tried to remove the thing. It was permanently attached to the wall. The pig hat sat below the lethal shards like Damocles be-throned beneath his Sword. I hugged the Moo Sisters, but they provided little comfort.

The time was nearing for my call with Bianca. Even though we were both in the Med, coordinating this was no small feat, what with differing time zones and her schedule. She still worked more or less every minute of her life as a waitress on Carnival Cruise Lines, and necessarily had to sleep whenever she wasn't. Only too well did I remember living the same; unending twelve-plus hour days of labor, catching snippets of rest that totaled a punishing five hours of sleep a day—if you were lucky.

I hate mind games and was loathe to resort to one, but couldn't resist the urge. After the Cannes debacle I was curious to see how long it would take Bianca to notice I didn't email her. It took three weeks. Then she had just sent a two word email in her frequent all caps:

"WHAT'S UP?"

Clever lass, summed up our relationship in two words! I had long since stopped stewing over the Cannes snub, because it just reinforced the Messina snub. After all we had been through to be together, one snub could be tolerated, but certainly not two.

Bianca didn't want to change her life. Focused so tightly on her own little corner of the world, she didn't see the obvious: the entire planet was evolving around her. Change was inevitable, but she couldn't handle it. So she ignored it—including her own changing. Europe had happened. She wanted to see it more than she wanted to see me. That marked a change in attitude, and motivations were important. I wasn't going to be taken for granted. She no longer earned the benefit of the doubt. She no longer earned my patience. Thus our relationship was over because I stopped fighting for it. For the longest time she'd been worth it. She still would have been worth it, if only she would let herself be. But she wouldn't. I had waited long enough.

And the time had come to tell her. I picked up the phone and dialed *Liberty*.

"This isn't working," I said to Bianca, via the freakishly dirty telephone. "And I don't think it's going to work."

"Why not?" she asked. "What's her name?"

"Whose name?"

"Who you're seeing, bamboclat! Obviously you have a ship squeeze."

"I do *not* have a ship squeeze."

"I don't believe it. Why else are you so cold all of a sudden?"

"You don't believe me?" I roared, suddenly angry. "You've accused me repeatedly of being too honest in everything I've ever been involved with. A sign of naïveté, you said. Well, I'm being honest now. I'm not seeing anyone and I'm not going to see anyone on ships. It doesn't work. It never works. Never has, never will."

"Lots of people have a ship squeeze," she continued on blithely. "So you fell for yours this time. It was bound to happen. Come back to Romania and I'll remind you why we've been together all this time."

That's about as close as we got to real communication, because I hung up.

***

Casablanca is an awful place. It is the largest city in Morocco—the largest in the entire North African Maghreb, in fact. It has many near superlatives; it is nearly the biggest economic center in all of Africa, nearly the most populous site in all of Africa, and hosts nearly the largest artificial port in the world. It is the setting of nearly the most famous movie in the world.

An elegant name, Casablanca: the Spanish term for 'White House', though none were to be seen. Stranger than the name itself was that the French left it in place after conquering North Africa. Block after block of dirty concrete buildings stewing in a brown coastal haze were apparently unworthy of transliteration to 'Maison Blanche'. What the place was called by the Almoravids and Almohads and Marinids and Wattasids before the French and Spanish is really rather pointless. The original Berber name from the 7th century B.C. was Anfa, which simply meant 'hill'. Prior to all that mess it was used by the Romans and, earlier still, the Phoenicians.

The weather was Atlantic cool. I was not warmed by walking the streets because I quickly stopped doing so. Lots of big business buildings did not make for interesting

249

sightseeing. Casablanca was just another big city. Take off the beards and swap the headgear and I could have been in Dallas—though as usual in the Arab world, when not in the market there were no women to be seen in public. Nothing evoked memories of Humphrey Bogart and Ingrid Bergman, which made sense considering none of the film was actually shot in the titular Casablanca.

I stopped at a café at the base of a nondescript building on a nondescript corner. Sipping from scalding hot mint tea—the first inspiring thing I'd encountered—I stared at all the men in turbans smoking and conducting business. I wanted to feel Gable "I don't give a damn" but, surprisingly, felt Bogart "We'll always have Paris."

I wasn't upset with Bianca. Rather, I was frustrated with my own conclusions upon our last visit together. On the surface my proposal to her in Greece had seemed to be the biggest success I could have hoped for. After being chased for years, Bianca allowed herself to be caught. Only upon setting foot on *Wind Surf,* and realizing it wasn't a Hollywood ending, did I realize I had pressed her too hard. By answering my ultimatum she had proved nothing.

She didn't belong to me. She belonged only to herself. Though you can try to influence with honest intentions for the best, you simply can't make decisions about life for other adults. You have to respect their decisions. I could not possibly relate to what Bianca had gone through in her life—wrestling with social mores not present in America, struggling through Communist deprivation and humiliation—though I understood it. Understanding can lead to empathy, but it is not—and cannot be—true relation.

Thus I did not fault Bianca for her choices. I had screamed inwardly for her to see things my way, even as outwardly we had discussed, planned, and schemed over three-plus years working the sea. In the end, however, she had to be true to the promises she made to herself about what she would and would not do in life. There was room in that plan for me, but not on terms I was willing to accept. I wanted her to break free from her past, saw a way we could do it together, and offered my entire life to help her do so. She kindly refused, fully in deed if only partly in words.

So it was time to continue on separately. Oh, we had been separated by literal oceans since the beginning, but had enjoyed and even nurtured a connection that transcended mere miles. The joy was still there, but the connection perhaps not. When I had made that fateful phone call, that terrible moment of realization upon gaining *Wind Surf*—that first time *I* had been the one to say 'no'—that was when it was over.

Yet here I was, still at sea. Should I remain? What was here for me, when I only set down this path for Bianca? Why not chalk it up to a good run, an unusual experience to cherish, but also ultimately to leave behind?

Home was ever tempting. Yet, strangely enough, *Wind Surf* was beginning to feel like home. And life was good. I was in the Mediterranean with oodles of free time and the most fascinating, ancient ports on the planet Earth. I could not share it with my loved ones, true, but couldn't fathom abandoning such an opportunity for personal experience, education, and expansion. I thought of Faye's wisdom: the best way to let my loved ones share the experience was to live it through me. I also thought of my own wisdom given to Cosmina: make yourself happy first and then find someone to share it with. I hadn't been following my own advice. Oh, the hunt for Bianca had been an exhilarating, wild ride. It made me who I am. In proving myself to her, I had been proving myself to me. I had no regrets, only stupendously awesome memories. And a tattoo.

Still, I was awash with disappointment. I'd tried so hard! I wanted it so badly! Why didn't the cosmos reward me for all the effort I put into this relationship? Oh, I knew life wasn't fair. I'd combatted that through the years with hope. But the habit of hope had been broken. A shame, that. It was a good habit. My mood didn't improve when the next day I saw my new family being broken. Specifically, one of my friends was escorted off the ship by security.

***

The dildo was huge, shiny, and black. Divina the purser, a petite and innocent lass from a small coastal village in the Philippines, had no idea what she held aloft. A small group of us happened upon Divina at her desk, curiously turning over in her hands a string of anal beads. They, too, were huge, shiny, and black—a matched set, apparently. Eddie, Susie, Yoyo, and myself had been en route to the ship's marina, but there was no way in hell we were going to miss this. The banana boat could wait!

"What kind of necklace is this?" Divina wondered aloud, perplexion furrowing her delicate brow. "It's very ugly."

"You don't know the half of it," I said delicately. Eddie sniggered.

"Oh my God!" Susie squawked. "Where did you get those?"

"Yes," Yoyo breathed. "Where did you get those?"

"They were put in the lost & found," she answered.

Yoyo was clearly mesmerized. The petite man—

smaller even than dinky Divina—watched, open-mouthed, pinky with its too-long nail tickling the corner of his mouth. When Divina placed the big dildo in a shoe box, his eyes never left it. Indeed, his entire head moved with the motions like a dog following a forkful all the way to his owner's mouth. Divina's face flushed furiously with embarrassment. She recognized what the dildo was, even if she had likely never seen one before, but of the beads she obviously had no clue. She hefted the string again, face repeating the query.

Everyone turned to me. I tried not to read too much into that. But while I love such mischief, I was loathe to explain the details to Divina. She was the sweetest thing ever. Something as carnal as sex play seemed somehow inappropriate around her. Divina fully embodied her name. I finally demurred, saying, "I don't think you really want to know, my dear. But no, that's not a necklace. And you might want to wash your hands."

"Who left those?" Susie wondered aloud.

"Nobody knows, dummy," Eddie teased. "That's why it's in lost & found. Divina, how long you keep 'em?"

Divina slinked the string into the box, and said, "One month, or until somebody calls Windstar Cruises."

"I doubt that'll happen," I predicted. "No doubt the owners were too embarrassed already, which is why they abandoned them."

"What happens when nobody claims them?" Yoyo asked hurriedly. Too hurriedly.

"Everything not claimed is discarded."

"Have you collected anything, uh, out of the ordinary?" Eddie pressed, grinning. Susie gave him a sour look.

"Yes," Divina answered brightly. "Francois' Rolex!"

"No way!" Eddie said. "I thought Francois was infallible."

"He did it on purpose," Divina admitted. "He left it in a cabin after the guests debarked. He wanted to make sure the stewards and security were doing their jobs. He claimed he wasn't nervous, but, you know what?"

She leaned in conspiratorially, and said, "I think he was lying! You know, about being nervous. How couldn't he be nervous?"

"Being superhuman helps," I suggested. "Anything else? You've got me hooked now."

"Sometimes people sign on early, when the stewards are still cleaning the cabins. They keep all the doors open and sometimes people walk into the wrong cabin. One lady complained that the stewardess stole her entire wardrobe. She was really mad and wanted to sue the company— American, of course. They found it all the next day in the neighbor's cabin."

Again Divina leaned forward to whisper something 'scandalous'. "You know what? The lady was really fat. As if the stewardesses would have stolen her clothes—you could fit three stewards in her pants!"

"That's the most common thing," Divina continued. "Except tip envelopes. Those get left in cabins all the time. You know what? Once they found a guy's false teeth!"

"How do you know it was a guy?" I teased. Then mused, "I wonder how he could have left without them? You'd think he'd notice."

"We also found a huge knife in a cabin. Like Rambo. I can't imagine how he got it on board."

"How do you know it was a guy?" I teased again.

"Could have been a pirate!" Yoyo added. "We have lots of those at home."

"Nah," I scoffed. "Harmless."

"Harmless?" Susie asked, shocked. "A Rambo knife?"

"I'd venture a guess that most people would get in worse trouble if they pulled out that dildo."

"Oh, and you know what?" Divina added. "They found a woman's string bikini in a room. She must have been even fatter than the lady with the missing clothes. I think she must have been three hundred pounds. Can you imagine if she wore that in the pool?"

"Nothing harmless about that!" I agreed.

Not surprisingly, the dildo story ran through the crew more thoroughly than a boat drill. While discussions of the intriguing items were frequent, requests to see them were not... with one notable exception. Yoyo lingered around Divina's desk at all hours, day and night, hoping to sneak a peek at the mysterious treasure. Though exceptionally shy, his wonder overcame all. Noting that he was the ship's photographer, I asked why he didn't take a picture of it. He blushed as badly as Divina.

And ever did Divina blush! When the fateful day arrived to dispose of the items, the *Surf* buzzed like a small town expectant of a parade. Everybody found a reason to sidle up to the purser's desk at some point or other, and 'innocently' inquire if the items had been claimed. Poor, poor Divina. She was red in the face every time. At the end of the night I, too, had to ask.

"You know what?" she said, again conspiratorially. "They disappeared!"

But something appeared off to me. Divina was adorably prone to deeming everything scandalous. Thus, I'd seen her confide many a time. This time seemed somehow forced. Something about her presentation was new. Then I realize it wasn't her presentation that was new, but her watch. It belonged to Yoyo. Or, rather, it *had* belonged to Yoyo. Methinks some high seas bartering was going on!

***

At sea, ship officers were judge, jury, and executioner. An accusation alone, regardless of whether proof was provided or not, was enough to dump a crew member. And dump is precisely what the officers of *Wind Surf* did: they abandoned a shocked and confused Janie in Arabic North Africa, leaving her to find her own way back to Saskatchewan. The surprise firing—no warnings, no discussions, just execution—left Janie in quite an emotional state.

I was setting up my desk in the starboard hall when Janie bounced over to see me. In fact, she actually ran across the hall to give me a huge hug. She squeezed much stronger than I expected. Only then did I notice, hovering in the background, the chief of security. Despite the flood of emotion, the Asian remained firmly professional, intentionally disinterested.

Pulling free from her mighty embrace, I asked, "What's going on here?"

"I've been fired!" Janie wailed. Tears streamed down her face, unchecked.

"Fired?" I said, surprised. "What for?"

"Stealing," she wailed. Tears exploded from her, and she visibly shivered. Janie was obviously suffering from shock. "They think I stole *cartons* of cigarettes! Can you believe that?"

I couldn't. While Janie was neither subtle nor street smart, she wasn't stupid. Certainly she wasn't stupid enough to steal entire cartons of cigarettes only one day after the

Mafia failed to do so. The tobacco inventory, both paperwork and physical count, had been scrutinized as thoroughly as if sniffed by a police dog. These ship officers had outmaneuvered and out-bullied the freakin' Mafia in their own homeland! Did they really think a small-town girl from rural Canada would try the very same crime the very next day?

"You'll have to talk to the hotel director about it," the security chief informed me quietly. He gently prodded Janie onward.

"*You know* that's not why!" Janie verbally slashed out at him. The chief avoided her gaze, but she kept right on attacking. "It's because I'm sleeping with Asians, that's why! The officers don't like to see a white girl sleeping with Asians."

I frowned less at the accusation than at the Asian chief's response to it. He obviously agreed with her. Clearly he was not happy about his duty.

"You know there aren't many women onboard," Janie continued with a snuffle. "Certain... people... want to keep the few white girls for themselves. Tell me that's not true!"

The chief only replied with a desultory, "Come on, let's go."

"Janie works for me," I interrupted. "Why was I not notified of this?"

"You'll have to take that up with the hotel director," the chief said. "Ship security takes precedence over everything else. Come on."

I watched them depart, then high-tailed it to Francois' office.

"There's nothing I can do," Francois said minutes later. The sunlight streamed into his office, making his too-black curls glisten. His posture was relaxed, his expression

257

unreadable, his hands clasped upon the desk.

"But she's my employee!" I protested. "Why was I not involved in this? I want to see the proof."

"She is *my* employee," Francois corrected calmly. "Your company owns the stock and rents the space. The staff is grandfathered in for the duration of their contracts —natural expiration or otherwise. At that time Sundance is free to bring on whomever they hire. That is why you were not notified."

"I see," I said slowly. Francois was one of the most professional and impressive men I had worked with. There was no way in hell I could outmaneuver him. If he had been behind this highly suspect firing, I would never know. In a much more subdued manner I asked, "Have you seen the proof?"

"I'm not at liberty to share any of the details," Francois said. "As far as you are concerned, you will continue in your honorary role overseeing the operations. Melanie will be taking over for the duration of her contract."

I didn't say anything for awhile. Francois did not seem pressed to fill silence. Only after several minutes had passed did he say gently, "Situations like this are hard on everybody. I'm sorry."

I didn't believe for one second that Janie had actually been stealing cartons of cigarettes. Something else was going on, and I agreed that most likely somebody had pushed her out for unprofessional reasons. Whether that was because she slept with Asians was merely Janie's interpretation. Strangely enough, her reasoning was not outside the realm of possibility. Most cruise ships not only tolerated interracial couples, they were in fact the norm. She and I were both used to that from working the big ships.

But this wasn't a big ship. *Wind Surf* was just a small town floating in the middle of nowhere. Everybody in charge on *Wind Surf* was European, and they had no universal claim of 'all men are created equal'. Taken as a whole, Europeans were heavily ethnocentric and just as racially prejudiced as Americans. I couldn't fathom anyone having any other issue with Janie. The numbers her gift shop put up were above board, if below expectation. I knew it well because I was tasked with double checking the damn thing every cruise. Further, she went above and beyond to keep her staff motivated and involved with shipboard activities. Down to her very core, Janie was a cheerleader. And every man wanted a cheerleader.

Was the culprit Francois, Barney, or Emmet? Only those three had the authority to fire Janie, other than the captain himself, who seemed above such things. My first thought was that Francois didn't particularly like Janie because she wasn't making her goals. But to falsely accuse her of theft seemed back-handed and insidious. That was not his style. He was a pit bull. Further, Janie had specifically accused the officers general of having ulterior motives. That led me to think of Barney. He was the young, handsome man who seemed to have his eye on the women. Emmet's only lady was obviously *Wind Surf*. I liked Barney a lot and it seemed odd that he would conspire to fire a fellow Canadian. None of it added up. But one thing was clear.

Something was rotten on *Wind Surf*.

TANGIERS
MOROCCO

AHH... MOROCCO! GATEWAY into Africa and the fabled sands of the Sahara; land of spices and carpets, of sweet tajines and orange-rubbed couscous; a multi-cultural land, conquered and reclaimed and conquered again. Yes, everybody wanted Morocco. And I wanted it, too: date palms, camels, and kasbahs. I wanted to see one of the most exotic spots on Earth.

Tangiers was the northernmost city of all of Africa. Want the Atlantic? On your left. Lookin' for hot

Mediterranean nights? Look right. Straight across rose the Rock, a scant seven miles across the Strait of Gibraltar. The amount of terror that has passed through that stretch defies imagination, from Nazi U-boat wolf packs to Napoleon's dread fleet, the Barbary pirates to the Spanish Armada.

Water hides its scars. Not so, the land: the successive waves of conquerors all left their mark. The sight of men wearing beards and turbans begat false ideas of Islamic isolationism. Morocco was a shockingly multi-cultural nation. In fact, when famed author George Orwell visited Tangiers in 1938, he noted post offices representing four distinctly different governments; he even bought British stamps using French coins.

The city started all messy, too. It was founded by none other than the son of Greek gods Poseidon and Earth. His name was Antaeus, but nobody cares about that. Of more interest is that he was killed by Hercules—by suffocation, no less. How one can suffocate the son of gods is logistically problematic, but stuff like that never bothered Hercules. He then proceeded to separate Africa and Europe —with a single blow, no less. The result of all this machismo was that Hercules took the city Antaeus founded. He also took the daughter he sired. But Hercules was a busy man, too busy even to enjoy such booty—pun intended—so he gave the woman to his son for a bride. Her name, Tinge, became the name Tangiers. All the best stories involved Greek gods and demigods. Or at least togas.

But for those who prefer a more secular history, know then that Phoenicians founded the place. After Carthage fell, Tingis—as it was then called—became a Roman outpost. Various rulers came and went after that, until the fateful year of 711. That's when Tarik ibn Zayid took his armies through Tangiers to conquer Spain. It took over 750 years to get them out. That's right: they remained undefeated for *three times longer* than the entire history of the United States.

So Tangiers was an old, old city with a surprising past. Some parts were strikingly modern, others not. Its high-rise buildings did not particularly interest me. Its three-millennia-old kasbah did. But if there was anything I had learned about travel, it was that you don't know what you don't know. That applies to everything in life, but particularly so in travel. I did not know what Tangiers, or Morocco itself, had to offer. I wanted to learn. Thus I hosted forty passengers from *Wind Surf* on a tour to find out.

It was hot outside. I figured it would be because we were, like, in the Sahara Desert. You know, the world's largest and most famous desert? Seeing nothing but sand and palms and Arabs was also a clue. Apparently such a supposition was not so obvious, based upon the gripes. Fortunately we were outfitted with a huge, modern bus with an effective air conditioner.

While the last passengers squeezed their collectively complaining bulk into the wide, cushy seats, I waited beside the guide. Hassan was a man who stood out in a crowd. He was tall and robustly chested, his skin dark, mustache wide, and face extremely handsome. His wardrobe was equally enchanting, with a floor-length jellaba flaunting grey and black vertical stripes, fez to match. His rich baritone voice fluently spoke five languages. I looked forward to hearing what this man had to share about his unique and world-famous home.

I was the only one. For within fifteen seconds of sitting down—almost as fast as Natalie gets bored in a train

—the entire front three rows of passengers began spewing racial slurs at our guide.

A few of the jokes were only light barbs, such as 'never trust a man in a dress.' Tacky and rude, to be sure, but not particularly hurtful. Those were the exception. The rule was downright evil. Only Osama bin Laden himself deserved such hate. Of course Hassan had done nothing to these middle-aged Americans of above average income and above average waistline. Through the lash of insults he sat quietly, eyes straight ahead. Hassan took each blow with tremendous dignity, only flinching when someone shouted, "Your mother fucks camels!"

Someone started singing "*Proud to be an American.*" Others joined in. Funny how at that moment I felt exactly opposite.

Our first stop was a nearby town called Tetouan: a creamy smear of white-washed cottages filling a valley of eucalyptus, cypress, and orange trees. It claimed the distinction of having been so over-run with corsairs that, in 1399, King Henry III of Spain said "screw it" and razed the entire city to the ground. It remained scorched earth for another two hundred years. Only when the Jews and Muslims together fled the Spanish Inquisition did it get rebuilt by the refugees.

Americans love pirate stories. Some of us are attracted by the ultimate expression of personal freedom. Who doesn't want to hack apart their cubicle with a cutlass, or punch the face of an irrational guest? That hell-may-care attitude lurks within us all. Yet America has little enough pirate history of our own. Hassan shared Morocco's, narrating the romantic tales of derring-do with a thundering voice. I thought it was fascinating to hear about real pirates and see real pirate coves. Alas, nobody else heard anything after Hassan said the 'I' word.

Inquisition.

The bus shook with righteous fury as all the men and women cheered and jeered. Oh, how proud they were of the Inquisition for torturing and slaughtering Muslims. The fact that the church did it almost entirely to Christians—whose property they intended to steal—didn't faze the crowd in the least. They were gleeful to be reminded of the good ol' days when Christianity scared the bejesus out of everyone, especially Christians. And now that it was 2005, by God, it was America's time to start it all over again. Booyah!

Hassan urged the bus driver to escape the hate by skirting the beautiful Bay of Tangiers. The blue waters did, indeed, calm the rhetoric. But the busload of Ugly Americans had become impatient. They were hot and they were hungry and they were thirsty. They were bored of the desert and bored of the ocean and bored of the history. They wanted a shopping mall. Hassan ordered the driver to return to the city.

We passed a school and Hassan explained that in Morocco students were required to learn three languages. Nobody cared because "American is the only language that matters." We passed the lush Mendoubia Gardens, but nobody cared because it was "just a big park." We toured the Spanish-built Grand Socco marketplace, but nobody cared because it "looked Mexican." Exasperated, Hassan asked me what the guests actually wanted to see. Before I could answer, a man shouted "anything but rag-heads playing big city."

Finally Hassan dumped everybody off at the medina. Here was something utterly unlike anything the crowd had back home. Here, crowded within walls 3,000 years old, were spice traders and rug merchants; here were fire eaters, snake charmers, and belly dancers. "Come with me to the kasbah," ran the famous line. Though originally used as a trailer for the film *Algiers*—which itself prompted the making of *Casablanca*—the line was arguably more famous for being used by the cartoon skunk Pepé le Pew. This was all pretty exotic stuff, but apparently it was a lot more fun to mock the lack of Western-style infrastructure.

"Oh, the Walmart is around the corner, I'm sure. Ha ha!"

"How dumb these people are! Who cares how many languages you know if you haven't heard of Krispy Kreme!"

We labored through streets labyrinthine and narrow, through cramped stairwells, and through thick crowds. The streets were intentionally not wide, not straight, and not on a grid. Hassan explained that this was because they were designed by Phoenicians—a thousand years before Christ —in an effort to protect against invaders. The Ugly Americans had a much simpler explanation: "Before Jesus, people were so stupid."

Everyone complained bitterly and viciously about the lack of elevators and escalators. Though the tour was advertised as 'extremely strenuous,' over a dozen from the group were incapable of walking up a single flight of steps because they were so overweight. They complained loudly the whole time about how "foreign countries just don't understand American needs." In their creative efforts to avoid even a handful of steps, people became separated from the group. I had extreme difficulty keeping them together. Fortunately their bitching was loud enough to stand out in the crowd.

A boy of about twelve, barefoot and shirtless but clean, tried selling a bottle of Coca Cola for a dollar. He presented it to a forty-something woman of monstrous proportions and monstrous demeanor. And how did this American lady react to the boy's entrepreneurship? As if he was deaf, she literally shouted at him, "Why can't you speak English, like the rest of the world? I don't care if you speak three languages! You want our money or not? America has more money then Spain or France... learn English!"

Eventually the loathsome tourists were returned to the ship. They jostled and shoved their way out the front of the bus. The final guest contemptuously complained about the lack of acceptable souvenirs: "Not a single T-shirt shop!"

Hassan remained on the bus. He sat in the front row, hands resting gently in his lap, staring straight ahead. To the window he spoke, as if in a daze, "Nobody even looked out the windows. We drove past the summer home of the King of Saudi Arabia. So many beautiful buildings. Nobody wanted to see the new soccer stadium or the university that features seven different languages. Not one person tried the food."

Finally he looked up at me, and asked, "Why did they come here? All they will remember is the old, dirty kasbah, which hasn't changed in 3,000 years. They will think this is all Morocco is. They will claim to know, but they don't know. They had a chance to learn. I just don't understand why they came here."

Mark Twain famously said, "Travel is fatal to prejudice, bigotry, and narrow-mindedness, and many of our people sorely need it on these accounts." But when you've already made up your mind, it doesn't matter where you are: you see what you expect to see. I had seen Ugly Americans before, but not like this. This wasn't ethnocentrism: this was hate for another way of life.

America was at war with 'terror'—a vague phrase intentionally never clarified. But everybody knew an Arab man hurt us on 9/11, thus Arab men were the enemy. It was really that simple. Most Americans were too ignorant to know that a turban does not an Arab make, any more than a beard does.

And that's what really had me fuming. Not just the blatant rudeness and belligerence, but the sheer stupidity.

We had the greatest volume of wealth on the planet Earth... so why were we so embarrassingly stupid? We had no excuse for such ignorance. These 'rag-heads playing big city' required their students to be *fluent* in three languages to graduate. 20% of American high school graduates can't even read—English or otherwise. In fact, nearly 1 in 4 Americans can only read at a childish 5th grade level. Our math skills rank 21 out of 23. That's not a slip from the top: that's a plummet. That's a pathetic display of effort.

Our forefathers worked their butts off to give us more opportunity than they had. After scratching out a meager existence during the entire decade of the Great Depression, they went on to win the greatest war in the history of all humankind. And their children, raised fat and happy in houses two and a half times bigger—*and* with access to computers—can't handle four lousy years of college? When I graduated in 1995, America ranked 2nd on the planet for college graduation. Twelve short years later we dropped to 13th.

People like to blame politicians, blame corporations. I blame reality TV. We are all wrong. The dumbing down of America rests squarely upon the shoulders of those who demand nothing of themselves and even less of their children. Who to blame stares us in the mirror every day. Effort became passé, comfort became king. These Ugly

Americans displayed the arrogance of spoiled children gloating over the accomplishments of their forefathers. I would argue that the privileged mocking the unprivileged is not an American virtue. But as has been so clearly demonstrated, I am wrong.

***

Terrorism struck the ship that day. Security wasn't technically breached because there was none. I can't fathom why that was. Usually a few security officers wander the pier to prevent any illicit boardings. Usually. But not today! I can imagine them letting security slide in, say, Monte Carlo... but in a third world Arabic port? That's a curious omission. But forget security they did, and into the ship someone got.

Emmet was the first to see the culprit. He'd been hanging over the side of the ship, painting the hull. Most ports did not allow the painting of moored vessels due to environmental concerns—dripping paint and whatnot—but Tangiers was not exactly enlightened. Thus Emmet was out in his boiler suit all day, paint dribbles streaking across his pretty face like Jackson Pollock touching up the Mona Lisa. From his vantage on high, he caught sight of someone shimmying up a mooring line to squeeze through a porthole. No, it wasn't Captain Turner. Security caught the man within minutes, of course, hiding in the dining room. He was not an Islamic jihadist baby-killing Devil, but just a desperate local boy willing to take a risk for a better life. He was escorted off without any hassles.

Because security—or lack thereof—had been breached, a full security sweep was warranted. I was ordered to complete a thorough check of everything under my jurisdiction, which meant searching for bombs in my art lockers, the gift shop, and all our storage. That didn't take long. Searching under all the animal hats in my cabin took forever. Interestingly, Eddie was asked to dive with Emmet to check the hull for explosives. Certainly Eddie was happy to undertake the task, knowing how good it would look on his application as diver for the Royal Canadian Mounted Police. Having the full faith of a senior officer in searching out bomb threats in foreign ports was nothing to sneeze at. They didn't find any bombs, of course.

Unfortunately for Eddie, that full faith didn't help when the hammer fell.

***

Mt. Capanne is the tallest mountain in all of Livorno province, Tuscany. At the top one is toe to toe with the gods. This may seem a bold claim for a peak standing only 3,343 feet (1,019 meters), but it is not one made blithely. I'd climbed dozens of mountains on multiple continents and never before felt so much like a Greek god atop Mt. Olympus—not even when I *was* atop Mt. Olympus! Part of the charm is that Mt. Capanne is not on the mainland, but actually rises from the Isle of Elba. The sea punctuates the experience, with islets dotting the I's and peninsulas crossing the T's. Perhaps the real reason for feeling so divine is how you get to the top: you fly.

Though dubbed a funicular, the ride more resembled a ski lift. But not just any ski lift, oh no. Those little cages didn't just soar above groves of chestnuts like other cable cars; they continued far out of sight, valley after peak after valley after peak. The stretches between ridges were isolated and lonely: just you in a tiny, open cage taking in the panorama. Or, rather, just me and Cosmina.

The cage itself was incredibly small—so small, in fact, that two 'American-sized' adults would not fit inside. Good thing Cosmina was dinky! Both facing outward, our bodies were pressed back-to-back. More accurately, cheek-to-cheek. Though supported by secured bottoms, we felt anything but stable. The cage bobbed and bounced merrily on the wires some thirty feet above the ground. I loved heights and thought it a delight, somewhat in the vein of an amusement park ride. There was little chance of us getting shaken out of the cage, but every surge felt like the cage itself was flinging off the track.

That's when Cosmina admitted she was terrified of heights.

I thought she was joking, maybe playing some sort of game for attention. One look confirmed she was on the verge of panic. She had turned to face inwards, both feet thrust outward and butt pressed against the cage to fully brace herself. She gripped the rail so tightly that her arms actually wavered under the strain.

"What the hell, Cosi," I said, looking at her pale face. "You really are scared of heights! So that's why you gave me the helicopter tour in Monaco!"

"Oh my God," she moaned. Her body swayed. The wind gusted, pushing us about. The cables jiggled up and down the mountain. Cosmina made a weird, squeaking noise and gripped ever tighter.

"Stop tensing," I commanded. "You're going to pass out if you keep your joints locked like that. You're in a cage, Cosi, you couldn't get out of this if you tried. You've got to relax."

Panting with eyes squeezed shut, Cosmina croaked, "Get my phone... out of my purse."

271

I pawed for her purse. Retrieving her cell phone was a difficult operation, considering our hips were locked together and there was no room for elbows. It was probably the most intimate I'd ever been with somebody while fully clothed. As a groping teen I hadn't the imagination to top this simple telephone retrieval. The tiny cage jostled along and we continued to play Twister in the sky. Finally I found the item and offered it to her. Because her eyes remained firmly shut, I tapped the phone on her body. But she would not release her death grip from the rail.

"Hold it up," she commanded through gritted teeth. I complied.

Peeling back one eyelid as little as necessary to see, Cosmina took in the situation. Finally she instructed me on the order of buttons to push. Again, I complied, finally finding the number for her mother—in Romania. When the phone began ringing, I pressed it to her ear. Soon Cosmina was yammering in lightning-fast Romanian. She spoke so quickly I understood nothing of what she said. Well, almost nothing. One word kept being repeated over and over, like a mantra. *Pula.*

"Okay," Cosmina finally said, indicating I could hang up. She took a deep, shaky breath, opened her eyes to look into mine. Hers were deadly earnest. Mine were amused.

"Did I really hear you say what I thought you said?" I asked, rather cryptically. "Pula... to your mother?"

"It was her advice," Cosmina clarified with puffed breaths. "To take my mind off it."

"But pula means—"

"A nice big dick," Cosmina confirmed. She was nothing if not her mother's daughter. Cosmina suddenly slid downward, collapsing to sit on the bottom with crossed legs. The maneuver quite literally pressed her face into my crotch. I hastily sat down, too. The floor of the cage was too small for us to both actually sit, so we squirmed and wiggled until fully entwined with each other. There was simply no other option.

"This is absurd," I said. "Why did you come up here if you're so scared of heights?"

"I wanted to talk to you about your Romanian woman," she answered carefully. "Now you can't get away."

"What, what, *what*?" I whined. "I'm tired of the whole thing."

Was that ever true. I hated talking about Bianca with Cosmina. I couldn't even remember how the conversations went because I never really knew how things stood. At several points I recalled telling Cosmina that Bianca and I were done. Until Cannes, I hadn't actually believed it was over. The ending had been a long time coming, yet sudden all the same. Cosmina called me on it.

"From the beginning you said it was over," Cosmina accused. "You made a big deal about being done with Romanian women. Yet you were still all bubbly and moony when talking about her. So it wasn't over, even though you told me it was. Three months go by and you started seeing her again, in Messina, in Cannes. But now you act different. Now you don't talk about her. So is it over, or what?"

"I hadn't realized all that," I admitted. I was never a good poker player, and Cosmina read me like a book. She knew damn good and well it was over between me and Bianca; a story told by my body language, my silence. I was loathe to tell her I was single. Being taken was an easy out and I was sick of ship life's Green Card crap. "It's over. And believe me, I'm finished with Romanian women.

Screw 'em all."

Cosmina eyed me warily.

"If you want out of Romania so bad," I finally said, "Why not go after Fabrice? France is nice."

"Oh, please," Cosmina chortled. "He's smaller than I am!"

"So what? It's not about love. It's about citizenship. Maybe go after an officer." With more than a little contempt, I added, "They're apparently suffering a shortage of white women."

***

That evening I was lured into the main lounge, near the cordoned-off casino. The casino itself was empty, barring Dimitar, who loitered at a blackjack table as sentry. He frequently allowed his employees a chance to drink coffee and smoke cigarettes, which they did with wild abandon. At a corner table nearby sat two blackjack dealers and Cosmina.

To my surprise, all three women conversed in Romanian. A svelte brunette with high cheekbones and a killer body was obviously Romanian, but I never would have pegged the petite blonde as such. I recognized her as the lady I'd seen at the Shipwreck Cathedral in Malta. I was again struck by her simple, delicate beauty. I was about to engage her when the brunette spoke.

"So you're the American who speaks Romanian," she said with a husky voice. "Say something!"

Waving the air clear of cigarette smoke, I replied with some banal pleasantry. She and Cosmina both burst into laughter. Seeing my frown, Cosmina patted me on the leg and said, "We don't say it like that in the capital. You say it

274

very old fashioned."

"Say something else!" the brunette continued, waving her cigarette excitedly. "Something a peasant would say."

"I learned that from a retired colonel," I snapped, annoyed. "I'm not a performing monkey."

Through it all the blonde merely sipped her coffee, utterly aloof. Suddenly the brunette groaned, saying, "He's back."

All eyes turned to the casino, where a nondescript guest entered and sat at a blackjack table.

"Rude player?" I asked.

"Not really," the brunette answered, stuffing out her cigarette. "But he doesn't tip. Aurelia, didn't you say last night he stayed until two o'clock?"

Suddenly, to everyone's surprise, the little blonde—Aurelia—began raging in an exceptionally high-pitched voice. She rose to her feet and launched into a fiery tirade of squeaky doom.

"Yes! Why doesn't he go to bed? Doesn't he want to sex his wife? What kind of man doesn't want to sex his wife? I've got more balls than him!"

I instantly took a liking to this suddenly not-so-quiet blonde. With her falsetto voice she could be as sassy as she wanted and get away with it—and was she ever sassy. A strangely alluring and amusing dichotomy, this mousy woman. Not done with her harangue, she turned to the lounge, shook her little fist in the air, and furiously cheeped, "I've got bigger balls than you! Look at my balls!"

***

Of equal height to Mt. Capanne, but much greater danger, was Stromboli. The island and the volcano were really one and the same, for there was nothing to the place but steep flanks rising up to the crater. Actually there were three craters. And actually there was something more to the island: a tiny community of bat-shit crazy fishermen hugging the shore. Stromboli erupted more regularly than Old Faithful in Yellowstone—every twenty or thirty minutes—with the added oomph of major explosions every few months. If living on the side of a live volcano that's erupted continuously since Christ isn't bat-shit crazy, I don't know what is.

Stromboli was famous for several reasons. It was probably the most visited volcano on Earth, lovingly called "the Lighthouse of the Mediterranean." Its eruptions were so distinctive that vulcanologists used the word 'Strombolian' to describe similar activity in other volcanoes around the world. So famous is Stromboli that Jules Verne mentioned it in his famed novel *Journey to the Center of the Earth*, when Axel and Otto Lidenbrock emerge from their subterranean journey via the volcano.

Wind Surf's arrival to Stromboli wasn't quite so exotic. We sailed past the peak just after the sun dipped below the horizon. The waters lost their gold-tipped turbulence and turned to black chop. The beast rose from the dark, black on black, silhouetted only by stars. Red vapors issued from the tip of the dark triangle, yet catching the sun swallowed by the sea.

I had wandered up to the top deck to watch Stromboli do his thing. Boy did he. The first eruption was simply huge, with fountains of molten rock hurled high, high into the air. I desperately wanted to know how high the lava was thrown. But to me it was nothing more than a flaring patch of orange floating in the black.

"Two hundred meters, I'd gauge," Emmet said from

beside me.

I started, having not known he was there. Nor did I realize I had spoken my thoughts aloud.

"I only know because I've climbed to the top," Emmet explained. "I've seen it dozens of times during the day, during the night. That was a big one."

I nodded in the dark, unable to tear my gaze from the frothing lava. Lava was awesome!

"The mountain's fitful tonight," he said. Clasping his hands behind his back, Emmet then strode off into the night.

I understood fitful, but no longer felt it. When I first signed on, I had reflected John Adams when he wrote in his diary, "I wander alone, and ponder. I muse, I mope, I ruminate." Ever had I done so over Bianca. But from such activity conclusion comes, followed by a sense of peace. At times I loved her more than anything else in the world, at times she vexed me beyond my capacity to tolerate. In the end, I could do nothing but thank her for showing me just how exciting life could be, and how to chase your dream. Sometimes you even catch it. Fortunately, more often than not the journey is its own reward.

Certainly my journey was rewarding now. Yet doubt lurked. I was disturbed by Janie's firing—disturbed by both her accusations and those of the officers. It could have been an isolated incident, yet seemed not. Mere days later another was fired. This time it was a Filipino named Juan, whom I'd enjoyed a casual acquaintance with. Like Janie, he was abandoned in Arabic North Africa, penniless and distraught. Perhaps he deserved it. Perhaps, as a security officer, he was responsible for letting the stowaway on board. But again, like with Janie, management refused to discuss anything with anyone. Nothing was certain, but one fact.

Crew members were dropping like flies.

My newfound joy was being stripped away. I had mistakenly thought the source of my newfound happiness was the magnificent ports. Certainly they helped. But I had to finally admit to myself that I'd seen many a fantastic spot alone and not been pleased by the experience. Joy didn't come from places, it came from sharing them with others. Oh, big ships had plenty of people—changing like underwear. Penetration was easily achieved and just as easily forgotten. Connection was the hard part. I had struggled to find my place with the various cliques, but never fit into any. On *Wind Surf*, I didn't just find a clique that fit: I found a family.

For the first time, I was feeling protective of my fellow crew members. I didn't want to see any more disappear. Well, maybe Yoyo, because he was annoying. But disappear many would, and there was nothing I could do to protect any of them... or myself.

SETE
FRANCE

I DO NOT hate Italians. I don't think they're *all* deceitful thieves—just all of them I'd ever personally met. In Pompeii the train conductor stole Rick's expensive pen. In Palermo the Mafia stole and extorted at will. Captain Bixby's wife stole my heart. But to be fair, I've never met any Romans and was perhaps hasty when criticizing their betrayal of the Carthaginians and subsequent slaughter of every last man, woman, and child. They didn't do it because they were Italians. They were just assholes.

There's a great deal in Italy to love. Courtesy of *Wind Surf*, I'd sailed into some of the most beautiful ports in the world. Courtesy of Cosmina, I'd been shuttled into some of the most beautiful countryside in the world. At a little roadside restaurant, hidden beneath the craning necks of a thousands-strong congregation of praying sunflowers, I'd reached enlightenment via pasta. Served by a little girl of perhaps ten years, the hand-made fusilli of freshly ground wheat was served al dente, wearing nothing but local olive oil and cracked pepper. That culinary masterpiece haunts me yet, for I shall never again find its like.

And architecture? I shopped for silver on the Ponte Vecchio: a bridge so fine that even the Nazis couldn't bring themselves to destroy it. In order to cover their retreat on August 4, 1944, they demolished every other bridge in Florence. But the commander could not bring himself to fire upon Ponte Vecchio. Ignoring orders, he instead blasted apart the buildings on either side to block access. Such was the power of Italian beauty, to humble even the Nazis.

Yes, I'd seen a great many treasures of Italy, but not the big daddy. It was time to see the Eternal City. Rome. Capital of one of the greatest empires in history. First city on Earth to reach one million residents. Home to the Vatican. Tomatoes named after it and everything. And saw it all, I did. Kinda. At least the pictures indicate I was there. I don't really remember any of it.

The mess began in Civitavecchia. The famous seven hills upon which Rome was founded were actually a ways inland, so the Port of Rome was actually in the township called Civitavecchia. There wasn't much to Civitavecchia, so it was Rome or bust.

Previously it had always been bust. We'd been hitting

up Civitavecchia for several months, but I'd never been able to head inland. Though *Wind Surf* was in port until very late at night, Francois always scheduled a meeting smack dab in the middle of the day, thus denying anyone access to the city. Only Rome was so denied, so he must have hated the city. Maybe he had an ex-boyfriend there or something. Regardless of reason, the results were maddening. Even worse was that I had no reason to be at the meetings. They were an employee discussion for department heads. I didn't have any employees! Neither did Eddie, but he didn't mind attending because Susie wasn't adventuresome enough to visit Rome, anyway. So while Janie—now Mel—bemoaned working with Nina, I just sat there, not being in Rome. It was hard not to glower.

But Rick convinced me to give Rome a go. As head of the spa, he was also required to attend the meeting, but he claimed to have a plan of some sort. Though highly dubious, I was desperate to see Rome. And Rick was an interesting dude to hang with.

Rick was an Englishman-turned-Aussie. He had served six years in the British Special Forces, predominantly in the greater Australian theatre, and decided to retire there. Thus he picked up enough Aussie slang to confuse people who analyzed his dialect. His physicality was equally confusing. When I had first met him in Croatia five months before—had it really been so long already?—he had been more or less slender. His powerful shoulders had since pooled into a belly. Though sagging in sloth, he was yet prone to bursts of intense energy.

Rick reminded me of words once written by Joseph Conrad, "When attentively considered [his behavior] seemed appalling at times. He was a strange beast. But maybe women liked it. Seen in that light he was well worth taming, and I suppose every woman at the bottom of her heart considers herself as a tamer of strange beasts." Certainly all the women of his spa would follow him anywhere.

Indeed, two of them followed us to Rome. Natalie's presence concerned me mightily, for if she couldn't handle the train ride to Pompeii, she would surely go nuts on this longer trip to Rome. The latest addition to the spa, a sassy Norwegian named Ingrid, seemed a bird of a feather. Those two sheilas—as Rick was wont to say—were his cheerleaders.

"But we've got to be back at three o'clock," I lamented on the train heading out of town. "That means leaving Rome at... what, one o'clock? We'll have less than four hours there. I can't bear the thought of being a hundred feet from the Sistine Chapel and not having time to see Michelangelo's work."

"I've got a plan," Rick repeated.

"Unless you have an extra hour in your pocket, I don't see how you can change anything."

"I can change *everything*," Rick stressed, eyes gleaming. He tugged the gold hoop in his ear: a sign of impending mischief. He nodded towards the imposing, yet soft figure approaching down the train's central aisle. "Behold the plan!"

I frowned up at six feet of beaming Natalie. She wore a black top with customized sleeves—that is, torn off— over painfully mauve sweatpants. She looked ready for Walmart, not Rome. Cradling four bottles of beer before most had even sipped their morning coffee only reinforced the impression. The beer titan extended a claw, offering me libation.

"Beer?" I said. "It's not even nine o'clock in the morning!"

"Better get a move on!" she agreed.

"At least you're not vivisecting a salami sandwich," I grumbled, snatching the bottle. Nails released it with a click. To Rick I asked, "*This* is your plan?"

He tugged once again upon the hoop of mischief and answered, "One beer at every stop! You won't get to see all you want anyway. This way I *guarantee* you'll have a story to tell!"

I thought his proposition highly dubious, yet found myself sipping the beer to completion. The others each downed an additional beer before we pulled into Rome. The ride was sunny and warm, with sweaters wrapped around waists. Setting foot on the platform changed all that. In Rome itself, the weather was cloudy and very cool. Well, not for Ingrid, but she was Norwegian. Not for the Aussies, either, because they were drunk. Maybe they had a good idea after all. We all gathered up a fresh beer and pushed into a double-decker tour bus—Ye Olde Hop-on Hop-off.

The first stop was nothing less than the Coliseum. This was the real deal; site of slaughtered Christians, slaughtered beasts, slaughtered everything, really. *This* was living history—er, dead history. And it was exactly what I thought it would look like. And why not? I'd studied the intricacies of the structure in depth during college, seen a zillion pictures of it in books, watched Maximus slay Commodus within on the big screen. We didn't have time to wait two hours just to see the interior—which I would surely recognize just as much as the exterior. Suddenly it occurred to me just how right Rick was. I spun on my heel and snapped off half a dozen pictures... of a beer stand.

Then I marched over to it and ordered a beer and a panini. This tour was about to get rocked.

From the top tier of the tour bus we drank and laughed and, sometimes, looked around. So many domes, so many pillars, so many statues, so many traffic lights. And they were intolerably long, too. We soon developed a game for each red light. If we spied a sandwich stand on the corner—which we always did—and if they sold beer—which they always did—one of us would rush off to purchase four beers. Drinking down the entire bottle before the next light was the hard part.

The Coliseum. The Forum. Circus Maximus. The Trevi Fountain. Oodles of monuments to dead saints, leaders, and Romans. The omelette panini. The mortadella panini. The porchetta panini. There were a bunch of churches and cathedrals, too, but since none of us were Catholic we skipped them. But not the sandwich carts, oh no. By ten o'clock I had already feasted on four sub sandwiches—for in Italy a panino means 'bread roll', not necessarily the small, machine pressed sandwich of the States.

The weather turned even cloudier and cooler. Rain threatened. Ingrid, being Norwegian—and drunk—cried aloud that if it rained she would strip naked and prance in Roman rain. Rick heartily encouraged the clouds to open up. I may have also indicated support for the idea.

Before we knew what was happening—not that we would understand what was happening at that point—we were standing before the Vatican. St. Peter's Square was one of the largest squares on the planet, but everything *else* was very large, too. No sense of scale was possible until one started looking at the tiny figures of people. The colonnades stretching out from the Basilica to form the

Square were a whopping four columns deep. It was an ostentatious display of wealth I'd only seen in one other place—Las Vegas. Go figure.

Ultimately, the line to enter the Vatican itself was approximately two hours in length. The Sistine queue was about four hours. We had one. But all was okay, because there was a beer stand right there. Even better, a tabacchi stand! Let us not forget that Italians all chain smoke cigarettes. Luckily, I was able to procure a cigar. And beer. And panini.

Lighting up, I blew a cloud of smoke in the air and regarded the majesty of St. Peter's Square. It wasn't square, of course, but round. The colonnades surrounding it were designed by the great Bernini. They extended far, far out from the main structure of the Vatican itself, angled outward to imply the wide embrace of the church. Regardless of one's spiritual orientation, St. Peter's Basilica and Square were most impressive. And speaking of spiritual orientation, Rick proved his lack thereof when he began thrusting his hips in the direction of the square's central feature, an Egyptian obelisk. More than a few tourists stopped and stared at him in wonder. Several Vatican gendarmes glared from afar.

"What are you doing?" Natalie asked, aghast at his suggestive dance. She slapped his arm and chided, "You're being disrespectful!"

"I'm doing a rain dance," he chortled.

Ingrid raised her eyebrows suggestively and blew him a kiss.

"We're not at Uluru," Natalie continued. "It's the Vatican, you heathen."

"Fine," Rick acquiesced via slur. He clapped his hands together and prayed, "I do beseech you, oh Lord, to let it rain."

By then I'd had five sandwiches and one hot dog. That was about the only thing I knew for certain, other than that it hadn't rained—more's the pity. I lost track of how many beers I'd had. So did the others. We argued over how many street vendors we'd stopped at. When did you get that candy? Stop four? Three. No way, three was when we all ordered a round of Peroni. Two, then. No, two was when Brian had the hot dog. Our drunken arguments were as sloppy as Rick's rain dance.

In a moment of sheer brilliance, Natalie suggested we use our cameras to go over our day. As one, all four of us pulled out our cameras and started flipping through photos. Each narrated the progression aloud, much to the consternation of those around us who had come seeking something a little more momentous than four babbling, blaspheming drunkards. Get past the Forum there... aha! Vendor four. How do I skip all those pics of the Trevi Fountain? Vendor five was that one—outside Circus Maximus. Oh yeah! All told, I had a blurry photo of the Coliseum, two of the Vatican, and about twenty of beers, cigars, and panini.

We had a grand ol' time circling Rome. We were flying high by the time the tour bus dropped us off at the train station. We tumbled out of the bus and seemed to roll right up to yet another sandwich stand. We ordered beers and sandwiches all around—for the road, of course. Then we sat down to wait for the train returning to Civitavecchia.

"When's the train coming?" Natalie asked. "I'm bored of Rome."

"Why, of course you are," I teased. I perused the train schedule intently. Because we had obtained a guide written in English, there was no need to translate. That did not mean it was easy to decipher the print, however, for it kept morphing and jumping across the page. "Says here there should be a train leaving in... we gotta go! It's leaving right now!"

We leapt to our feet and started running. We must have been quite a sight: an American, an Australian, an Englishman, and a Norwegian running across platform after platform, shrieking, a beer sloshing in one hand and panini flapping in the other. Yet it was all for naught. There was no such train. In fact, the guide had been incorrect. As if in our drunken state we needed more challenges! After asking around, we were informed of a direct train to Civitavecchia arriving in twenty minutes. Assuming we didn't miss that one, Rick and I would still make our stupid meeting with Francois. So panting, wheezing, and dizzy, we sat our thick bodies and thicker minds on a bench to wait.

The train finally arrived and we shuffled aboard. While selecting our seats, I noticed a small Asian man sitting alone. His eyes were mere slits, and he stared dreamily into space. I couldn't blame him: after the crisp air outside, inside the train was stuffy and moist.

"Yoyo!" I said in recognition. "I'll be damned. You went to Rome alone? What, d'you see the Coliseum?"

"Hmm?" Yoyo said, looking up slowly. "Oh, hi Brian. No, I visited a friend."

"He looks like he's been to a whorehouse," Rick observed.

"Rick!" Natalie cried, giving him her usual slap on the arm. This caused him to spill his beer, prompting a growl.

"He's like you," Yoyo defended lightly. "He gives massages for a living. I fell asleep!"

"People do that all the time," Rick muttered,

unwrapping his sandwich. Taking a huge bite, he continued talking with his mouth full. "Just last week I had this middle-aged guy fall asleep in just five minutes. I left him there and finished my paperwork."

"You what?" Natalie asked, shocked. "You left him there?"

"Charged him, too," Rick continued, still chewing. "I checked on him every few minutes, but he was still out."

"What if he woke up?" Natalie demanded. Though his employee, she was ever his conscience.

Rick shrugged, took another bite, and said, "I'd have told him I stepped out for a second, that's all. He didn't know any better. He felt great, he said. Uptight bastard needed a good nap."

"Did you get a good tip?" Ingrid asked with a smirk.

"Always," Rick replied.

"The other day I had a client with a *huge* erection," Ingrid popped up. "And I do mean huge. Freaked me out."

"Did you get a good tip?" Rick shot back.

"Oh my God," Natalie said, suddenly remembering something. "When I first started with Steiner's, I was cutting this guy's hair one day. He started moving his hand up and down under the gown—a lot. I slapped him with the comb, called him a dirty effer, and pulled off the gown. Turns out he was just polishing his glasses. I think I would have been less embarrassed if he'd actually been wanking off."

"Bah," Rick scoffed. "That'd do you some good. I still can't believe I have a virgin working for me."

I raised an eyebrow and teased, "A virginal Steiner? Isn't that an oxymoron?"

"You mean a *virgin* virgin?" Ingrid asked, slightly surprised, "Or just a virgin to a naked guy's hard on in the spa?"

"Both," Natalie answered. "I'd freak if I saw some guy's hard on at work."

"Bah," Rick scoffed again. "One cruise I had this gay guy come in every day and pay double if I'd give him a massage fully naked. Him being naked, I mean, not me. Anyway, he was very polite and made it clear he didn't want any sex or anything. He just didn't want to wear a towel and didn't want me freakin' out that he was hard the whole time."

"So you did it?" Yoyo piped up suddenly. We thought he'd fallen back asleep.

"Of course! After six years in the military I've seen a million guys naked. I don't care. Made a killing."

"I hate it when people fart," Natalie suddenly declared. "I'm sure in some places they're rubbing oil on sexy bodies, but not on ships. Here it's just lots of fat, middle-aged people farting. It's gross."

"Spa shop talk is interesting," I commented lightly. "But I gotta tell you, my first massage was a freakin' nightmare."

Laughing at the memory, I share the story.

"The first massage I ever had was in Las Vegas. I was with my girlfriend. We didn't have much money in those days so we went to Chinatown. We hadn't asked for a couples massage, but they put us in the same room with two beds. I guess they're supposed to be relaxing and romantic or whatever, but not this time! The two Chinese ladies started yammering at each other and didn't stop until the massage was done. I mean, really, do you have any idea how obnoxious Chinese can sound? Some languages are pretty, and some are not. These two had high-pitched voices that were penetratingly loud. They crawled all over us, too. I know you guys use your elbows, but these chicks literally crawled on top to dig their knees into our backs. I think their knees were sharper than their elbows. An hour of that, squawking in our ears, kneeing in our backs. At the end my masseuse shouted in this wangy voice, 'You want happy ending? I give happy ending!'"

"Oh my God!" Natalie said, throwing her hands over her mouth. "She actually said that with your girlfriend there?"

"Yes," I answered. "I'm sure she could've cared less about my girlfriend being there. She was just going through the motions. In hindsight, I should have said yes, just to see my girlfriend's reaction. Instead I said 'Not today, I have a headache,' which was true enough."

The train began to slow. This prompted immediate worry.

"There's no way we're there yet," I said. "We didn't get on the wrong train, did we?"

We peered out the window as the train pulled up to a station. Bodies came and went, and the train throttled up again. So much for our direct train to Civitavecchia—damned Italians were incorrect *again.* Ultimately we stopped half a dozen times. We arrived in Civitavecchia just as Francois' staff meeting started. Rick and I left the others and sprinted across the platform and out of the station. We shared a groan upon observing not a taxi in sight.

"Come on, mate," Rick said gamely.

We rushed out of the station, down a hill, and through the streets. With no sloshing beer and flapping sandwich to encumber us, we made good time—but not good enough. Sweaty and panting, we rushed through the *Wind Surf* to the dining room. There, Francois sat about a cleared, round table with the ship's management. When we thundered in, everybody looked up in surprise. Rick collapsed onto his knees before he even reached a chair, gawping madly for air. A hand wavered up from behind the chair back, and Rick called weakly, "We're here."

Eddie of the sports deck, Mel of the gift shop, Dimitar of the casino, the bar manager, the restaurant manager—all were amused. All but Francois.

Calmly looking at his watch, the hotel director finished Rick's statement by adding, "With two minutes remaining."

Needless to say, we got in trouble. As much as I hated to disappoint Francois, I had to admit it was a helluva good time!

***

The coastal town of Sete was France's Venice, or so they liked to call it. They were the only ones to do so. Anyone having visited Venice would scoff heartily at such a comparison. For Sete was not a sprawl of wondrous, crumbling palaces rising from a labyrinth of canals, a collection of bridges and backwaters and whispers, of forgotten fountains, of moldy statues. No, Sete was—and had been for millennia—a fishing village. Sure, it had canals. It also had dozens of smelly fishing trawlers.

So Sete was not the coolest of ports. *Wind Surf* made it into one. The head chef, a Frenchman named Neill, personally led an excursion into Sete's market. Because the market was so chaotic, the two dozen guests required four chaperones to keep them from getting lost or, more likely, bought and sold. Thus it was that Cosmina and I joined the Frenchmen Neill and Fabrice into the madhouse of fish,

291

flowers, cheese, and produce. Neill didn't know what he was going to buy, but promised to come up with something special from whatever looked best.

I am ever a fan of farmer's markets. The only thing better than the people watching was the food watching. Though from the farming hub of America, I had to admit I'd never seen anything even remotely compare to the produce plied in Europe. They had centuries of focus on perfecting taste. We had decades of focus on maximizing profit. Agribusiness was a dirty word in Europe, and even just dipping your toe into the culture explained why they were so vehemently against genetically modifying foods. America, by contrast, didn't even bother labeling Frankenveggies. Maybe it was because most Americans don't eat vegetables!

The market was a large warehouse-style building, inside of which was row upon row of heaped, fresh awesomeness. Entire schools of fish crowded mounds of ice, pyramids of multicolored onions rose to glorious peaks, and refrigerated cases held carved wheels of cheese from cow, sheep, and goat milk. And the baked baguettes? They looked so sexy I would have robbed an old lady for one.

A morning in the Sete market with Chef Neill was vastly enlightening. Though a classically trained French chef—meaning lots of heavy cream and perfumed liquors—he personally preferred simple items. His first order of business was to show us how quality can make the simplest items sublime.

First he approached a vendor selling radishes. After a mere glance at the heap of finger-long icicle radishes, he began mercilessly interrogating the tiny, ancient grandmother who sold them. She seemed utterly unfazed by his barrage of questions. Satisfied by her answers, Neill then began painstakingly selecting the goods. Each radish was the size and shape of a man's finger. Below the thick tangle of green they shifted from a fat purple to a white tip. He handed each of us a radish, then moved on.

"He's not going to make us eat this, is he?" a rather portly American lady asked, aghast.

Overhearing her, Fabrice reassured her, "*Not to worry, eez already washed.*"

"How do you know?" she challenged with growing alarm. She held the offending vegetable at arm's length, staring at it with nothing short of dread.

"*Do you see any dirt?*" Fabrice asked lightly.

"Pesticides! Chemical fertilizers!"

"*From ze French countryside?*" Fabrice scoffed lightly. "*Ze only fertilizair eez manure. Eez as natural as yoo can get.*"

"Manure! Oh my God!"

"*Eez been washed,*" Fabrice repeated, growing annoyed but doing a very admirable job of hiding it.

"Says you," she huffed. Then she reaffirmed with a jiggle of determination. "How do I know she didn't spit on it?"

Fabrice glanced at the little old lady in her crocheted shawl. She smiled back up at him. Fortunately he didn't have to say anything further, for another man—Mr. Portly, presumably—shushed her.

Next Chef Neill went to a salt peddler. Here he rubbed into his palms samples of crystals ranging in color from clear all the way to black. After narrowing it down to three, he delicately tasted each. Finally he purchased a small bag of a coarse, frosty-white salt. Again, he moved on.

The last vendor sold butter. I had no idea there was

such a wide variety of something as simple as butter. I'm not talking about butter vs. margarine or any other processed spreads—I'm talking about plain old butter. That vendor was nothing less than the Baskin Robbins of butter. Eventually Neill selected a freshly churned, non-salted, cow's-milk butter. Then he led us away from the crowds and into a relatively quiet corner.

Everyone was ordered to line up and hold out their hands. Into each outstretched palm Neil delivered a small, circular scoop of frigid butter.

"I didn't wash my hands!" proclaimed Mrs. Portly. Chef Neill ignored her to move back down the line again, adding a pinch of salt. We were ordered to take a bite of the radish and then a bite of the salted butter. The combination did not sound particularly engaging, and more than a few people hesitated. But after looking at the almost orgasmic faces of those who ventured forth, soon all hurried to obey. The radish was arresting in its sharpness, yet the tongue was soothed by the creamy butter. After swallowing, the boldness of the radish faded into a delicate tingling of salt. The combination was so astounding that one woman blasphemed by saying she'd take it over chocolate.

But not all French culinary ideas were so successful that day. Cosmina and I discovered this to our chagrin that afternoon. Alas, there was no room for us in the kitchen, nor at the tour's dinner table. We had gotten all hot and bothered at the prospect of real French cuisine prepared by real French chefs. As a consolation, Fabrice recommended his favorite restaurant. Right on the canal, he said. The real deal, he said. Methinks the restaurant, like Sete itself, was perhaps viewed by the French through rose-colored glasses. The restaurant was not a hidden treasure of fantastical culinary delights, but rather a place of sardines and mackerel, of heavy oil fish that could keep your heart pumping smoothly despite an overabundance of heavy cream and cheese.

We sat at a table right on the sidewalk, overlooking the canal. The water was just low enough where we couldn't see its algae. Too bad we could smell it. It took the waiter a long time to arrive, which was good because it took us a long time to figure out the menu. Neither of us knew French, though Cosmina claimed to. She was not particularly pleased at having her bluff called. Because the waiter did not speak English, we merely pointed at the largest selection of seafood. It seemed to cover everything wet, so surely we'd find something we liked.

Cosmina immediately launched into a long narrative of why everybody was stupid. She rattled off so many names, so fast, I quickly lost track. I stared at the canal, wondering which would get her to shut up faster: me jumping in or throwing her in.

"Are you listening to me?"

"Yes! Yes, of course. Susie is a bitch."

"That's not what I said," she chided, blowing out deep from her cigarette. The smoke rushed to the neighboring table, where it curled around a steaming bowl of bouillabaisse. I marveled at how the patrons didn't mind.

"Susie's not a bitch," I corrected.

"No, dummy, she's a total bitch," Cosmina snapped. "I was talking about Rick. I knew you weren't listening. Why do men never listen?"

"What's wrong with Rick?" I asked. "Besides the obvious, I mean."

"Oh, you mean besides his beer belly? He's stupid, that's what. I don't know how he got to be manager of the spa. He must have bribed Steiners or something. God! I can't believe the stupid things he says."

"Like what?"

Cosmina shot me a dangerous look, so I just shrugged and dropped it. She's the one who brought it up, but, well, whatever. Once more I gazed to the dirty canal with longing. To my surprise Yoyo walked by.

"Yoyo!" I said, waving him over. Delighting in the noise that Cosmina made, I added, "Care to join us?"

"Oh, thanks, Brian," Yoyo said, "but I can't. I'm meeting someone."

"You know somebody in Sete, too?" I asked, surprised. "Rome's huge, but in tiny Sete? For being from a small village on a small island in Indonesia, you sure know a lot of people."

"He's an... internet friend," Yoyo explained. Seeing Cosmina openly glaring daggers at him, he waved goodbye and skipped off.

"God I hate him," Cosmina spat. "I hate gays."

I rolled my eyes, not really sure I wanted to bother discussing the subject with her. Her culture was fatally macho and ignorant about social issues like sexual orientation. If you didn't beat your woman, you were gay. If you didn't look manly enough to beat your woman, you were gay. If you weren't a male whore—whether married or not—you were gay. To a Romanian, it was really that simple.

"You don't even know for sure Yoyo's gay," I challenged. "And what about Francois? You like him."

"Oh, I love Francois," Cosmina agreed. "He doesn't take crap from anybody."

"You hate Yoyo because he's effeminate, but love Francois?" I protested. "I agree Francois is tough as nails, but he's flaming gay!"

Looking at me like I was a complete idiot, Cosmina easily explained away the incongruity by saying, "He's French!"

The food came, which I thought would save me from an unpleasant lunch. Was I ever wrong. We had ordered the big mixed seafood platter for two, which cost the equivalent of about a hundred bucks. At that price, I thought it had to be fairly good. Wrong, wrong.

"What the hell...?" Cosmina gasped, cigarette dangling dangerously from her lips. "It's all raw!"

The oysters were raw, yes, and not very good. The mussels were raw, too, which I had never before encountered. So were the clams. Both had a strange, metallic tanginess, so they tasted as gross as they looked. The remaining seafood was cooked, but was downright menacing. I'd never before noticed that crustaceans looked like aliens. The lobster's antennae were over a foot long and jabbed outward to probe things even in death. The beast had been split in half down the middle, revealing that no one had bothered cleaning out any of the inedible innards. The guts were startling multi-colored and waxy, like eating a box of melted crayons. An entire crab sat crookedly atop the pile of seafood. It was whole, and we had no idea how to open the shell. Once we figured it out, we wish we hadn't. There was all sorts of creepy stuff in there. I was reminded of dissecting a frog in biology class. The escargot —in their snail shell, of course—were obviously boiled in salt water, rather than the garlic butter or anything else I'd been expecting.

"I got to pop off the heads and tear off all the slimy shit? I don't think so," Cosmina said, grimacing, as she dropped a large shrimp to her plate in disgust. Its three-inch antenna stuck out over the edge of the table to tickle her belly. There we were, the whole freakin' restaurant around us loaded with beautifully prepared mussels in nice broths, or rich crab bisques and crusty French bread. We had the only raw—or at least horrendously boring—food in the restaurant. No doubt we were just culinary barbarians.

"And don't you go looking into my paisana," Cosmina suddenly said. "Talk about a bitch."

"What?" I asked, confused. I'd been focused on the seafood. "Your paisana?"

"Don't play stupid with me. I expect it from everybody else, but not you."

"You mean Aurelia?" I asked. "What about her?"

"Don't go there. That skinny little girl's got nothing for you. Stick with me, and I'll show you amazing things. In fact, tomorrow you're coming with me. I've got the whole day planned. An offer you can't refuse."

I wondered if she was aware of the menace those words implied.

MALAGA
SPAIN

THE DAY SHALL forever be known as the "Spain in the Ass." It was one bitch fest after another. I thought I'd had an earful during the "Raw Meal of Sete," but that was nothing compared to the waves of discontent I weathered the next day. Neither Cosmina nor I particularly liked Sete, so bitching seemed rather par for the course. But that big day in Spain was different. We weren't visiting some crappy little fishing village with delusions of grandeur—oh no. I had been promised amazing things, world class things.

Cosmina had made me an offer I couldn't refuse.

The *Surf* moored just off the pier of Malaga. I was always fond of Malaga, being as it was the birthplace of the greatest artist who ever lived. Thusly its Pablo Picasso Museum, unlike its counterparts in Paris and Barcelona, featured a tremendous amount of his earlier work. In Picasso's case, earlier meant hornier—as if that was possible. Good ol' Picasso: not only did he change the very definition of art for all time, he was also delightfully pornographic.

But our destination was not on the shores of the Mediterranean. Our destination was inland hills west of Granada; the site where Queen Isabella finally defeated the occupying Moors, the site where she met Christopher Columbus and gave him the go-ahead for the New World, the site where Cosmina vomited in the garden.

We were going to Alhambra!

The problem—for there was always a problem with Cosmina involved—was that she was sick. I wasn't particularly surprised, seeing that she was a chain-smoking, bitter misanthrope. That much sourness sooner or later comes to the surface. As nice and tidy as that theory sounded to me, it didn't explain her diarrhea. No, her problem was eating all that nasty raw seafood in Sete.

The drive wasn't two hours: it was eternity. We sat together in the front of a packed tour bus. The whole time Cosmina was sneezing on me, blowing her nose on me, hacking on me, farting on me. At first I felt bad for her. Then I felt bad for me. It wasn't necessarily her fault—though some vegetables other than cocktail onions would have done her some good—but she should have remained on the ship.

"Why didn't you go to the doctor?" I asked, grimacing

as she fidgeted and farted with wild abandon.

"And have the witch doctor put me in quarantine?" she scoffed. Hack! Sniff! "No way. The tour operator said this place was amazing, so here we are."

"You don't even want to see this place, do you?" I asked.

"My job is to get you off," she said in a pathetic attempt to sound naughty. Wiping her nose simultaneously undermined the effort. "You get off on old rocks."

Eventually the great fortress rose before us. A veritable forest of cypress trees jut above the parapets to poke the sky, proving this was no mere battle stronghold. Though the dry hill overlooking Granada was first fortified in the 9th century, it wasn't until the 13th century that the royal residence and gardens were built. They took well over a hundred years to perfect—time well spent. Centuries of visitors have been seduced by the unique combination of columned arcades, fountains, and light-reflecting water basins found in garden after garden, courtyard after courtyard, level upon level. Certainly it was one of the most beautiful palaces I had ever seen, and was a superlative for Islamic architecture. Indeed, it is considered the finest example in all of Europe and one of the top two in the world.

What really blew me away were the intricacies of geometric patterns in the architecture. Walls, alcoves, niches, columns, and doors—you name it—all were hand-carved with a mesmerizing mesh of geometric patterns and Arabic calligraphy. Inside some chambers I was reminded strikingly of the tombs of Egyptian pharaohs, as flickering light illuminated ancient, sacred messages cut into walls, floor to ceiling.

Geometric decor was not merely stamped onto the

surface, but fully integrated into the architecture. Cavernous domes reared overhead, dripping mathematically perfect stalactites by the thousands. It was like walking into a beehive built by a mad geometrist. Dome after dome, fountain after fountain, pool after pool; all were astounding. America had nothing like it, for even our most accomplished buildings were completed quickly. We simply cannot understand what it means to continually craft a building over centuries. How could we? To Europe a hundred years is a blink, to us it's an epoch. America's superlatives—and we have many—invariably revolve around innovation.

The really stunning thing was that Queen Isabella didn't raze it all to the ground. She who expunged all Muslims; she who exiled all Jews; she who started the Inquisition; she who tortured thousands of Christians; she who oppressed thousands of Native Americans—she thought the Alhambra simply too marvelous to destroy. She bucked centuries of Christian/Muslim tradition of destroying each others' places of worship.

Ultimately then, and ironically, the Alhambra was a lesson in humility. The reign of the Moors lasted a whopping seven centuries. Nobody thought it could fall. Isabella, while victorious, realized her place was not absolute. I was reminded strongly that America, by comparison, has only been on top of the world for seven decades. Don't get cocky, my dear America: time tells all.

Most of the attitude that day, however, came from Cosmina. She thought she was sophisticated simply because she was from the capital city. There she had learned how to work the system, any system, to get ahead —not *far* ahead, mind you, just ahead. She watched the bottlenecks and lines and instinctively knew when to cut in front or when to get an *almost* equal view for a fraction of the wait. For each obligatory snapshot in front of whatever thing it was the people were into—a fountain, a window, a pool—Cosmina would pose. In standard European format, she didn't smile. Being sick just added to her looking like hell. On the plus side, she stank so badly that most people gave us a wide berth.

What Cosmina didn't get—and I heartily argue most tourists don't—is the vibe of a place. It isn't about the perfect picture moment, it isn't about proof you were there. The Alhambra was a pasha's pleasure palace, where his harem lived and cavorted. Tall hedges exploding with flowers had once hidden musicians who'd been blinded so they were unable to see the Pasha being intimate with his 300 wives. Personally, I would hate to be in a place dominated by hundreds of bickering women fighting over rank. Then I discovered that the Pasha's mother was in charge of them all. Who's going to mess with *that* mother in law? The women were gone, but the romance remained, visible in every intimate meeting of stone and sand, every tryst of flowers and water. Yet while I was enchanted by a kitten quietly lapping water from a mirror pool, Cosmina waited impatiently in line for a photo op with a crowded fountain.

Cosmina's not caring about anything did not bother me, of course. Her loud complaining did. She was louder than the guide. I would shush her, she would sneeze on me. Repeat. In all, the three hours at Alhambra were more nauseating than the two hours in the bus. I was so inured to her abrasiveness—be it verbal or olfactory—that I didn't care about the return anymore. But one of her gripes set me off. It had nothing to do with the Alhambra. No doubt she only dropped it because I had begun ignoring her. She said somebody was going to get fired from *Wind Surf.*

"What?" I said, surprised. "What did you say?"

"Nothing." Sniff!

"You said you knew somebody was going to get fired from the *Surf.*"

"Did I?" Hack! Cough! "Maybe I know something. I've got the ear of some high level people."

"Who?" I pressed.

But Cosmina was not playing. At that point, neither was I. With great disdain I snapped, "Anyone who drops a hint like that and doesn't follow through is either lying or a bitch."

Cosmina was about to retort, but suddenly stopped up short. She held up a finger as if to make a point, then released a horrid, violent belch. Several passersby were so shocked they stumbled into each other. Cosmina abruptly began running. She pushed aside two Japanese tourists and buried her face into the nearest shrubbery—in this case, roses. She promptly vomited, long and hard. Several people snapped photos of her raised backside. I tried not to laugh at that.

When she was finally through, she pushed herself up slowly. She staggered a bit, looking around sheepishly. I started laughing. I couldn't help it. Of all the shrubbery she could have chosen... she'd cut her cheeks on the thorns!

***

The Spain in the Ass was not over upon returning to *Wind Surf,* however. Oh no, things were just getting started. I decided to head down to the Marina and help out Eddie and Susie. Thought I'd be a team player. Boy, was that ever a mistake.

Like Cosmina, Susie had suffered a rather nasty stomach issue. Doctor Faye was 90% sure it was just a bug from a local meal in port somewhere, but ships never take chances with a stomach virus. Thus Susie was quarantined. For three days she was trapped in that tiny little cabin. No fresh air, no exercise, no choice. Food was delivered. That was bad enough. But what was really bad was that Eddie—being her cabin-mate—was quarantined with her. Three days locked in that tiny cell with a volatile, cramping Susie. Poor bastard.

The Spain in the Ass was Susie's first day out, and boy did she lay into everyone. She'd had a huge argument with Cosmina in the morning before the excursions left. Apparently Susie thought Cosmina was nothing but a spoiled princess. That was a no-brainer, but did it really need to be said? But for whatever reason Susie felt the need to launch into Cosmina about how she was a petty, selfish, arrogant, manipulative slut. Susie highlighted each item with great emphasis and clarity, overlooking the rather obvious fact that she was listing all of her own faults—obvious to the rest of us, anyway. Of course Cosmina, too, was feeling under the weather. She retaliated with great fury. Watching those two duke it out would have been a spectacle worthy of buttered popcorn, had Eddie and I not been stuck with the fallout.

But that had just been the beginning. Susie then swept through the spa and nearly reduced Natalie to tears. Natalie took no offense at being called petty, but was astounded to hear she was also a slut—especially considering she was a virgin. After one look at his dark countenance, Susie carefully avoided sparring with Rick. Alas, gift shop manager Mel had no such luck. She received a particularly nasty rebuke about her life because she was also Canadian

—apparently that meant she should know better. Better than what Susie never bothered explaining. We need not mention the grisly details of Susie's encounter with Yoyo.

I was not above a hearty bitching, either. I had shamefully organized an excursion of crew friends while she'd been in quarantine. This, apparently, was the height of selfishness. I had replied that I was unaware mourning was required and added, rather drily, that next time she was under the weather I would smear mud over my head, shred my clothes, and wail funeral dirges. That had not gone over well. The fact that I was volunteering my time to help them that afternoon did not blunt her fury in the slightest. She was only assuaged when I told her she was in charge of the get-together in St. Tropez tomorrow. To save my skin I was also required to invite her to a traditional Flamenco dance that evening.

And so, as the sun snuggled with the dry mountains on the western horizon, four of us from *Wind Surf*—Eddie, Susie, Yoyo and myself—went ashore to see the Flamenco dance. I had only seen such things in movies. I knew it would involve acoustic guitar and clapping. I hoped it would involve hot chicks. Then again, I hope everything involves hot chicks.

In a night club just opening up for business, a large area was cleared for the event. The spectators sat cross-legged behind a large ring formed by a dozen male musicians. Though varying from young to old, all wore a look of intense concentration, or perhaps self-importance. All wore a black vest over a black shirt over black pants. All were unshaven. Two had guitars.

The lights shifted, dropping the hushed audience into darkness. A spotlight struck the center of the circle, intensified white-hot. The black silhouettes of the musicians, combined with the blazing light from above, emphasized the emptiness of the circle, the loneliness, the expectation. The guitars began strumming together, tickling the air, teasing. It was a coy sound, yet stirring. We fidgeted in the dark, feeling summoned by the light.

Into the circle strut two figures, a man and a woman. Both were in their late fifties and fairly heavyset—the woman particularly so. But these two were not merely Mom and Dad. He moved with a smooth grace, a simple confidence, but wore simple black signifying he was meant to be overlooked. She was a flower vibrating in the wind before a storm, her voluminous skirts nothing short of a blossoming rose garden. Gold hoops flashed before the tightly controlled waves of her black tresses. Separately, they were nothing. But together....

To the strumming beat they circled each other, wary at first, but inching closer. Courage grew with arousal. Their eyes shared volumes of expectation and they read voraciously of each other.

The strumming guitars strengthened and a drum began in earnest. The air thumped with the increasing heartbeat, and suddenly exploded with hand clapping. The two dancers smashed together, greedy, lustful, then spun away. Their singular focus on passion overwhelmed them, overwhelmed us. The drums pounded harder and the syncopated hand clapping became astonishingly complex. As the musicians danced their own part, spectators strained to see past their black silhouettes, over the empty space, to the two lovers in the white-hot spotlight snapping and smoldering like a bonfire.

Then Mom spun away, skirts flaring in an arc of fire, to begin moving her massive hips in ways to make a grown man cry. The man watched, as we all did, and was overcome. He rushed back in, swept her off her feet, and carried her out of the circle—presumably to ravish her.

Together they shared a stunning display of raw passion in dance, and I was thoroughly caught up in it. I had never before been moved by dance, but this was all that and more. Next to their grace, their passion and beauty, I felt like a potato. Susie, too, felt out-classed. Perhaps not surprisingly, she chose to take it out on Eddie.

"Why don't you look at me like that?" she challenged. She was not wistful, but sour.

"Like what?"

"Like them!" she snapped. "Can't you see how they look at each other? They're in love!"

Before Eddie could answer, she continued wistfully, "They're *still* in love, like it's their first dance. They've never tired of each other, but grow more impassioned with each year."

Eddie said nothing.

Into the circle stepped a barrel-chested man with sparse, wispy hair slicked back over his tanned scalp. Unlike his predecessors, he hardly moved at all—he was pure attitude. He strut like a peacock around the edges of the empty circle, eyes scanning the dark crowd.

"I hope he doesn't pick me," Susie whined under her breath. "God, please don't pick me."

"Maybe a macho man is what you need," Eddie muttered. "Or a big linebacker."

Eddie was a brave man.

Suddenly the man snapped an arm out, pointing to a trio of American girls. They were extremely attractive and extremely young—probably sixteen.

"Of course he chose *them*," Susie complained. "Creep."

The dancer pulled them up one at a time, each time taking the dance one step further. In the end he always grabbed the girl, flung her over his shoulders, and spun her around his head a few spins. They shrieked in terror, but once set down could not hide their smiles.

The funniest thing happened next. The performers began pairing with members of the audience. In perhaps the most disparate match in the history of dance, the Spanish mom selected Yoyo. I will never forget the look of abject terror in his eyes. Taking his hand, she led him into the circle. The spotlight glowed on his tiny body twitching in fear. He looked like a mouse preparing to dance with a cat.

The music began, and she began gyrating her thick hips in his direction. He had absolutely no idea what to do. Then, no doubt recalling how the manly man had danced with the trio of teens, Yoyo felt emboldened. His chest puffed up and he flung himself into her. He could barely reach around Flamenco Mom's thick middle, but he tried nonetheless. With a great surge of effort, Yoyo hefted her up to swirl her around his head—or tried to. He only got her about a foot off the ground. With agonizing slowness, they leaned back further and further, then completely collapsed. Down they plummeted, crashing to the floor with an explosion of ruffled skirts and flailing limbs. For one horrible moment they looked like Picasso's *Guernica*.

Good-natured laughter filled the chamber, and the two would-be dancers awkwardly rose and untangled themselves. She kissed Yoyo on the forehead and pushed him back towards his seat with a pat on his rump.

***

Halloween on *Wind Surf* was a momentous night. It

was one of the better parties I'd enjoyed working on a cruise ship. There was less of the usual suspects than on, say, Carnival Cruise Lines—no public sex, no alcohol poisoning—but there was enough flirtation with both to make the night just right. The beauty of a small ship was that it wasn't a mass gathering of strung-out strangers. We were family. Well, that would make us incestuous, so we'll just say everyone was intimate. Yes, Halloween was momentous.

It didn't start that way, though. It started very chill. After sunset, but before festivities, I met Rick on the top deck for a cigar. I snuggled in a sweatshirt, shivering slightly from the night breeze. He wore nothing but a T-shirt. This was less from acclimation to the cold and more from being too drunk to feel it. He had been sitting up there alone for hours. We lay back on the chaise-lounges, staring up at the tall, empty masts. Beyond twinkled the cosmos. Unlike big cruise ships, *Wind Surf* did not emit much light pollution, so we could see the Milky Way.

"What are you dressing up as?" I asked, blowing smoke up to the stars.

"Not, mate," Rick answered. "I don't do parties."

I made noises pretending great offense and said, "Not even for Halloween?"

Rick said nothing. We sat in silence, pondering. The stars did the same. A gentle swell rocked the ship. It would have been imperceptible had we not been staring directly at the stars past two hundred feet of ramrod-straight mast. The stars spun lazily. I thought about how differently the *Surf* ran the waves compared to the big ships. She danced on the top, just like Ardin had said. Rick had a completely different reaction to the swell. He freaked out.

"Look at that!" he exclaimed, pointing up. "I bloody

knew it!"

"Look at what?" I asked, scanning the dark skies.

"Right in front of your face, mate!" he pressed. "A bloody UFO!"

I snorted in amusement, but realized quickly that he was in earnest.

"That's a star, dumb ass," I scoffed.

"Spinning in place?" Rick protested, rising from his lounge to pace excitedly. "Look how it's moving! That's no bloody shooting star."

"Are you serious?" I asked, exasperated. "*We're* the ones moving."

"I don't feel the ship moving."

"That's because you live on it. You're used to it. Come on, man, you're killing me. That's obviously a star."

Just then a figure of white emerged from the darkness. In our escalating exasperation we hadn't heard him approach. To my surprise, it was Chief Officer Emmet. He seemed preoccupied with something to port. He squinted, paced, squinted again, and scanned the black waves with binoculars.

"Hello, Emmet," I said. "Everything all right?"

"Hmm? Oh, yes," he said, lowering his binoculars. "I'm just... well, just be extra careful."

"Of?"

"Bloody UFO's, that's what!" Rick exclaimed.

Emmet's handsome face smiled, and he asked, "UFO's?"

"Will you please tell this idiot that's a star up there," I said, pointing to the spinning point of light.

"It's not a star," Emmet said.

Even in the dark he could see my surprise at this statement. He explained, "All officers are trained in celestial navigation, and I can assure you that is not a star."

"See?" Rick exploded in satisfaction.

"It's Venus."

Now it was Rick's turn to scoff. He marched back to his chaise lounge and plunked back down heavily. He grabbed a half-empty six-pack from the deck and ripped off another can.

"We thought we saw a distress signal in the dark," Emmet continued. "I'm pretty sure we didn't, but I thought I'd come up for a higher vantage to see if there was a repeat. We're just outside Spanish waters and there's a lot of Algerians trying to get into the country. They are frequently preyed upon and left to drown."

"Whoa," I said. "That sounds serious."

"Probably nothing," Emmet reassured me. Returning to his duty, he wandered off, bidding us a pleasant night.

"You gonna get on Cosi tonight?" Rick asked suddenly.

I snorted in derision, saying, "Wasn't planning on it. Why, should I? Anything you wanna tell me?"

Now it was Rick's turn to snort.

"She tried to entrap me for a life in Australia. Tried to get on me and I told her I didn't like her butt. You see that pineapple ass? She can keep her bloody socks."

"Socks?" I asked. "You're the third person to mention socks. What's that all about?"

"Be glad you don't know," he said with a dismissive wave. "Forget it. But I'm not here for a woman. Certainly not a bloody wife."

At least that explained why Cosmina was so mad at him back in Sete. I could just imagine her reaction to being called 'pineapple ass'. But he opened up another curiosity. As innocently as possible, I asked, "Why *are* you here, then?"

Rick glugged down more beer in noisy, necking gulps. He didn't answer for a good long while, but finally just said, "Let's not talk about that, mate."

I did not press it. The hour had come to ready my costume, yet I was hesitant to leave him alone up there. There was something unsettling about his behavior. Not just his silly UFO tirade but... something. "You sure you don't want to come to the party?"

"Naw, you go on," Rick said, desultorily. "I'm gonna stay here awhile."

Turmoil emanated from him in waves. I felt tempted to stay, but I didn't know Rick that well. I didn't want to be intrusive. I walked away, leaving him alone with the night.

Assembling a Halloween costume while in the Mediterranean was not particularly easy. We were in a different city every day of the week, or a different nation— none of which celebrated the holiday. There were no seasonal costume shops in a strip mall, no aisle end-caps featuring discounted holiday fare. Before I knew it, the holiday was upon me and I didn't have a costume. Blasphemy! I was so desperate I seriously considered wearing the previous auctioneer's pig hat and nothing else —it *was* a cruise ship party, after all.

Luckily for everyone, at the last moment I got what I needed in Toulon, France. I'd been wandering the farmer's market with the feisty blackjack dealer, Aurelia, when we found a wig shop. Because it was a real wig shop designed for folks with real needs, there was little enough inspiration. No comical green tresses were to be found. But it did sell dirty blonde. An idea was born.

Later, on the *Surf*, I accosted Natalie.

"I gotta get in your dress, baby."

"Every man says that," she responded playfully. "Not gonna happen! But do try. I need a good laugh."

"No," I said, "I mean I literally need to get in your dress. Who else has a dress that'll fit a man almost six foot two?"

"Only if I get to do your makeup," she countered.

And so it was that before the Halloween party, I found myself in Natalie and Ingrid's cabin. It was an intriguing peek into how women work, and it was utterly unlike the way men cohabitate. They pranced around in mixed states of half-dress and half-nude. There was much touching. There was sharing of clothing, accessories, makeup. Things were tried, judged, discarded, reapplied. It was all staggeringly complicated, and made worse by not having a plan at all. No, men weren't like that at all. Men tolerated each other's presence during toiletries, whereas women embraced it. But for one glorious night, I was one of the girls.

Natalie offered up several items for me to wear. We pondered whether or not to stuff a bra, but eventually settled on a black dress that made it unnecessary. It had a plunging neckline, which revealed my startlingly hairy chest. To shave, or not to shave? That applied to my goatee, as well. After careful consideration, we decided the effect would be more pronounced if I remained shaggy. A beast, I said. A monkey, they corrected. The amount of laughter over our antics was almost debilitating.

It was then time for makeup. I got it all: foundation, blush, eyeliner, mascara, and whatever other eldritch secrets women use to make themselves beautiful. The process was both long and involved, every second made tense by Natalie's sharp claws in my face. I thought for sure she was going to skewer one of my eyeballs. Capping it all off was a trashy red on my fingernails and toenails.

A hirsute hussy was born.

Natalie and Ingrid both wore togas to the party, proving that only I had difficulty coming up with a costume. Indeed, everybody else had no troubles at all. The nurse and her husband were the Incredibles, Eddie was a gondolier, Susie was Raggedy Ann. Dr. Faye dressed as a surprisingly sexy pirate. Even more suggestive was Cosmina, who wore a greasy boiler suit and played a 'dirty mechanic'. The keyboard player, Nigel, looked positively dapper in a three-piece suit and long-nosed Venetian mask.

Because I was in a dress, everybody assumed I was gay. No less than three crew members commented upon it. I was a little annoyed they didn't seem in on the joke, but even more so at the two officers who noted 'they knew it all along.'

As mentioned, the party was a momentous one. Alcohol and laughter flowed freely, but not obnoxiously. One who was perhaps on the borderline of public decency was Fabrice. He was one of the few attendees to abstain from a costume. That did not mean he wasn't festive, however. Bottle of champagne in one hand and glass in the other, he rushed over to hug me. After sloshing a good dose of bubbly down my back, he motioned me over to a corner conspiratorially.

"*As far as ze othairs know, I brought two bottles of champagne,*" he screamed over the music, belying his covert mannerisms. He revealed a third bottle and said, "*But I saved zees for us, knowing yoo would appreciate eet!*" I loved how people saw me work in a suit and assumed I was classy and stuff.

We drank champagne and watched the crew dance, cavort, and be merry. After awhile, Barney pushed his way through the revelers to join us. He was wearing a giant bear suit. Where that came from was truly a mystery. He gratefully accepted a glass of 'champagne for the masses.' Fabrice winked at me so copiously I feared a grand mal seizure.

"To Romanian women!" Barney offered, holding up his glass.

I stared at him, uncomprehending, and maybe a little scared.

"I finally got what I wanted," Barney explained. "I've been wanting to ask Cosi out for a long time. Honestly, I'd been too shy. And you two were together, of course."

I opened my mouth to deny it, but he waved any protestations away. "I know you two had your fling and all —that's fine. But I finally mustered the courage to ask her out. She's a handful, as you know."

"Temperamental is a kind word for it," I noted.

Barney laughed. "I think it's exciting. You never know what you're going to get with Cosi. But after seeing her and Rick together, well, I wanted something more for her than that. I wanted her to keep her socks on forever, you know?"

"What the hell is going on with Cosmina's socks?" I cried, exasperated.

"You mean you don't know?" he said, shocked. "I just assumed...."

Embarrassed, he made a hasty excuse and disappeared into the party.

Suddenly a commotion pulled all eyes to the dance floor. A very drunk Yoyo—wearing only body paint, for the most part—screamed and crashed the dance. He began spinning around a support pole in a most suggestive manner. Fabrice topped off my glass with a wavering hand,

and continued with the conspiratorial tone.

"*'E ees now undair Francois' protection,*" he said.

"What does that mean?"

"*Yoo didn't 'ear? 'E upset one of ze offisairs.*"

"What did he do?"

"*I don't know,*" Fabrice admitted. "*I only know Francois saved 'is job. 'E likes Yoyo. Look!*"

We both glanced over to where the hotel director—conspicuously the only man in full dress uniform—was watching Yoyo dance. His eyes flashed with desire. Francois set his drink down, marched into the crowd, pointed a finger at Yoyo, and then towards the door. As directed, Yoyo hopped and skipped that way. Francois followed. Nope, there was no mistaking what that was all about!

But who had been intent on getting Yoyo fired? He was such an awful employee, there could have been a million reasons to sack him. But which officer wanted to? Was it Barney? If he'd hooked up with Cosmina, that may explain how she knew Yoyo was going to be fired. Surely it had been Yoyo she was referring to in the Alhambra. But it was hard to imagine Barney trying to get people fired, people like Janie and now Yoyo. He was so nice! But then again, that's what they say about most serial killers.

The party drew to a reluctant close. Fortunately for many, Francois and Yoyo were not the only ones to hook up. Cosmina and Barney left early, she all but hanging off his bearish body. Eddie and Susie, too, seemed to be feeling the love. Or, perhaps in Eddie's case, feeling the alcohol. She was full of giggles herself. Maybe there was hope for them yet! After nearly an hour of dirty dancing, Ingrid hooked up with the singer of the band, Neil.

The big surprise of the night was when Natalie

departed with an Asian sailor none of us recognized. No, that's not true. The biggest surprise was when the middle-aged pianist Nigel started making out hot and heavy with the delectable Nina. No, that's not true, either. The biggest surprise of all was that I left with someone.

The casino had closed early. There weren't any gamblers and Dimitar wanted to join the party. Thus he cast loose the feisty mouse Aurelia. She wore a particularly tight but highly complimentary red outfit with devilishly sharp lapels. She looked great. We'd been seeing each other a fair amount lately and, after a few drinks, one thing led to another.

We retired to her cabin, which she luckily enjoyed alone. It was fortunate nobody else lived there. No, not because we wanted privacy, but because any cabin mate surely would have died. It was hotter than a sauna in there! Just opening the door released a flood of hot air into the corridor. As if that weren't enough, on her bed were heavy winter blankets. Aurelia was like a small burrowing mammal, sleeping twelve hours a day in her dark, steamy little den. At one point in the night I woke and had to stick my head in the corridor just to breathe.

The next morning was nothing short of hilarious. I had to make it back to my cabin—through the guest hallway—wearing the dress. Makeup was smeared into my stubble from a night of passion and agonizing heat. In true female fashion, I had lost my shoes after having taken them off at some point in the night. My painted toenails looked marvelous, if nothing else did. Guests were freaking out. The walk of shame, indeed!

ST. TROPEZ
FRANCE

IN A.D. 68 the decapitated body of a Christian named Tropez, martyred in Rome and thrown into the sea, washed up in southern France. All these years later, the place is still known for body parts: toned and tanned and half-naked on beach towels, that is. For St. Tropez's Pampelonne is the beach for body parts, as it was here in the 1960's that Europe was introduced to topless sunbathing.

Ironically, the French Riviera favorite isn't just known for nudity but its opposite, too. Fashion forecasters, merchants, and designers are drawn by its reputation for cutting-edge chic. They shop its skinny, cobbled streets lined with expensive boutiques.

St. Tropez (pronounced san tropay) was one of the coolest villages *Wind Surf* lay anchor to. You didn't have to be an exhibitionist or celebrity to walk its beaches, but you felt like one. Certainly Aurelia and I did. The weather was great. We'd never have guessed it was November. Work was great. I'd never have guessed I was in the auctioneer's doghouse. Life was great. Without making too big a deal about it, Aurelia and I were enjoying each other. But we had nothin' on the three legged dog.

While walking toes in the sand we were nearly bowled over by a large, shaggy dog as he raced into the sea. He didn't see us at all, so intent was he on a stick thrown by his humans. He leapt into the mild surf and splashed and surged and yipped and yapped. Once snapping his jaws onto the errant stick, he came trotting excitedly back out for more. Only then did we notice he had only three legs. That didn't slow him down at all! He bid his humans to repeat, and they obeyed. We hustled out of there, lest we be caught in the maelstrom of smiling, perky puppy.

After the early morning stroll, we returned to the *Surf* —Aurelia to her oven for sleep, I to the lounge for tours. Cosmina had a busload of tourists who wanted to see the countryside of Provence. Not surprisingly, she didn't want Yoyo in charge. So I spent the whole day wandering the streets of various villages in Provence, such as Ramatuelle, Gassin, and Grimaud. It was an entirely different world, Provence. The people, the pace, even the hours lazed away like on island time.

While I thought St. Tropez the stuff of dreams, others did not. Some thought it a horrible place. Susie, in particular, thought so and was very vocal about it. A group of us had tendered into town after dark: Eddie and Susie, Cosmina and myself—Barney and Aurelia were both working—and Natalie and Yoyo. While Susie led us around the quay she was nothing short of disgusted by what she saw. Or, rather, what she didn't see.

As is the French style, the quay was artificially angular and lined with tall structures. Over the centuries they'd gotten crammed so shoulder-to-shoulder they became one giant wall of apartment. Borrowing from their Italian neighbors, each section of the 'wall' was painted a different color. This eased the burden on the eye but did nothing to ease the burden on the soul. The quay, while fascinating, felt entrapped. Above the wall rose the pointed yellow dome of a church. Just as the Eiffel Tower was the sole structure to pierce the uniform Parisian landscape, so, too, did the Church of Saint-Tropez break the monotony of standardized rooftops. Surely only a royal decree sometime past could explain such complete parity of height.

"Doesn't this awful place have any restaurants?" Susie spat. Her eyes scanned the length of the quay, glancing over and passing by a dozen eating establishments. Indeed, the first floor of every structure in the 'wall' was either a boutique or a café.

"We've passed a bunch," I answered, confused.

"I don't want a French restaurant," she answered snidely. Obviously I was being stupid.

"Well, what do you want, then? McDonald's?"

"Yes."

"Are you serious?" I asked, stunned. "We're in freakin' Provence and you want McDonald's?"

"You don't like McDonald's?"

"No, I don't," I responded. "But that's not the point.

Live a little! You're half-way around the world. Why not try something new?"

"Are you in charge tonight, or am I?" she retorted. Eddie gave me a glance that implored retreat. I gave her a mock bow and acquiesced.

That evening was indeed Susie's turn to run the show. Oh, did she lord it over us. When someone else happened to select the itinerary or organize an outing, she claimed to think nothing of their role. But with her in charge? She was in *charge*. Or so she thought, anyway, and reminded all of us—continually.

She also couldn't stop reminding us how tough she was. Vicious, in fact. That's what Francois had said. So Susie said it, too. Again and again and again. Now, I'm no stranger to self-glorifying stories about how tough I am and stuff, but this chick was completely desperate for attention. Is that what everybody thought when I opened my mouth? Perish the thought.

All that had happened was that Francois had taken some paperwork from her and, in the process, messed up her personal system. This caused her more work, so next time she guarded it from him. He laughed and called her vicious. That's it. That was the story. Yet before we'd even left the tender she had dropped the word 'vicious' at least twenty times.

It didn't help that her narration kept getting interrupted. So Susie returned to the subject of her viciousness again and again. Far worse than logistical interruptions, such as boarding the crowded tender, was Natalie and Yoyo. Seeing that they were with two couples that night, they took it upon themselves to play couple, too. Considering Yoyo was about five feet high and Natalie was over six, they were an arresting sight.

"Vicious! That's what Francois said after he messed up my paperwork, and—what are you doing?"

Yoyo had hopped into Natalie's arms and flung his skinny arms around her neck.

"I have my own system," Susie continued. "I know what I'm doing, and he just—are you two kissing?"

Yoyo began peppering Natalie with kisses.

"I know what I'm doing, and he messed up my paperwork, so I—will you two stop it?"

Nibbling of ears. Giggles. They began comparing long fingernails. Of course, Yoyo had them only on his pinkies.

"Oh my God, stop!"

Those of us unable to hide our snickers received a nasty glare from Ms. Vicious. In exasperation, Susie flung a hand out at the very next restaurant and declared authoritatively, "We're here!"

"Here?" Cosmina challenged, surprised. "You sure? It looks—"

"Yes, I'm sure!" Susie interrupted (viciously).

What Cosmina was no doubt going to say was 'expensive'. In Susie's haste to take back control of the situation, she'd obviously figured any port in the storm. This was perhaps unwise. But she marched in as if she were Prince Albert of Monaco—who'd dined there quite recently, in fact. She gave orders like royalty, too.

"There will be six of us. Well, then put those two tables together! Yes, those two. No, we will not be needing the wine list. Bring some water. Yes, we'll have cocktails. What do you mean you don't have Miller Lite?"

We situated ourselves around a long table along a brick wall heavy with photographs of celebrities. Sylvester Stallone. Michael Douglas. I seriously thought I was the only American to have ever sat there who hadn't won an Oscar. We shared uneasy glances. Susie didn't notice, having made a point of not meeting anyone's gaze.

Only then did she look at the menu. She couldn't read French, of course, but she could readily identify behind each item a helluva lot of zeroes. Alas, Susie may have thought she was a princess, but her budget did not share her confidence. She looked exceedingly nervous. She motioned everybody closer. We all leaned in.

"Okay," she whispered. "When I give the order, do what I say."

The waiter returned. Everybody leaned back and began conspicuously lounging, glancing at anything but each other. A giant basket of bread was served: gorgeous, steaming, fresh-baked loaves of crusty French bread. Susie stared at them as if they were baked gold. She looked like she was about to panic.

As the waiter finished his action, Susie whispered, "Ready..."

Cosmina, not appreciating being ordered around, opened her mouth to protest. But just then the waiter walked away. Susie pounced on the opportunity, hoarsely whispering, "Run."

"What?" I said, surprised.

"Run!" Susie repeated urgently. She pushed Eddie out of his chair with great force. He tumbled out awkwardly, then hastened out the front door. We fled. So fast did Susie bolt from the table, she kicked over her chair. We ended up sharing a bowl of olives at a neighboring bar.

Susie continued with her self-congratulatory talk about being vicious, while the rest of us politely ignored her restaurant misstep. All but Eddie, that is. Whenever Susie wasn't looking, he shook his head in disgust. After two or three times, and two or three beers, he suddenly declared, "Tomorrow! Boy's day out. Who's with me?"

Susie stared at him, shocked. Eddie didn't let her retort, but pressed onward.

"Brian? Yoyo? You guys in?"

"I'm photographing a tour," Yoyo said.

"Unfortunately," Cosmina muttered.

Recognizing this as a cry for help, I quickly agreed to join Eddie. For the rest of the night Eddie wasn't the only one avoiding Susie's angry glare.

So the next day Eddie and I tendered into Marseilles. Surprisingly, the first order of business was going to McDonald's. While the Golden Arches were an American creation, it was foolhardy to think they'd only enslaved the 'natives'. Eddie insisted upon such fare and I acquiesced.

"Please don't tell Susie," Eddie begged. "She'll be furious if she knows I did this without her."

"We could always tell her we went to a strip club," I offered.

"She'd take that better," Eddie agreed grimly.

Afterwards we hopped on a ferry, bound for some exceptionally unique places. First we toured the quarantine islands of southern France, the Iles du Frioul. They were a series of gnarly-shaped islands two miles offshore of Marseilles. The rugged, bare rock was ignored for millennia, but eventually deemed the perfect place to quarantine plague victims. While it is unknown how many men and women succumbed to their disease—real or suspected—certainly nobody lives there now. Dotted here and there about the islands are the ruins of the quarantine hospital and even an old fortress used by the conquering Nazis in WWII. As interesting as the rugged islands were, they were nothing compared to what awaited us on the island of If.

Chateau D'if (pronounced *deef*) was startlingly similar to San Francisco's famous Alcatraz. Both were heavily fortified, hardcore prisons on a rock in a bay just outside a major port city. Both were constructed to house particularly bad or celebrity inmates. Because Alcatraz rose from the frigid, lethal waters of San Francisco Bay, it was considered escape proof. Ironically, Chateau D'if—lapped by the welcoming, beautiful waters of the French Riviera—proved to be more so. Why? Because Chateau D'if was not about rehabilitation, but retribution. They shackled you to a wall in a tiny stone room with no windows and watched you writhe until you died.

The prison itself was originally a fortress built to defend Marseille. It looked exactly like you'd expect with sheer walls, round towers, and battlements. Storms of angry waves and angry men were rebuffed by a thick stone sea wall. This protected the one landing on the small island, more or less. Even so sheltered, the waves made disembarking tough business. This was in no way a place for ease or comfort. This was a brutal place of stone and iron built by men of the same.

Upon entering the fortress, fascination sours into nothing short of horror. The cells are tiny, dismal, and filled with a chill that can only come from centuries of torture and death. The courtyard is small and cobbled. A dramatic stone staircase spirals tightly up to the second level. The mezzanine is lined with the awful cells, each its own shape and configuration. The only uniformity is shackles and the desperate scratchings of fingernails in the rock.

I'd never heard of Chateau D'if, even though the literary great, Alexandre Dumas, wrote extensivly about it.

Not only did he write *The Three Musketeers*, but also *The Man in the Iron Mask*. The latter swashbuckling affair was inspired by real life, with Chateau D'if being home to the poor bastard in the title. His 'suite' was a vaulted brick tomb with a small fireplace, a table and chair, a bitter breeze for companionship, and no hope of escape. Another notable inmate of Chateau Di'f was the Count of Monte Cristo. Unlike the mysterious Man in the Iron Mask—who was probably in reality the twin brother of King Louis XIV— the Count was fictional.

After wandering the fortress prison awhile, Eddie and I moved to a table sitting crookedly upon a rock overlooking the sea. The wind whipped by forcefully on its way to the keep, where it whistled through the arrow slits and battlements. Even out in the sun I suffered a chill. I couldn't even imagine being locked in that breezy, damp hell hole. It was weird to sip cappuccinos and play civilized while gazing upon such a Medieval atrocity.

"The irony of this is killing me," Eddie commented. "I was in quarantine for three days and felt like I was in jail. I finally get out and what do I do? Tour a quarantine island and a prison."

"We're all creatures of habit," I consoled with a smile.

"I'm officially running from my girlfriend today," he added.

Recognizing that this was the moment Eddie had been waiting for, I lent an ear.

"I wanted to die in there, man. Three days locked in a room with somebody you like is tough, but when you're at each others' throats all day? Awful. The funny thing is that we didn't even talk."

"Then why was it so bad?" I prompted gently.

"Silence is worse. I guess there's so much to talk

about we didn't want to bother starting. I don't know. All I know is that my sense of adventure is growing and hers is gone. Being a dive master is awesome. But Susie just wants to go home."

"Home has a strong pull for many," I agreed.

"She just wants to be the princess again," Eddie scoffed. "We're both from a small country town where her dad owns a bunch of things. When we first started dating back in high school everybody called *me* the gold digger! I wanted out of that town big time. In the beginning Susie was kind of swept up in my sense of adventure, I think. When the opportunity to become a diver in St. Maarten came up, she came with me. I think she only agreed because she knew it was a short term thing. But we stayed for over a year. And why not? We were living in paradise, making money, diving. It wasn't just play, either, because it was great for my getting into the RCMP as a diver. I didn't want it to end, so I convinced her to join me for a contract on *Surf*."

"The *Wind Surf* seems to spell doom for many a relationship," I commented lightly. "Yet I find myself loving it here."

"Me, too!" Eddie agreed. "What's not to love? We're seeing the entire Mediterranean! But Susie hates it. I'm getting sick of her bullshit. I think she's just scared of not being in control. She wants everything familiar, all the time. That's why she wanted to find a McDonald's yesterday: so she wouldn't have to try something new and risk not liking it. You saw what happened when she was forced to step outside her comfort zone. She made a fool of herself."

"Well, we've all done that," I offered. Eddie shrugged, recognizing the remark for false chivalry.

"We're growing apart and Susie's getting desperate to stay together. She squeezes tighter and I pull back harder. A downward spiral, eh? We only got together because it's what you do. I'm not feeling the love and don't know how to break it to her. She was always high maintenance, but she's never been so bitchy before. I don't think she realizes she's driving the wedge deeper."

Eddie scanned the sexy blue of the Mediterranean, breathed in the salt air, and smiled.

"An entire afternoon with no drama," he sighed. "I'm so glad Susie's not here."

"I'm glad Cosmina isn't!" I joked. "We're not even a couple but seem tied together at the hip. Still, imagine how much worse it would be if they were both here."

Eddie laughed and said, "We'd push 'em in a cell and throw away the key. I'd think Cosi would lighten up now that you're with Aurelia."

"Oh, we're not really a couple or anything," I said. "Just a ship squeeze, I guess."

"Well, Susie's mad at you because of it. She sees us growing apart and sees you two happy and fresh."

I nodded, musing.

"I'm going to keep going," Eddie finally admitted. "Farther and farther. It's what I want to do, but also because I know sooner or later Susie will drop out."

Eddie finished his coffee and added with a mischievous smile, "And it's easier than confronting her."

***

Though I happily toss out some good-natured grumbling about going into port with Cosmina, the truth is that more often than not we manage to have a good time.

Every time *Wind Surf* docked on the party island of Ibiza, Spain, for example, we had fun. Sometimes that meant getting wildly drunk on sangria and gorging ourselves on tapas. Sometimes it meant getting a tattoo. And sometimes it was all about a sex shop.

"Won't Barney be upset?" I asked her as we walked through the cobbled streets to the small sex shop we knew was hiding among the ancient multi-level stone labyrinth. Ibiza was a bizarre place built up over a millennium of war. Where cannonballs were once stored now boomed world-class discos. Ramps once kept clear for rolling cannon up to parapets were now laden with passed out ravers. Many had been up for so long, dancing night and day and night again, courtesy of drugs, they had finally exited to the fresh air and passed out wherever they were.

"He's huge," I continued. "I don't want to make him mad."

"You know how laid back he is about these things," Cosmina answered. "It takes a lot to get him angry. Of course you don't want to be around when you do. Anyway, he knows there's nothing between us. Plus I said I'd pick up something nice."

"Now we're talking!" I teased.

The shop was very small but packed with merchandise. While the walls dripped all manner of sex toys, the center was dominated by bins overflowing with discount porn DVDs. So large were the DVD containers that shoppers were pushed into narrow aisles along the walls. This brought them nose-to-nose with dildos, vibrators, latex masks, and all sorts less mainstream amusements. Anyone uncomfortable about the subject matter got over it real quick, or fled screaming into the night.

"I saw Yoyo here earlier," Cosmina suddenly said.

I looked at her in surprise and said, "You came here earlier? You told me you were too embarrassed to come alone."

"Not exactly true," she admitted with a shrug. "I had just arrived when Yoyo came in. At first I freaked when I saw him. I don't want to even think about what he's buying here. When he saw me he tried to pretend he was all straight and stuff. I don't know why he bothers. It was funny, though. Anyway, as soon as he saw me, I ran as fast as Susie in a French restaurant."

"Nice," I said.

"Oh my God," Cosmina cried, bringing her hands to her mouth. "I recognize something!"

I raised an inquisitive eyebrow. She burst out laughing.

"You have no idea how proud of you I am," I said earnestly. "Please, do tell."

"I saw it in Sex and the City," she replied. She tried to say it flatly, but her wriggling lips gave away her joyous mood. "It's called the Rabbit."

My eyes scanned the multitude of offerings, but spotting a specific toy was like finding a needle in a stack of needles.

"Here," she said, reaching up to pull a box from a peg on the wall.

When she presented the sex toy, my eyes widened in surprise. My needle analogy was sadly insufficient. This thing was, well, humbling in its size. Behold: the Vibratex Rabbit Pearl!

"I've got to get this!" she exclaimed. Then, realizing she said that aloud, she suddenly grew embarrassed. "Oh my God, I can't pay for this. What if someone sees me?"

"Well, I'm looking at you right now," I replied. "In a whole new light, I might add."

"Stop it," she chided. "I'm serious. I can't have any passengers seeing me with this."

"There's nobody here but us," I pointed out. "Look, I'll buy it for you. No biggie."

Though it was obvious Cosmina wanted to purchase the Rabbit, doing so still required much coaxing. In the end I had to buy several German porn DVDs—enough so that she felt I deserved to be more embarrassed than her. With her shiny, new, naughty item tucked safely away in a nondescript shopping bag, I figured the matter was closed. As it turned out, it was just getting started.

"Oh my God!" Cosmina suddenly cried, aghast. She came to a dead stop in the middle of the sidewalk. "How will I get this through security on the ship?"

"Why would they mind a vibrator?" I asked, confused.

"They have to scan my bag," Cosmina explained. "That means everyone will see its X-ray on the screen!"

I started chuckling.

"Honestly, I'd like to see that," I admitted. "But can't you request a personal search instead?"

"And have the chief know it was mine? No way! At least if I'm in line there could be confusion over whose bag it is."

"You need to embrace your sexuality," I teased. "I say scan that thing!"

"Everyone else will see it, too," she lamented. Her brow furrowed deeply and she eyed the nearby sea. She was apparently considering chucking the offending item into the drink.

"Fine, fine," I said. "Give it to me. I'll pretend it's

mine."

"No," she said slowly. "I'll just board last—very last. That way I get to see it, too. You know how the last image remains up until they scan something else."

And so it was we boarded the ship very last. Just before placing her bag on the X-ray machine, Cosmina nearly made a run past the guards. At the last moment she composed herself by lighting a cigarette.

"You know you can't light up here," the security guard grunted, surprised.

"Oh, sorry," she said. She dropped her shopping bag on the machine and ran back down the gangway to dispose of her cigarette. Now at a safe distance, better to gauge the guards' reactions, she watched her bag slide into the machine. Instantly the monitor was emblazoned with the brilliant halo of a gargantuan mechanized dildo. It was fascinating, actually. The individual pearls—which I presume spin around inside the shaft—radiated like a tumor.

Creepy analogy aside, the whole situation was quite hilarious. I couldn't stop laughing. Neither could the security guards. Cosmina was so embarrassed that she nearly ran away into the night, forgetting about the ship entirely. Only reluctantly did she set foot back aboard. This time she *did* run past the guards, forgoing the usual pat-down. They watched her go, laughing even louder.

But the joke was far from over. Because nothing was scanned afterwards, the embarrassing image remained on the monitor *all night long.* We had assumed security would power off the machine and the image would disappear forever. Alas, they kept it going all night. Whether this was standard operating procedure or sheer malice, I don't know.

Even worse, the image was up half the next day, too,

for *Wind Surf* arrived in port late after twelve o'clock noon. As the passengers queued up to tender out, they had loads of time to regard the X-ray in great, glowing detail. Cosmina led the first batch of tour guests down to security and saw it. She nearly swooned upon recognizing her Rabbit Pearl vibrator.

Oh, it was precious. But the laughing died soon after, when Eddie sent two kids to the hospital with broken skulls.

Alas, falling badly while riding a banana boat happens a lot. In fact, it's part of the fun. But that day just off the shores of Lipari Island, Italy, two young men fell not just badly, but devastatingly so. The teens had been riding the banana boat with their parents. The raft hit a rogue wave and all four were smashed into each other. The timing was just right and the momentum just wrong; the two boys knocked heads.

The younger teen suffered a mild concussion. His older brother appeared to have broken an eardrum. Blood trickled out of his ear. Dr. Faye gave him a full review, but was unable to identify to her satisfaction where the blood was coming from. She insisted both boys have full scans on the shore. A good thing, too: he had a cracked skull and internal brain hemorrhage. Fortunately, having identified the issue early, he was treated and was ultimately just fine.

Late that night I found Eddie in the ship's library. I'd been looking for him for hours, unaware he'd gone ashore to the hospital with the family and Faye. I didn't know what to say, but knew what needed to be said. It wasn't his fault. I knew Eddie well enough to know he'd feel completely responsible for potentially killing that boy. But just because he was driving the boat did not mean he could predict—let alone stop—a rogue wave. The sea had been glassy smooth prior to the accident. Certainly he wasn't driving too fast because the Zodiac boat was old and literally incapable of speeding. No, it was not Eddie's fault in the least. In fact, it had been his cool demeanor under pressure that had gotten both semi-conscious boys safely out of the water and to the doctor. But like all real heroes, he didn't think of himself that way.

The library was small, appropriately bookish, and quiet. Though inside were only Eddie and Susie, the atmosphere was crowded—crowded with regret. Eddie was just staring ahead, overwhelmed by it all. It was painful to see him being so hard on himself. It was even worse seeing Susie be selfish in Eddie's moment of need. As I entered the room, she was using his lack of protest as an opportunity to push her agenda.

"This is proof we shouldn't be here," Susie was saying, "Just another reason. One of many."

Eddie ignored her.

"It's a sign from above," she pressed.

Eddie slowly turned to look at her. His expression was unreadable, but his tone was most clear.

"A sign?" he rebuked sharply. "A sign from above? You think God had me nearly kill two boys as a reminder that you wanna go home?"

She leaned back, surprised. She began fussing and said, "Well—"

"Get the fuck out of here!" he seethed.

Susie did as ordered. She ran towards the door, tears streaming down her face. In her effort to escape she collided with me, nearly knocking me off my feet. I watched her run down the corridor, then turned back to look at Eddie. He sat alone among the books, now quiet, now composed. I decided to let him be and closed the door.

MARRAKECH
MOROCCO

A WEEK LATER, a minor miracle occurred. Two, actually, if you count my not going to a Moroccan prison. But the real miracle happened in a place and manner that was most surprising. It involved monkeys. That, in and of itself, is not surprising. Everybody knows a good story must have monkeys.

The passengers had changed, but Eddie still felt haunted by the two injured boys. When with others he was his usual chipper self, but would grow uncharacteristically quiet when he thought others weren't looking. I desperately wanted to cheer him up. It was a rare moment of accord between Susie and myself. Working together, we even succeeded. It happened at Gibraltar.

If you've heard of Gibraltar, you probably know it has a rock. Boy, does it. The Rock of Gibraltar is the stuff of legend. It's impossible to not be impressed by at least one aspect of the Rock. Even Cosmina would get off on that old rock.

The history was staggering. After all, the sole access to all of the Mediterranean to the outside world was through the Strait of Gibraltar. He who ruled a mere seven miles of waterway—from the tip of Morocco to the tip of Spain—ruled the Mediterranean. As if the Strait wasn't easy enough to defend, the north shore was anchored by the famed, impregnable Rock. This natural, solid stone fortress rose a thousand feet high. Well, not solid—it was riddled with no less than 350 miles of tunnels and oodles of caverns.

In fact, the interior of the Rock was more interesting than the exterior. One chamber was so big they made it into a theater. Behind the stage were natural rock formations stunningly lit in several colors. Pavarotti himself sang there. Most amazing of all was the underground lake in the Rock—still five hundred feet above sea level! But, really, it wasn't about the history or the caverns. It's all about the monkeys.

The Rock of Gibraltar is home to Barbary Macaques. They are the only wild population of monkeys in Europe. They were most likely brought over from north Africa by the Moors during their seven hundred year reign. There is considerable debate about how that happened and why. What is undisputed, however, is that they were already a

338

problem when the British took over the area in 1713. Also undisputed is that they are feisty, thieving little bastards.

Several hundred monkeys live on the Rock, divided into five troops that live at the top of the Rock. Once in a while a few might make a brief foray into town at the base of the Rock. This results in a bit of hassle to protect property from theft or damage, but most locals believe the presence of the monkeys is worth the trouble.

Certainly the British monarchy would agree. According to legend, as long as the monkeys are on the Rock the British will own it and keep their monarchy alive. Legend or not, the British take it seriously enough to keep tabs on the monkeys at all times. In 1942 the population dwindled to just seven, and the great British Prime Minister Sir Winston Churchill ordered the numbers of monkeys be replenished immediately from both Morocco and Algeria. The order was enacted in what was surely an efficient, if loud and exasperating, military manner.

In fact, for centuries the entire monkey population was taken care of by the British Army. The military controlled their population and even appointed an officer to supervise their welfare. This included disciplined food allowances of such items as fruit, vegetables and nuts—all included in the monkey budget. Yes, the British military had a monkey budget. The officers recorded the births of the macaques and, in proper military fashion, named every single new infant, usually after some high ranking official or other. Should any macaque fall ill, it was taken to the Royal Naval Hospital. In fact, Gibraltar Monkeys received treatment equal to that of any other enlisted person.

Tourists loved the monkeys, of course. The feeling was quite mutual. How else would the monkeys get their greedy little hands on treats like sandwiches and candy bars? Obesity was the leading cause of death among

Gibraltar Monkeys.

Our tour van chugged up the steep road that wound higher, ever higher, to the Upper Rock. Just off the road was a plummet straight down to the sea. Those of us on the passenger side of the van—or driver side, rather, since it was British territory and a British vehicle—tried not to look down. Susie and Aurelia both hunkered down over their tour-provided boxed lunches. Cheetos were safer to contemplate than a vertical cliff of 1,000 feet. Eddie and I, however, strained to see past them and into the great abyss of sky. The driver, a small, middle-aged Englishman in a hat, stared straight ahead at the long, long line of brake lights. There was only one road to the top and everybody was on it.

We heard a thunderous thump. Something large hit the roof of the van. It was so loud that several of us nearly dropped our lunches.

"Stow your food," the driver ordered. "Put it away good."

"What was *that*?" Susie asked, rather alarmed.

"Him," the driver answered, gesturing a thumb out his window.

There, sitting complacently on the driver's side rearview mirror, was a big monkey. He was a burly animal with cocoa-colored fur covering his entire body. His face was 'clean shaven' and a lighter brown. He had no tail. He seemed quite complacent. Another heavy thump rattled our roof and our nerves, and this time we heard a scrambling. We could follow the sound from the back of the roof all the way to the front. Then the antenna began waving madly. Occasional flashes of a small, hairy paw could be seen playfully batting at it, exactly as a cat would paw a length of string.

We exited the vehicle and oodles of monkeys were immediately all over us. They jumped into our not-so-waiting arms and onto our backs. Susie, being a rather sturdy lass, was the target of a particularly big and ugly varmint. It leaped onto her back and immediately scrambled onto her head. With the living, squirming monkey mask blocking her vision, she began flailing her hands and running around. This would have been hilarious, had she not been several steps from a precipice a thousand feet down. Eddie rushed over and steadied her. Though he tugged on the beast, it refused to budge. It absolutely loved being on Susie's head. Indeed, it even began batting Eddie's hands away as he reached for it.

And then the miracle happened. Susie suddenly composed herself, consciously setting aside her knee-jerk reaction of fear. She stood a little taller. Peering from beneath the protruding, hairy belly of the monkey, she smiled. It was a radiant smile, reflected in her eyes. They'd never looked so pretty.

Eddie smiled, too, and exclaimed, "It's about time!"

All three of my companions were targeted for monkey business, though I was avoided for some reason. But my moment of intimacy came soon enough. A baby monkey leapt up onto Aurelia's back and—no doubt having watched others of his kind —began grooming her sweater. It was adorable. Delicate little fingers poked and prodded through the weave of her sweater. Perhaps he wanted to smooth the patterns into the uniform elegance he found on his family. More likely he wanted to find a bug to snack on. He had yet to grow up into a sugar and fat addicted, corpulent freeloader like the others. Aurelia thought it was cute, but grew mildly alarmed when he wouldn't stop. Try as she might, she couldn't shoo it off. Finally I held out my hand and the baby monkey took it just like any little kid, and jumped down. The skin on his palm was not rough, as I suspected, but quite soft and supple.

Leaving the van behind—it would catch up, as there was only a single one-way road—we walked to the top of the Rock. The views of dry Spain and even drier Morocco were stunning. Unfortunately, the weather was not dry. The thick clouds above had begun to spit at us. Meanwhile, monkeys bounced all over the place.

Eddie seemed truly happy. He was having a blast and, amazingly, so was Susie. Not all things were perfect, however. When Susie saw Aurelia and I cuddling—Aurelia was very clingy—she tried the same with Eddie. It didn't work.

After a while we'd seen our fill. The van came easing up to us, a monkey sneaking a ride on each side mirror. When we approached the vehicle, they scrambled up onto the roof. I opened the door and suddenly a monkey struck. It was astoundingly fast. In the bat of an eye, the animal swooped into the van, reached deep into the seat back pocket, fished out Aurelia's bag of chips, and leapt back out. The whole maneuver literally took about two seconds. Even if he'd seen the chips in advance, that would have been amazing. Obviously he knew what people did with their uneaten food. I thought it was amazing. Aurelia didn't.

"Hey!" she shouted, leaping half-way out the van after him. She shook her little fist in the air and squeaked furiously, "Those are *my* Cheetos! You give them back!"

Laughing, Eddie said, "I think he's scared of you, Aurelia."

"He better be," she smoldered adorably. "He comes back here I'm gonna pop a cap in his ass."

Lest we risk thinking that life was looking up, reality

came crashing down upon us like a ton of manure. Eddie somehow managed to join me for a drink after dinner, where he told me about the stink of it.

"Well, it happened," he said simply. "I got fired."

I stared at him in shock.

"Susie's packing right now. I had to lie to get away for a bit. I just wanted to be away from her for a little bit tonight."

"How...?"

"The family sued Windstar Cruises and the knee-jerk reaction was to fire me," Eddie explained. "What can you do?"

"Goddamn ships," I complained bitterly. "You did everything possible for them, everything by the book. You saved their lives! Hell, you even went to the freakin' hospital in Italy with them. I guess I'm not surprised they're suing the cruise line, but did they really have to put it on you? The family didn't give you any credit?"

"Actually, I heard they did," Eddie said. "All the officers backed me up, too. All but one. That was enough. So I'm gone."

All of the officers backed him up, but one. That sounded familiar.

"Who?" I asked. "Who didn't back you up? I thought you got along with everybody."

"I don't want to talk about it," Eddie said, waving off the subject. "It's done. I feel stabbed in the back, to be honest."

I desperately wanted to press the matter. This did not feel like an isolated incident at all. In all my years of ships, and all the hundreds I'd worked with on a daily basis, I'd never known so many to get fired so fast. It all seemed to come down to one mystery officer, too. I had no proof of that, of course, but could not deny the feeling that death stalked the decks of *Wind Surf*. Was it the same mysterious officer who had Janie fired, took a shot at Yoyo, and now stabbed Eddie in the back? Like Eddie, I got along very well with all the officers aboard. I couldn't imagine any of them being so petty. Only one thing was clear: someone on *Wind Surf* was a closet asshole. A phantom firer.

"Guess I'll have to deal with Susie after all," Eddie added. "I can't stay on ships anymore."

"Sure you can," I disagreed. "Getting fired on one cruise line doesn't matter to the others. Any first worlder who's survived ships is hot property. But you're right about one thing: you'll have to deal with Susie."

Eddie smiled ruefully and added, "Easier to jump ship in port."

"I'm going to miss you, buddy," I said earnestly, and we clinked glasses.

***

I have wanted to see Marrakech for many years. My ex-wife and I planned on a trip for years. Somehow I have a feeling I beat her there. Ha ha, bitch! Just kidding. Anyway, Marrakech was all that I hoped and more. There were snake charmers in the massive square, theatrical water carriers plying the bazaar, and spice markets with piles of saffron three feet high. For Marrakech was truly the gateway to the mighty Sahara, the world's greatest desert. Camel trains came in daily. I heard the Muslim prayers five times a day broadcast over the air. I saw the veils, the djellabas, the donkeys, the monkeys. I very nearly saw the jails. Yes, really.

The tour was rather complicated. The ship dropped us

off in Casablanca and two busses would drive the 300 kilometers into the desert, right up to the Atlas mountains, to the fabled city of Marrakech. Once the tour of the city was complete, the busses would drive through the Sahara to the western coast of Morocco to meet up with *Wind Surf* at a small port called Essaouira. The dual port action wasn't the worry, so much as Marrakech itself. That promised to be most tricky.

We would have to herd eighty utterly overwhelmed suburban Americans single file through crowds of screaming hawkers, rug sellers, spice merchants, snake charmers, barefoot children, laden donkeys, and spitting camels. That would be hard enough to accomplish in the open, but we had to keep everyone together through a warren of streets, alleys, stalls, tents, niches, alcoves, and mosques unchanged since the 12th century. Safety was such a concern that three local guides were hired for each bus, as well as two crew members.

Therein lay the trouble.

The day before Cosmina and I retired to our usual table in the Compass Rose to work out the details. Cosmina smoked like a fiend. She was understandably concerned. She would be on one bus, of course, and I would be on the other. But who else? How many reliable crew members could we find who were off duty long enough to join a twelve hour tour? Fabrice was too busy for that, as was Barney. The marina remained open, which meant Eddie and Susie had to stay aboard on this, their last chance for a port before leaving. After the accident the previous week, that meant Faye had port duty, as well. The spa was open all day, thus negating Rick, Natalie, or Ingrid. That left who?

"Yoyo, of course," I said.

The eruption of tobacco smoke enveloped her head as if her temper had exploded like gunpowder.

"He lost eight guests in Italy doing a tour safely done by millions every year, for Christ's sake," she snorted. "Can you imagine him taking control if something goes wrong?"

"Well, you already said no to all the shop girls," I retorted. "That's the only department closed all day. Except the casino."

Cosmina's eyes narrowed.

"Fine," she finally said. "But she'll be on my bus. I don't want you two making out when you're supposed to be watching passengers. You get Yoyo."

And so it was.

Going so far from shore, so deep into a non-Western culture, required some guidance. Prior to departure Cosmina gave a ten minute lecture on what to expect. Her speech was an odd mixture of prevention and tarnation. It began with cultural attitudes about getting along with locals. Being a Muslim nation, most rules fell on the shoulders of women, of course. Photographs: it was extremely rude to take someone's picture without asking permission, especially of women. Eye contact: women, keep your eyes to the pavement to avoid confrontations with men who feel challenged by you. "La, shukran"—no, thank you—needed to be said forcefully at any invitation or approach.

As Cosmina continued, she grew heated. Being from a distinctly macho culture like Romania, her ire was not directed at the inequality of the sexes. She was used to that, and even agreed with an alarming amount of it. Rather, Cosmina began frothing at the mouth over the fact that, well, we were going into Morocco. She was scared she was going to lose some tourists. Her nerves crackled with such ferocity that her speech was nothing less than fire and brimstone.

"Stay in the group at all times!" she cried. "Women, especially, will find things uncomfortable. Men will glare or leer at you if you're alone. And for God's sake, don't show any skin! Do you have any idea what will happen if you show skin? You will get eye-raped, for sure, but probably worse. Wear long pants and long sleeves at all times, or else! Men, too! You go in there wearing shorts and a T-shirt and I can't protect you. They have people juggling fire, for Christ's sake, and snake charmers. If you leave the group, I cannot guarantee your safety. I've hired three local guides to assist each busload, but what can they do against the masses of angry Muslims wielding fire and commanding poisonous snakes? You've got fifteen minutes before the busses leave. So go back to your cabins, dress appropriately, say your prayers, whatever you need to do. Because once you get on the bus, it'll be too late."

"Very inspiring," I congratulated as she stepped off the stage. "Look, you made Yoyo cry."

The petite photographer stared up at Cosmina with huge, terror-filled eyes.

"I need a cigarette," she muttered, then stormed past the crowd of awe-struck passengers—each and every one thinking they'd made a horrible, horrible mistake.

The drive to Marrakech took three hours. Once we left the city, the desert yawned deep and wide. It was hard to imagine that we were heading directly into a desert waste stretching a whopping 2,800 miles. That was the distance between Los Angeles and New York City! Imagine driving across the entire breadth of the continental United States— the world's fourth-largest nation—and never seeing anything grow. The Sahara was crazy desolation. Even the cowboys, riding atop exhausted and dehydrated horses through the scrubby Old West, got to see the occasional buzzard circling above. Not in the Sahara. Maybe things had lived there once, but it's been an unending circle of death for millions of years. Indeed, there were sections of the Sahara where not even insects lived.

The city of Marrakech was deceiving to the core. At a glance, there wasn't much to appreciate. Oh, there were plenty of gardens boasting date palms and several very fine mosque towers, but if driving through one might not take much notice of the place. When staring at drab, patched walls, it's easy to yawn and move on. Yet just behind the mortar, sheltered in a courtyard surrounded on all sides for ultimate privacy, are secret gardens of the lushest beauty. Peppered throughout the seemingly dirty and downtrodden streets, tucked inside and just out of view, were moments as wondrous as anything the pasha could boast of in the Alhambra. Then again, it could also just be a utilitarian, mud-brick courtyard festooned with dripping laundry. And that was the magic of Morocco: it was impossible to imagine what was just out of sight. It was a mesmerizing land where wealth of all types, be it monetary or cultural, abuts illiteracy and subsistence.

But we were not explorers. We were suburban Americans. That meant shopping. And what better place to shop than the ancient medina? For the medina, while overwhelmed with acrobats and actors and magicians, was really about shopping. Morocco was a land of fantastic handcrafts, a wonder of woven cloth and rugs of all colors. Leatherwork was everywhere, tanned in a startling variety of colors from tanning pits in use since antiquity. Anything and everything could be found among the tents and stalls, from pounds of real saffron to bottles of not-so real magical potions. In short, the Medina was everything you'd imagine from a bazaar in the Sahara. I was expecting Disney's Aladdin to run by at any moment, having stolen a loaf of bread.

But behind the wonder lay danger. The place was chaotic. The sights, the sounds, the smells: all were overwhelming. Even experienced travelers get lost in a place like that. Luckily, the guides on my busload of tourists were top notch. They kept the guests organized and moving smoothly. The only difficulty was with Yoyo. He was supposed to stay at the front of the tour with the main guide, in order to photograph the tourists oohing and aahing. Invariably I found him wandering aimlessly on his own, playing with a brass trinket or following a camel. I was very, very glad I had chosen to bring up the rear. Otherwise Yoyo would never have made it back.

No, the real drama came during lunch. For it was here that both busloads of tourists met up. The eighty-odd passengers took over a restaurant in a gorgeous outdoor courtyard. A dozen round tables mingled with countless giant urns pregnant with lush plants and even palm trees. Everywhere were fountains whose water overflowed with rose petals, lending the air a soft, lush quality. The hard desert sun was diffused by shady palms and flapping canopies, leaving the mosaic-covered floor cool. Each table was hosted by a local guide to educate the passengers on the unique cuisine of Morocco. To each table was brought a huge tajine filled with steaming cinnamon and pepper chicken and an extremely delicate hand-rubbed orange couscous.

All that was awesome. Sitting at the table with Yoyo, Cosmina, and Aurelia was not. The two women had been fighting all morning. It was epic. Actually, as feisty as

Aurelia was, she rarely directed her energies towards actual confrontation. She took the passive in passive aggressive quite literally. In other words, she utterly blew Cosmina off. And therein lay the problem.

It all started with wardrobe. Though Aurelia had been in attendance for Cosmina's fire and brimstone speech, she felt no compulsion whatsoever to wear long sleeves or even pants. Cosmina had been too busy freaking out—I mean 'being efficient'—to notice. Once the bus took off and the two were finally sitting next to each other, Cosmina nearly had a heart attack. Aurelia was wearing a pink T-shirt— tight enough to show no bra—and cargo shorts with a decidedly feminine cut. She had also brought a sweater, which she tied around her waist. When challenged by Cosmina, she merely shrugged. The vitriol had been building ever since. And finally, during lunch, it erupted.

"What the Hell is wrong with you?" Cosmina seethed to Aurelia.

"What?" Aurelia asked, nonchalantly dropping several sugar cubes into her mint tea.

"You ordered American food? Why did you order American food? You can't order American food!"

"Why not?"

"Because we're on a tour!" Cosmina viciously whispered. "We have to lead by example."

"But I don't like tajines," Aurelia said simply.

"How do you know?" Cosmina retorted. "How could you *possibly* know what a real tajine tastes like? We're not in the Moroccan restaurant in Bucharest. What do you know about Morocco? I've studied Morocco because it's my job. It's what I do for a living, learning about other cultures. *I'm* the professional here. You're not. You'd be totally lost here without me."

Aurelia didn't say anything. Cosmina gladly filled in the silence with angry, repetitive mutterings.

"...tell me she doesn't like tajines! She doesn't know anything. Nothing. She knows nothing!"

"I know I don't like tajines," Aurelia finally sassed back, sipping her tea.

"You don't know shit!" Cosmina exploded. Several guests turned to look, so she hunkered down and continued with a fierce whispering.

"Look at what you're wearing! How stupid can you be to wear that? I should just leave you here. How would you like that? Just leave you here to get along by yourself in this strange land in your wet T-shirt."

Cosmina leaned in close to Aurelia's face and taunted, "What do you think of that?"

Aurelia, unfazed, replied, "I lived in Morocco for three years."

Then, turning to a passing waiter, Aurelia proceeded to converse with him in a mix of French and Arabic a long, long time. The waiter, delighted with the surprise conversation, eventually bowed and walked away. He wasn't the only one surprised, actually. I think it was the most I'd ever heard the aloof Aurelia speak.

Cosmina sat and watched the whole conversation, dumbfounded. The moment Aurelia turned back to her mint tea, Cosmina took a final jab. With great—if hushed—authority, she declared, "My word is law!"

Aurelia shrugged her delicate shoulders and then proceeded to actively ignore her. Cosmina was furious. I was impressed. I recalled the dinky blackjack dealer when she was shaking her fist in the lounge and screaming, "Look at my balls!" I sensed I could learn something from this little one about defying expectations.

Trying to diffuse the tension at the table, I suggested to Cosmina, "Perhaps we should switch on the way back."

"Shut up!" she snapped. "I'm keeping you with Yoyo forever!"

It didn't turn out that way, however. Yoyo missed the bus and only at the last second hopped onto Cosmina's. A good thing for him, too, as the drive home was nothing short of ruinous.

It all started when our bus driver got pulled over by the Moroccan Royal Gendarmerie for speeding. That, in and of itself, was not the problem. It was amusing, in fact. Of course, we've all heard horror stories of reckless tour bus drivers driving off cliff-side roads in the Andes or something, but our driver was nothing of the sort. He was driving down a ramrod straight road through the middle of hours and hours of empty desert. I guess cops had speed traps everywhere.

Alas, the driver did not have all his papers. I don't know what kind of papers that involves in an Arabic country, but he didn't have 'em. A quick bribe of the officer solved that problem. That should have been the end of it. But it wasn't the end of it.

The gendarme waved a hand to indicate all the passengers and spouted something in Arabic. Sometimes Arabic language sounds very ugly. With the night creeping over the Saharan wasteland and a gendarme in blue military fatigues carrying a machine gun yelling at us, it was ugly indeed. I leaned across the aisle and asked our guide, Yousef, if we should be getting nervous.

"He wants to know who is on the bus," Yousef informed me.

"No problem," I said. I stood up and called out to the passengers to pass their passports up to the front. Booklets were passed from hand to hand, back to front, sometimes dropping in the darkening bus. Annoyances were muttered, as well as a few curses, but mostly people were hushed. A pile of passports rose from my seat. The officer took his sweet time picking them up one by one, flipping through them, peering in detail with his flashlight, and finally comparing each to the bus driver's list. The process took so long that the passengers began speaking amongst themselves, quietly at first, but with growing casualness. Soon the entire bus was talking. A nasty bark from the gendarme shut everybody up immediately.

The list did not correspond to the passports. Heated words were exchanged between the gendarme and the driver, then the gendarme and the guide. One need not speak the language to recognize accusations or defenses. After several minutes of heated debate, which appeared to include references to another bribe, the gendarme stuck a thumb at me.

"What's going on?" I asked Yousef.

"Your passport isn't here."

"Of course not," I said. "It's on the ship."

"I told him that. He wants to know why."

"I assume it's to stop crew from jumping ship in foreign ports."

Yousef spoke, the gendarme responded. The atmosphere was getting more heated, not less. Finally Yousef turned back to me again and asked, "How do you justify going so far into Morocco without a passport?"

"A crew ID is a legally accepted form of identification," I replied, growing nervous. I couldn't help but dwell on the irony that every other cruise line I'd worked for allowed American employees to keep their passports. Only on Windstar Cruises did I have to relinquish the document and rely on my cheap plastic crew ID. That was a perk that had annoyed many of my fellow crew members.

The gendarme barked orders at me and gestured outside. His hard posture and impatient stare made it clear he wanted me to exit the bus.

My throat got dry.

"No way," I said. To Yousef I repeated several times, rather urgently, "No way. Please tell him I am staying with the group."

The gendarme was not happy. He began insisting for me to obey in a manner that intimidated me and scared the bejesus out of the driver—which in turn scared the bejesus out of me. It was a nasty spiral. The driver urged me to go outside, begging with clasped hands. He was visibly sweating. Soon I was, too. In heavily accented English, the driver implored, "Please go. He no take you unless... stay in light. Stay in light."

"Now I'm really freakin' out," I commented, only half in jest. To Yousef, I asked, "What the hell does he mean?"

"I go with you," Yousef said. "He will not arrest you without taking me, as well."

"Tell me what the driver means by 'stay in the light,'" I insisted. "If that's some sort of *Poltergeist* reference, I'm running. You hear me? I'm running."

"Stay in the headlights," Yousef explained. "If the gendarme tries to take you away, stay visible to the driver and the passengers."

With great reluctance I stepped off the bus. Yousef quickly interjected himself between me and the gendarme. Stepping onto the hard-packed dirt of the roadside, I glanced around nervously.

The sun had set and the air was cooling. A strong

breeze blew from the east, from the rugged Atlas Mountains behind us. Some distance away, the dunes piled up to the side of a rocky outcropping. The silhouette of date palms teased at life, yet atop the rocky promontory sat only the blasted, bleached ruins of an ancient fortress. This desert was dead, dead, dead. Nothing lived here at all except miraculous flies the size of swallows. The stupid things went straight for my eyes, presumably for the moisture. They kept thumping into my face. As if I didn't have enough problems...

We stalked over to the front of the bus and stood firmly in the blast of the headlights. The gendarme motioned towards his patrol car sitting in the dark, but I shook my head. He marched up and began yelling at me. It was not pleasant, and even more disconcerting because I had no idea what he was saying. I was distracted mightily by the headlights flashing on the fully automatic assault rifle he wore over his shoulder. I know everybody else in the world thinks to be American means to sleep with an M-16, but that is obviously not true. An angry man with an assault rifle yelling at you in a foreign tongue is the stuff of nightmares.

I did not want to end up in a Moroccan prison. Being in the country without a legal form of ID was enough to warrant it. Despite what I said, what the hell did I know about my ship ID's legal status? I just assumed I was legal —and we all know what happens when we assume. I could easily have been in breach of some provision of international law, or Moroccan law. Even the suspicion of it was enough to justify being arrested and processed. And if that occurred, well, *anything* could happen....

Yousef was a godsend. He didn't bother translating everything, which was probably a good thing. For nearly an hour they shouted back and forth. An hour! Finally the vibe changed. The gendarme, unable to separate me from the group, seemed to realize his limits. Unless he was willing to truly escalate the situation—a risky proposition with the driver and forty-odd passengers watching—all he had was intimidation.

In the end all was cleared. In fact, we didn't even have to bribe the guy. No doubt he knew that you just don't harass tourists or they don't come back. To be honest, he probably just wanted a little retribution for the fact that America was currently invading two of his fellow Arabic nations. The gendarme drove off, and we did, too. Or tried to. We got about ten miles before the bus broke down.

Needless to say, there was no cell phone reception out in the middle of the Sahara. Fortunately the bus had a CB radio, which was used to call in for a new bus. None were available. What they were all doing after dark on a weekday remained a mystery. A repair vehicle was sent out. The passengers were allowed to wander outside the bus, of course, but none did. Considering what they'd just witnessed with me and the gendarme, nobody felt like stretching their legs—or even peeing. Eventually the repairman came and replaced the fan belt. We limped back to Essaouira, a whopping four hours late. A mortified Cosmina nearly swooned with relief.

IBIZA
SPAIN

THOUGH IT HAD been a long day, after the Marrakech debacle I felt the need for a drink to unwind. Cosmina joined me, wanting to hear about all the sordid details. Our usual table in the Compass Rose was occupied so she invited me to her cabin for a drink. Kicking off our shoes, we sat on the bed and shared a bottle of wine. Cosmina, to my astonishment, didn't smoke too much. Perhaps that's because she smoked two whole packs while waiting for our bus to return. Reminiscing about the day, we managed quite a few laughs about it all—the arguments with Aurelia, the bus being pulled over, the bus breaking down, the thought of Yoyo trying to handle it all. Now that it was over, it was easy to laugh. Or maybe we were just getting tipsy.

"Looks like you and Aurelia are really getting along," Cosmina said in an obviously leading manner.

At first I shrugged, but after a moment nodded and said, "We're not like you and Barney or anything, but we enjoy each other's company."

"Because you're done with Romanian women," she offered, laughing.

Chuckling, I admitted, "Can't live with 'em, can't live without 'em."

"Well, I'm sorry about lunch," Cosmina said.

I waved it off, saying, "Aurelia can be quite vexing."

She wasn't apologizing to Aurelia, whom she had wronged, but to me. Cosmina did the same thing with Susie, way back when she snubbed her on the gondola tour in Venice. Even when apologizing Cosmina seemed to have an agenda. I asked her if she knew anything about Eddie's getting fired, and she nodded. I then asked if she knew anything about an officer not sticking up for Eddie, and she shrugged.

Obviously Cosmina had the ear of the ship's officers. I had hoped she'd feel free to spread a bit of gossip on this issue. It's not like these were military or insider secrets or anything! But I was concerned by some mystery officer dealing death blows to careers, especially to a man who was liked by all. Not only was Eddie liked, but he went out of his way to help senior officers. He dove with Emmet all the time, checking for explosives and whatnot. Barney, too, was a fan of the dive team. He and Susie both grew up in the same small town in Canada. Eddie hadn't moved there until his teens. But while Barney had a connection with the diving couple, he was in deeper with Cosmina, who abhorred Susie. Had he been the one who didn't support Eddie? Was he the phantom firer?

We finished the first bottle of wine and moved on to a second. It was getting late and we were getting tired, but one more glass seemed warranted. I yawned even as I poured the glass. Cosmina tugged off her socks and wiggled her toes.

"No luck for you," she said. "My socks are off."

"Mmph," I mmphed. I was too tired to articulate.

Cosmina was quiet for a moment, wiggling her toes, then blindsided me.

"When I was younger," she said simply, "I was raped."

Though surprised, I managed not to stare. I immediately felt awkward. How selfish was that? She was the one who'd just admitted something deeply, deeply personal, yet I was the one feeling uncomfortable? Was I supposed to say something? I couldn't for the life of me think of an appropriate response. So I set my wine down and listened.

Still staring at her feet, Cosmina continued, "It was raining and muddy. All I could focus on was how cold my feet were. They were so cold. So cold and wet. That's all I could think about through the whole thing. It's all I can remember of it, even now. So now I can't make love if my feet are cold."

Looking up at me, she asked, "Makes me weird, doesn't it?"

"Not at all," I said. "Not at all."

Many aspects of Cosmina's character suddenly

became clear. Psychology wasn't the only thing that made people act they way they did, but it certainly contributed. Rape was never about sex, but control. Control had been taken away from her, leaving nothing to fill the void except feelings of inadequacy. Now, years later, she fought tenaciously for control over the most meagre of situations. She was a tyrant when she could be, and bitter and petty when she could not. She had grown to covet strength and to admire it in others, even as she grew to hate weakness. That helped explain, for example, why she liked Francois and hated Yoyo.

Though her admission shocked me, she was very pragmatic about it. She dropped the bomb, shrugged, and moved on. Happily, this was because she'd finally found someone sock-worthy. I had already liked Barney, but now I liked him even more. Though a gentle soul himself, he knew the toughest people to deal with were usually the ones most in need of someone to try.

***

Café del Mar was the leading chill out lounge on the island of Ibiza, which meant it was probably the leading chill out lounge in the world. Ibiza was the party capital of Europe—even over perennial favorites like London, Paris, and Amsterdam—with more clubs per square meter than probably anywhere else in Europe. Unlike all those hyperactive pits of electronic dance music, Café del Mar was all about chillin' out. To aid in this, the club was positioned over a westward facing beach. The sun never went down alone, but was attended nightly by vast, adoring crowds. The music selected by the DJs to commemorate the moment was very eclectic, representing all aspects of music from all corners of the globe. They had produced about forty major hit CDs in the past 25 years.

"I must touch sacred ground," Nigel said. "You with me?"

"A pilgrimage it is!" I agreed.

The trip took a full month to plan. Mainly this was because *Surf* didn't hit Ibiza regularly and schedules were conflicting. By the time the stars did align for the trip, a whopping ten people wanted to go. Appropriate for a world-renowned club playing world-wide music, the pilgrims represented America, Australia, Bulgaria, Canada, England, Poland, and Romania. As our numbers swelled so, too, did our anticipation. Certainly music was a huge part of my life, though I never gave it enough credit. Rather, I was a gluttonous consumer, greedily snarfing it down while utterly failing to acknowledge the effort behind it.

The fateful day arrived. The weather was overcast, but we shone brightly with enthusiasm. By ten o'clock in the morning all of us had gathered but one. Twenty minutes later Rick showed up. Huffing and puffing, he dropped a heavy duffel bag to the ground. A cigarette bobbed from his mouth. Smoking was a habit he'd taken up recently.

"Sorry I'm late!" he panted. "Busy morning."

He began tugging the gold hoop in his ear. This, of course, meant he was planning mischief.

"Lots of paperwork?" Nigel asked with an Englishman's polite, if false, empathy.

"Lots of beer," Rick corrected. Sure enough, out of the duffel came a six pack of beer.

The walk to the car rental agency in Ibiza Town was short, and soon two cars were procured. In that time we learned that Rick had not been exaggerating. His staggering indicated he was already quite drunk. This was different than our previous drunken escapade, the circuit of Rome. Both Natalie and I sensed it from the very beginning. The vibe was way off. This was not a happy, silly little romp. This was serious drinking. Nobody just 'playfully' drank that much that early all alone. Despite his obvious inebriation, he was terribly excited to drive on the right side of the road in an American manner. He'd never done so before. Needless to say, I didn't relinquish the keys. He was angry but made a big, blustery show of dropping the subject.

The ten of us piled into our two cars. I drove one, hauling Aurelia, Rick, Natalie, and the ship's fitness god, Daniel. Nigel drove the other car with his bandmate Neil and three gals from the gift shop: Mel, Nina, and the new girl, Vikki. In our car, Rick glugged down another beer in record time, then dropped the empty can back in the duffel. Beer dribbled over two large CD cases, which prompted a curse from him.

"Dammit!" he blurted. "Got beer on me music."

"What the hell, Rick," Natalie chastised, looking over his shoulder—rather easily, I might add, since she was so tall. "Why did you bring so many CDs?"

"Cruising music!" he answered proudly. He fumbled through the selection—spilling more beer upon it in the process—until he found what he was looking for. "I've been collecting Café del Mar music for years! Not a single store bought disk here, mate. No way! These are all custom CDs carefully assembled—hic! Custom."

"Why did you bring so many?" Daniel asked lightly in his rather strong Polish accent. "It's only an hour drive."

"An hour?" Natalie cried, horrified. "Nobody told me it'd be an hour. That's it, I'm bored already."

We made it across the island in good time and had to

poke at the back yards of about a dozen houses before we found access to the beach. We followed the jagged, rocky shores until we came upon the club. It was closed.

"I expected it to be closed for the morning," Nigel observed, "But I didn't expect it to be closed for the season! This is off season? The weather's better than an English summer!"

Sure enough, our continual wait to make the trip happen had taken too long, and the season came to an end. As Nigel noted, the weather was still actually quite nice. We took our photos of the original Café del Mar building—there's a dozen around the world now—touched the sacred, puffy clouds painted on its walls, and had a laugh over the whole thing. Most of us had really come to lay on the famous beach. To our shock, however, it wasn't a beach at all, but a rough slag of rocks! It hurt like hell just walking on it. How people could relax upon those crags for hours in anticipation of the sunset was clearly evidence of mass drug abuse. So much for the great pilgrimage.

We wandered on foot awhile, until we found a place for lunch. We managed to chew up a lot of time. There were laughs aplenty at our bad luck. Little did we know just how bad it was about to get.

Upon returning to the cars, we discovered ours with the front passenger door wide open. That had been Rick's seat. Apparently, in his drunken stupor, he had forgotten to lock his door. His duffel bag was gone and, with it, all sixty-plus of his CDs.

Rick was furious. He immediately began blaming me for not locking the car. Why it was my responsibility to lock his door was not explained. He raged at the sky, raged at the car, raged at me. His face became splotchy and red. Waves of discontent rolled off him almost visibly. Natalie tried to console him, but was roughly disabused of the idea.

"It's not about the money!" he snapped. "It's about an era of my life that some bloody bastard *stole*! I'll never get that part of my life back, you understand? What the bloody hell would you know? You're just a child."

"Hey, now," I warned. Rick spun on me and began raging anew. "Why didn't you lock the bloody car, you bloody wanker? You told me it was locked!"

"It's not my job to lock your door," I retorted. "It's not my fault you showed up drunk—at ten o'clock in the morning!"

"How 'bout we just find a real beach?" Nigel interjected.

"Fine," Rick seethed. Sulking like a child, he stomped over to the car and slammed the door shut with tremendous force. Indeed, he yanked the handle so hard he tore it from the door. As we shuffled into our places, I was given some nice moral support from the others. As we drove off, Rick ripped off the end of a cigar with his teeth. He spit the butt at me, snarled, then lit up. I ignored his taunt. Soon the back of the vehicle was obscured in a haze of white cigar smoke, much to the chagrin of the ladies.

We drove along the coast of the island of Ibiza, just south of the town of Sant Antoni. After awhile we spotted a particularly attractive jut of the beach. The coastline, long battered by the sea, had been eaten into a twenty foot cliff. The exposed rock was a buttery golden brown, and deep like a perfectly baked Chicago-style pizza crust. At the bottom the restless sea tossed over smoothed pebbles and sand. The beach was rugged but inviting. The sun crept low early, creating a light soothing and seductive. Catching the soft, horizontal rays, the cliffs glowed like the brick of a fireplace.

We pulled our cars right up to the edge of the cliff, for at that point there was no road but a broad expanse of rocky plateau. The ten of us pushed out of the cars eagerly. Some of us wanted to play in the waves, others to gaze upon them, still others to stroll along them. Rick wasn't in the mood for any of it, not surprisingly, and didn't follow the others down a side slope that led down to the water. Natalie bravely volunteered to stay with him.

"Gimme the keys," she ordered, holding out a clawed hand.

"Why?" I asked, glancing furtively atop the plateau. Rick stood perilously close to the cliff's edge. Seeing me look up, he flipped me off.

"He wants to listen to his last CD. The one that was in the player."

Before I handed over the keys, I gave her explicit instructions to not let Rick drive. "I mean it, he's obviously very drunk and very dangerous."

"No kidding," Natalie said sarcastically.

"I'm serious, Natalie," I admonished, holding back the keys. "You're only eighteen. You ever know anybody killed from drunk driving? I do, and he wasn't nearly as far gone as Rick. I'll go swimming with these..."

"Okay, okay," she relented. She clicked her fingers together, the long nails of her outstretched hand sounding like a crab clacking its claws. Reluctantly I handed the keys over.

But the beach was calling. The ladies were already tiptoeing through the sand and surf. Aurelia, who hadn't brought a bathing suit, wanted to walk along the beach for a ways. She took my hand and we strolled along the dunes and hillocks of long grass. It was nice to be with Aurelia and stuff, but mostly I wanted to get away from Daniel.

The fitness instructor wore tight little swimming trunks that revealed a physique to make the statue of David jealous. Bastard. And speaking of godlike bodies, Nina was mercifully wearing a bikini. She and Nigel wandered off to find a quiet spot somewhere. Lucky bastard.

Eventually we returned to the group. Next to Vikki, who was sprawled across the pebbles and snoring, Aurelia wiggled her little bottom into the sand and watched the afternoon laze by. I stripped to my trunks and plunged into the mild surf. I was only in the sea for about two minutes before blinding pain ripped across my shoulder. It was a freakish amount of pain, quite possibly the worst I'd ever encountered in my life. This wasn't just some sting or a jab, either, but wave after wave of scalding hot pain. I looked around, assuming a shark had ripped off my arm or something. There, just chillin' in true Café del Mar fashion, was a little jellyfish.

Though my brain told me it was not so, I insisted the six-inch critter was nothing less than a Portuguese Man-of-War. I also convinced myself that, upon leaping out of the water, I actually rose straight up and ran on top of the waves all the way to the beach. Aurelia said I waded. Whatever. All I know for sure was that the ball of my shoulder was slashed with three distinct red streaks. Before my eyes they swelled and raged ever hotter. I rushed up to the car, intent on some towels, some fresh water, something, anything—only to discover the car was gone.

So was Rick.

I was furious. I had left Natalie with explicit instructions to not let Rick drive. The hour was getting late and we needed to get going soon. There was no way we could fit eight of us in Nigel's sub-compact rental car. An entire hour passed, but Rick and Natalie did not return.

Meanwhile, I paced in pain. With each puff of wind upon my shoulder the pain flared ever hotter, ever higher. I'd heard you can urinate on a jellyfish sting to take away the pain. I asked for volunteers, but none were forthcoming. Though I tried to jest about my burning shoulder, the reality was that none of us were laughing about anything. We all felt the vibe. Rick was so emotional at that point, and so drunk and so low, we all looked at the sandy cliff from below and honestly expected to see the vehicle careening over the edge to plunge into the sea. Even a sober driver was in danger of doing so.

An hour of stewing passed and the sun began pushing into the sea. Nigel, an introspective man ever in search of the elusive melody, approached me and quietly asked, "You don't think Natalie's driving do you?"

I didn't reply, but just stared up at the plateau.

"You know how this could end, right?"

I knew. Danger was in the air. Like humidity, it was tangible, cloying, unavoidable. I felt like we were living in a thriller and had been listening to the music build up all day. The ladies' faces were lined with tension, and they were not alone. Neil, a small and happy-go-lucky lad, was genuinely intimidated by the whole thing. He just wanted to go back to work, singing Neil Diamond songs. Daniel, while a visual feast for the eyes, was also a yoga instructor who embodied pacifism. The reality was that everybody expected me to handle Rick upon his return. I tried not to think about a physical confrontation with Rick. Though I was not a small man, that didn't matter one whit against Rick. He was a six-year English Army veteran. Regardless, we had to get those keys from him.

We heard the revving of the engine first. It roared far louder than the tickling surf. Then we saw the headlights.

They sawed back and forth through the damp air. Obviously whoever was driving was beyond reckless. The engine revved so high it rattled.

"Get away from the cliff!" Neil shouted, even as he shooed everybody from the scene. Nigel and I started running up the slope to the plateau. We reached the top just as the car zoomed past us. Shrubs flapped from the front grill and dirt streamed off the car, clumps scattering and tumbling after. We were showered with gravel. The car, a tiny blue sub-compact, looked ludicrous as it swerved and skidded like a sports car in an action movie. The car stopped, facing the cliff. Dust rose. Hearts pounded.

All was silent for one long, tense second. Then the engine started revving again. It revved louder and louder until it shrieked like a steaming tea kettle. With a start, the car charged full speed towards the cliff's edge. Even over the high-pitched whine of the engine we heard Natalie's scream. Rick was going to intentionally drive right off the plateau and into the sea.

The car was going too fast to stop. There was nowhere to turn. It was too late. Then, at that very moment, the very threshold of tragedy, Rick locked the breaks and cranked hard on the wheel. The car arched sideways almost instantly and, still sideways, slid damn near the very lip of the cliff. The whole maneuver was unexpectedly silent. The turn was so sharp it was astounding the car didn't roll and tumble right off the plateau anyway.

The dust began to settle. Nigel and I both ran to the car. The passenger door kicked open, and Natalie came lurching out. Tears streaming down her face and sobbing, she floundered away, to safety. The passenger door remained ajar, leaving the open door alert impotently calling. The driver's door remained closed. Rick remained within.

Now it was my turn.

I felt Nigel's eyes on my back while stalking to the driver-side door. I heard the others whispering at the edge of the slope. It only added to my nerves. Finally at the car, I looked through the window. Rick sat motionless, hands on the wheel. I knocked on the window. He didn't seem to notice. I gripped the handle and yanked the door open.

"Get out," I said firmly. There didn't seem any need to shout. In that rarified air, all felt the gravity of what was about to happen.

Rick turned off the car. Keys in hand, he slowly complied. He pulled himself out of the vehicle and stood tall. He stepped right up into my face. Our eyes met. I didn't recognize the man.

"Give me the keys, Rick," I said evenly. My gut tensed.

He did not comply. The moment dragged on. The alarm beeped incessantly, maddeningly.

Rick opened his mouth to say something, but suddenly was overwhelmed by the flailing fists of Natalie!

"All I wanted was to listen to music!" Natalie screeched as she beat him. He cringed and protected himself, but she continued hammering away. "You son of a bitch! You son of a bitch!"

After a minute of attack, Rick had dropped the keys and began just accepting the blows. I pulled her back as gently as one can gently pull back an hysterically violent giantess with two-inch claws. She stopped her assault and buried her face into my shoulder—my *jellyfish* shoulder. I tried not to cry out, but it was impossible. The pain was excruciating. It didn't help that I was angry with her for letting Rick have the keys. But I was just glad they were safe. Through sobs she explained everything that had happened. They were laying on the hood, listening to music, when Rick offered to teach her how to drive donuts. The moment he got the keys he took off like a bat out of hell. Scared her to death, but she didn't know what to do.

As for the drunk asshole himself, after the beating from Natalie he walked to the edge of the cliff. Nigel hovered nearby, but all Rick did was stare out at the darkening sea. The car's open door alert beeped annoyingly. Natalie wept. The surf ebbed quietly, and the wind whistled gently. The sun had set. It was over.

Despite the absurdity of the idea, Rick suddenly insisted upon driving us home. Ah, alcohol, how you can utterly destroy common sense! On the drive back to the other side of the island, I insisted on being in the backseat with Rick. Neil drove, making it just the three of us. Thus all seven of the others—including the extra-sized Natalie— crammed into the car with Nigel. That was how scary Rick was being. Fortunately he was so drunk he didn't even notice the new arrangement. He mumbled and blubbered about his lost CDs over and over and over. Considering how badly Rick had battered the little car, it drove well.

That is, until one of the tires exploded.

I've had my fair share of flat tires, but had never seen a blowout like that. Miraculously, Neil had no difficulty pulling the car over safely. We got out and whistled over the sight of it: the sidewalls had completely disintegrated— just vanished, as if abducted by a UFO! Heat radiated off the rim like a grate in a fireplace. Rick must have really driven the hell out of that poor, poor Peugeot. Nigel's car pulled up behind as I fished the spare tire from the trunk. Interestingly, not only Neil, but also Nigel and Daniel fought over changing the tire. None would allow me to do so.

"You've had to deal with enough issues today," Nigel said. "Plus, if Rick goes off again you're the only one who can handle him. I don't think Natalie's got it in her anymore. You know women, once they vent, it's gone forever."

So we made it back. Some pilgrimage. The real kicker was that night Aurelia and I had an argument for some reason I still don't understand and parted badly. To say it was a crappy day was a grand understatement. Further, I was informed in the morning that the bright red scars blazing across my shoulder were likely permanent, unless I went to a doctor and got some sort of shot to bleach them out. Lovely. I vowed from then on to keep my Ibiza visits to simple, wholesome things... like Vibratex Rabbit Pearl vibrators and stuff.

***

Aurelia and I didn't exactly break up because we were never exactly together. Regardless of labels—friends with benefits, ship squeeze, what have you—we patched things up within a few days. Also in need of a patch was the rift between Rick and I. That was addressed several days later when he invited me to his cabin for an 'apology drink'. That he would choose to pair his apology with alcohol was not surprising. But that's not to say the experience didn't hold surprises. Chock full, it was.

As spa manager, Rick had his own cabin. It was the same size and design as any of the other ship managers that brought in revenue. Well, I brought in more revenue than the entire spa and lived in a closet with a broken sink and rusted toilet, but nobody cared about that. Rick had procured for his cabin a small refrigerator which he kept stocked with beer. His desk groaned under a mess of bottles of harder stuff, filling the space right up to the edge. Considering how *Wind Surf* was wont to list, my obsessive-compulsive need to keep things ship shape cried bloody murder.

He offered me a beer and we sat on the bed. Recognizing a poster on the wall with a flying saucer, I read the tag aloud, "I want to believe. You're an *X-Files* fan, too? Good boy."

"What's that?" he asked, sloshing his beer around before downing it. He'd obviously already had quite a few, for his words seemed to slosh, too. "Some porn thing?"

"Not triple X," I laughed. "*The X-Files*. That poster is from the show."

"It is?" he said, frowning at it with bleary eyes. "I just like the message. They tell us there's no such thing as UFOs. They tell us there is such thing as God. They tell us a lot of things. It's important to question authority."

"I quite agree," I said.

Having finished his beer, Rick rose and stumbled over to his desk. He shoved a meaty hand into a hotel-style ice bucket and dropped a fistful of cubes into a disposable plastic cup. He then filled it to the brim with cheap vodka. He had already slugged down half before he made it back to the bed. I watched this with concern, but both the topic and his manner seemed harmless—for the moment.

"You're hitting the sauce pretty hard," I observed.

"No kidding, mate?" he said, then toasted me before chugging the vodka.

We discussed UFOs for a while, which is a topic I've always found enjoyable. I'd read many books on the subject and devoured any silly documentary I could find. I guess like Fox Mulder from *The X-Files*, I, too, wanted to believe. But didn't. Rick and I had a lively, fun debate about it. We both continued to talk—and he continued to drink—until finally he crossed the threshold of absurdity.

"A hole in the South Pole!" he exclaimed. "There is a hole in the exact South Pole to the center of the Earth. The UFOs fly in and out of there all the time, mate!"

"That is the stupidest thing I've ever heard."

"You don't believe because authority *told* you not to believe."

"I don't believe because that's the stupidest thing I've ever heard," I retorted. "You ever heard of the Amundson-Scott station? It's a research station built right on the South Pole."

"So they tell you," Rick pointed out, tugging on his earring. "You are believing the lies of authority."

"What authority? Antarctica isn't owned by anyone. There's dozens of scientists from all over the world there."

"How do you know?" he challenged. "Have you seen them? Have you met any?"

"I've seen documentaries."

"Produced by the government?" Rick stressed. "Have *you* ever been to the South Pole?"

"No, but I know a lot about it. I have an entire library on the early excursions to the South Pole."

"Published by your government!" Rick pressed. He downed another full cup of vodka.

"Published in several countries," I replied. "The first guy to the South Pole was Norwegian. The British sent loads of people, too."

"Of course the bloody British sent people!" Rick spat. "That's what they bloody do!"

Rick suddenly rose to his feet and began pacing. His

body pulsed with energy, like a predator in a cage, moving back and forth, back and forth. I had wondered why he was pushing the anti-authority point so hard. Suddenly I was nervous to find out. The energy in the room turned chill and quiet. Like the calm of a deep, frosty night, I felt keenly aware that I wasn't safe and secure at home where I belonged. I was exposed and feeling lost—and under the threat of a predator.

Though hidden behind a layer of fat, Rick's muscles popped back into form. He shivered and raged, veins bulging in his neck, his face turning splotchy. He raged to himself as he paced, raged about how authority was always lying, always lying. He'd been downing drinks hard throughout the conversation. Who knows how many he had before I arrived. I grew concerned, fearing a repeat of Ibiza. We had been dangerously close to violence. It had smoldered and raged just below the surface. Now it looked like it was going to blow.

"They denied all of it!" he seethed, clenching his fists and curling his lips with ultimate disdain.

"All of what? Who?" I asked. I resolved at that moment to embrace whatever cockamamie story he came up with, even if it involved a UFO.

"They denied all of what they knew, all of what I saw! They forced us to remove it all from the reports. No reports, no proof," he snarled. "They think that means no truth! But they're wrong."

Rick's energy suddenly drained, spilling away to reveal a soggy mess of a man. He grew quiet, so quiet. Then Rick moved into the corner. He sat on the floor, his back to the bed. He stared at the corner. No longer did his muscles snap and tense. They drooped in defeat, then began to shake.

Rick was crying.

He began recalling memories—memories he'd pushed down deep. He bared them to the corner, not me.

"I saw it all," he sobbed. "They say it never happened in East Timor, but I *know* it did. I saw it. They killed thousands, they raped thousands. They raped bodies before they got cold. They raped nuns. They *crucified* nuns. They held people over volcanic steam pits on bamboo racks... their skin just dropping off..."

He fell into silence. He no longer sobbed, but just stared into the corner.

After a while, he asked gently to be left alone. I placed a reassuring hand on his shoulder, gave him a squeeze, then did as requested. Trudging back to my cabin, his words haunted me. I remembered the first hint of Rick's buried horror. He had thrown a fit in Pompeii at Janie's cheers about the eruption of Vesuvius. Now it made sense.

Rick just wanted to forget. He couldn't work anymore in a real job with real authority, not after they officially denied all the horrors he had seen. So he escaped to the sea. Even there, in a semi-autonomous place as head of the spa, he felt the need to self-medicate. All too common, all too useless. Alcohol didn't solve anything. It just pushed problems off until later. This guy was in serious turmoil and it was struggling to surface. Something would set him off beyond the point of no return, and it wouldn't be pretty when it happened. Rick had been able to postpone dealing with his issues plenty, what with seven ports a week. But eventually *Wind Surf* would stop offering up distraction.

I was reminded of the words of the great adventure writer, Joseph Conrad, when he wrote: *"His agitation was impressive and alarming in the little cabin, like the floundering of a great whale driven into a shallow cover in a coast. The whole ship seemed to feel the shock of his despair.* "

To date, the ship had not felt Rick's despair. But it would. For *Wind Surf* was setting sail for a Transatlantic crossing—fourteen days at sea.

WIND SURF
TRANSATLANTIC

ENDLESS SEA, endless time.

Fourteen days at sea was a long time. I planned three auctions during the span, though honestly didn't have enough art onboard to justify even two. I'd been selling off the good stuff for months. I'd requested many art reloads from Sundance, but had yet to hear back from them. No doubt they were waiting for the *Surf* to hit the Caribbean before shipping out several tons of art. Luckily, even with my short supply, on the very first auction I cleared all my goals. Thus I had a week and a half of leisurely cruising with not much to do.

Life under sail in the trade winds was so blissfully uneventful that sunset became the most dramatic moment of the day. Nothing but blue in all directions. Blue up, blue down. No clouds. No ships. I'd never been at sea for more than a day and not seen another ship. But *Wind Surf* was sailing the old trade wind route, first used by Columbus himself. The trade winds, first discovered by the Portuguese, began beyond the western edge of the Iberian peninsula. The winds reliably lifted a sailing vessel southward and west. The route was longer than the northward parabola that modern ships used to cross the Atlantic, but still the better choice. For *Wind Surf* sailed faster under sail than on engine. That's still not saying much, by modern standards of impatience. *Wind Surf* maxed out her engines at a measly twelve knots. Under sail she could push as high as fourteen. Still beats the hell out of Columbus' month-long journey.

"But for seamen, change comes with port. It boards suddenly, from the shore. Any sea voyage is an emotional whole, with a beginning, a middle, and an end. At the middle there is a solid center of self-sufficient life at sea into which everyone on the ships I have known settles comfortably; so comfortably, at times, that poses drop and psychological armor slips. It is hard to keep up every affectation on an ocean."

So said Joseph Conrad. He was quite right. For the first time drifting the high seas, I was truly comfortable in every sense of the word. And, with the next port, it would come to an end. All good things must come to an end. After nearly three years of auctioneering, I had finally found a ship that was unmistakably mine. I had stayed on her longer than the usual contract for auctioneers, so organizing my vacation seemed prudent. Sundance was happy to send me back to the world's largest sailing vessel, 'cause I was killin' it. So how cool was that? A week and a half to relax before my vacation. After six weeks I'd be back with the family. Yes, I unabashedly referred to my fellow *Wind Surfers* as family.

Nothing but blue, blue, blue. It's like being in a prison cell: nothing to change the view, hour after hour, day after day, week after week. Some people just couldn't handle the lack of distraction. One such person was Jeff, the auctioneer I'd taken *Wind Surf* from. He had worked two week-long cruises in the Caribbean, then the two-week crossing. After only seven sea days he'd already sent in his resignation.

One poor soul who had trouble handling the confining crossing was Nigel. Oh, he had no problem whatsoever with the quiet. In fact, that's all he wanted. He just couldn't get it. For poor, poor Nigel was hounded day and night by Mr. 101. This bizarre passenger made his presence known on the very first day of the cruise. During a pause between sets, the heavyset, balding man rushed up to the keyboard and jabbed his hand into Nigel's face.

"You're the keyboard player?" he asked—stating the obvious—"I'm something of a musician myself. I have composed one hundred and one songs."

"That's wonderful," Nigel said. "I'm always happy to meet a fellow music enthus—"

"A hundred and one!"

"Indeed."

"We should get together and listen to them," the rotund man said. "Where is the band's after party?"

Nigel was a proper Englishman, which meant he was

unfailingly polite. He tried desperately to parry Mr. 101's blustering self-invitations, but was unable to shake him. By the end of that first night he had already accepted a CD of songs and promised to find a way to integrate them into their musical sets. To say that the music was amateurish was an understatement of gross proportions. It was so incredibly horrible that it brought the listener to tears. The next day Nigel, who always shared music with me, played the first track of the CD for me.

"Listen to the whole thing in its entirety," Nigel guided. "You'll think it's hideously repetitive and boring—which it is—but at the end... well, listen."

One didn't need to be a musician to see just how right Nigel was. The odd mixture of synthesized sounds were indeed repetitive—and noisy. It was like a child had thrown a tantrum on an electronic keyboard, then hit repeat. It was so absurd I couldn't help but laugh. But it got worse. Just when the stupid thing was over, Mr. 101 added his special touch: duck quacks. I'm not kidding. It was freakin' hilarious.

"I promised to use some of his music for the fashion show," Nigel sighed. "It was the only way to get him out of my face. Needless to say, I won't."

Nigel never told me how he got out of it—for Mr. 101 was in attendance, puffed up and proudly waiting for his moment to shine. When I later pressed him, Nigel just smiled.

Yes, Mel did another fashion show, another 'look your fantasy life'. She was incredibly nervous, just as Janie was before her. Alas, Barney was not available for Mr. Cool, so this time I played it. What did I wear? What else? What I wore every day, accoutered complete with cigar and martini. Mel showed me exactly as I was. That's when it really struck me.

I was living my fantasy life. Whoa!

My time at sea had been filled with so many different types of trials and tribulations, I'd rarely had a chance to slow down and reflect on whether or not I was happy. Had I been pressed, most of the time I'd have probably admitted 'no'. I'm not a negative person, by any stretch of the imagination, but was always struggling for loftier goals, always just out of reach. But not any more. On *Wind Surf* I was really, truly happy. I loved what I was doing—for a change—and certainly loved where I was doing it. And I felt loved.

Love, of course, is what got me here in the first place. I would not have gone out to sea for anything less. After four years, I finally found it. Not in the way I had hoped, but as part of a family. Can't complain about that!

No, no longer was I chasing a woman who made me happy. True, our highs were higher than anything I'd seen outside of Hollywood, and our lows commensurate. Actually, after the initial horror of being a political pawn in the restaurants of Carnival Cruise Lines, there really weren't any lows. Just gaps. Long gaps. In the end, they were too long. So while I started out at sea for Bianca, I ended up at sea for me. That's what let me heal, and heal quickly. I didn't regret a minute of my journey, though certainly the chase was not a way to live a life. Happiness cannot be given, though it must be accepted. And now, finally, I was following my own advice: make yourself happy first, *then* find someone to share it with.

Whodathunkit?

While the fashion show was silly fun enjoyed by all, the great highlight of the Transatlantic cruise was surely the Captain's Ball. Captain Turner himself, having recently returned from vacation and in the company of Mrs. Turner, was to personally host the gathering. Everyone came out in their finest formalwear. This was only the second time I'd worn my tuxedo—a good thing, too, because it was in sore need of justifying its expense. The main lounge managed to somehow pack in every guest aboard. In that chaos, a small cluster of the ship's elite hovered near the bar.

"Brian!" Francois called to me from the crowd. He waved me over with a flash of gold. "Join us for something special."

Noting how he was attended by Captain and Mrs. Turner, Chief Officer Emmet, and the cruise director, Fabrice, it was hard to refuse such an invitation.

"I presume you've never tasted Rémy Martin's Louis XIII cognac," Francois said. He indicated a gorgeous bottle cradled gently in the white gloved hands of the bartender. "A blend of France's very best grapes from the Champagne region, aged in centuries-old oak casks. Named after the king enthroned at the time Rémy Martin first moved to Champagne, King Louis XIII."

With great flair, Francois took up a snifter from the bar and, tapping it with a nail, held it up to my ear. The sound resonating was the most pure note I'd ever heard in my entire life.

"Only the best crystal," Francois said proudly, "For a cognac designed and blended for kings—who, incidentally, are about the only ones who can afford it!"

The bartender poured me a glass. I swirled it lovingly, noting the legs were thick and delicious to the eyes. The flavor was stunning. There was no mistaking that it was designed for royalty. It was head and shoulders better than anything I had ever imagined. I had been sure Francois only invited me over because I was in my tuxedo.

Now I could definitely say it had paid for itself, fitting and all.

"*Note zee bottle,*" Fabrice said. "*Zee crystal notches on zee side deter theft. Ze bottle alone is worth many hundreds of dollars.*"

Captain Turner nosed his snifter delicately. After a moment, he mused, "Being that this is not single malt scotch, I defer to the nose of our resident Frenchmen."

"*Ees vairy complicated bouquet,*" Fabrice offered. "*Ze tongue ees vairy sweet, vairy mellow. But ze parfoom ees bold, with 'ints of jasmine and sandalwood.*"

"What do you think, love?" Captain Turner asked his wife.

"It does remind me of jasmine," Mrs. Turner agreed. With a self-effacing laugh, she added, "But only because Fabrice said it first!"

Suddenly Rick materialized from the crowd. He was not dressed in formalwear, but in an old T-shirt that barely stretched over his beer belly. He moved with the greatly emphasized gestures of someone three sheets to the wind and trying to hide it. Every gesture was grandly—and comically—overcompensated. He marched stiffly right up to the bar, no doubt unaware of elbowing us all out of the way. He reached out and plucked the crystal bottle off the bar. As he pulled back, his entire body wavered alarmingly. All eyes were on the expensive bottle as Rick careened backward. Several of us tensed, ready to make a grab for it should he let it fall.

But Rick didn't let it fall. He brought the bottle up to sniff the bouquet, even accidentally sticking his nose in it. When he pulled back, nose dripping with cognac, he raised his eyebrows all the way up into his hairline in an effort to appear reflective.

"Amazing!" he blurted. "I detect leather. Yes, leather, but with a hint of something else... something special."

He closed his eyes and inhaled very, very deeply.

"Yeeessss," he breathed, as if in a trance. "*Lady saddle.*"

Mrs. Turner gasped. Without missing a beat Captain Turner, placing an arm around her, guided his wife away. They disappeared into the crowd, leaving the rest of us staring at Rick in shock. He was about to guzzle some Louis XIII straight from the bottle when Francois snatched it from his hand. Though the hotel director was obviously furious, he managed to control his temper.

"What is the meaning of this?" he demanded of the gleefully unaware drunkard.

"I don't do parties," Rick slurred back happily, "Least not any I've been invited to!"

Emmet, meanwhile, had quietly motioned for security. Moments later Rick was being escorted away. I watched them go and Emmet, on his way past, said contemptuously to me, "Next time control your friend."

I stared after them, almost as aghast as Mrs. Turner. Francois recapped the cognac and handed it over to the bartender. After giving me a meaningful look, he, too, walked away. I wasn't sure what had just happened. Was I somehow being held responsible for this incident? Turns out, yes. The mysterious lurker of *Wind Surf* was about to reach out from the shadows to strike again—to strike me.

***

The following morning Francois called me to his office. Though I was absolutely comfortable with Francois, being called into his office gave me a hint of nerves.

Whenever a figure with authority called me into their inner sanctum, something was triggered, something deep in the reptilian part of my brain: fight or flight. Of course he was going to talk about last night. But was I going to be somehow held accountable? That's what it felt like. But I wasn't the drunk, crass idiot who came uninvited!

Francois sat behind his desk casually. He motioned for me to take a seat. After a rattle of golden bracelets, he clasped his hands and leaned forward.

"I need your help," he said. "I'm having trouble communicating with Rick. I've been watching him for awhile, but last night was an unacceptable escalation."

"I quite agree, but I'm not sure how I can help you."

After a moment of musing, Francois leaned back and said, "Unlike some of my colleagues, I don't think Rick is just an undisciplined child. I don't know exactly why. He's pathetic, yes, but not a man to be dismissed. To do so would be to dismiss whatever so haunted him, and he is indeed a man haunted. All that said, though, have you any idea how to handle him? You're his friend."

"Friend?" I said, surprised. "I wouldn't go that far."

"I see you drinking with him a lot," Francois pointed out.

"Well, I'll have a social drink with him, for sure. And obviously he has begun continuing on toward excess. I have nothing to do with that, and have never really understood alcoholism. I don't like being around it any more than any other man."

"Yet you judge a man by the company he keeps."

There it was again. Emmet had said something the night before in a very similar vein. I didn't like being classified in such a manner. Why not judge me on my work performance? My volunteerism? Why must I be judged by something I can't control and doesn't adversely affect anything?

"I wish I could help you," I said, rather dismissively. "I don't know how to reach Rick. All I know is that someone with an alcohol problem on ships is like a bull in a china shop."

"Or a lamb to the slaughter," Francois corrected.

I left, swallowing hard. For the first time I was worried Francois didn't think much of me. That was a shame. Yet I, too, judged a man by the company he kept. I resolved to stop doing that because, upon reflection, I'd spent most of my ship time with a rogue's gallery! But flirting with the dark side, and being surrounded by others who succumb to it, doesn't mean I was out of control. Since escaping the Carnival Cruise Lines restaurants, I was a social drinker; nothing more. In the words of the great Sir Winston Churchill, "I've gotten more out of alcohol than alcohol's gotten out of me." Yet, as stated, those around me did succumb. Rick cracked during the Transatlantic. Upon setting foot ashore, he shattered.

Rick didn't make it back from our first port of call, Barbados. He'd gone on a bender and passed out. *Wind Surf* sailed without him. Oh, he got aboard the next day by taking a ferry to the next port, St. Lucia, but it was too late by then. He was fired on the spot. His departure wasn't cause for concern. It was inevitable. This wasn't like the mysterious firing of Janie and Eddie and the attempted firing of Yoyo. No, Rick wasn't a victim of the phantom firer.

I was.

The chief officer ordered me into his office at six o'clock in the morning. At first I thought it might have something to do with Rick as well, but why would he call me in so early? Six sharp in the a.m. could easily be considered punishment. His office was not large, though it was significantly bigger than anyone else's save Francois'. Unlike the hotel director, however, Emmet shared his office with two other senior officers. They were not present at the early hour, though their inhabitance was clearly visible from all the dirty coffee mugs. Emmet's desk was overwhelmed with paperwork filed, paperwork not filed, and stacked binders of still more paper.

"Good morning, Emmet," I said cheerily. I was always at my most chipper in the morning.

"Have a seat," he said, indicating a small wooden chair. "You missed boat drill."

"Boat drill?" I repeated, surprised. "I've never done boat drill."

"Your predecessor surely informed you that it is required prior to transferring to a new part of the world?"

"I see," I replied. "No, he didn't. His handover was an insult. I'm sorry."

"I'm sure you can understand why someone in your position needs to be certified," Emmet explained with his usual kindness. "Well, not certified, but on a small ship we need everyone. You obviously understand that because you help out with fire drills and shore excursions and such. Not to mention a lot of the guys here are foreigners and having a native English speaker is a huge asset in a crisis."

"Of course, of course," I said. "When I return I'll make sure I'm on top of it."

I wasn't particularly happy to do boat drill—who was? But Emmet was being cool about the whole thing. No big deal. I waited for him to continue, but he paused to ponder. After a few moments I tentatively asked, "... is there anything I need to do? Or is that all?"

Emmet's expression turned sour. His entire demeanor

changed before my very eyes. In a tight voice he commented, "I'm tired of you shirking your duties."

"Shirking my duties?" I repeated, surprised. "I'm not aware—"

"How could you be?" Emmet interjected. "How could you be aware of anything when you're busy playing video games?"

Now with obvious confusion, I asked, "Video games? I haven't played a video game in years. I have no idea what you're talking about."

"So many things you could be doing and aren't," Emmet continued with an incredibly derogatory tone. I was sure he wasn't talking about failure to eat my vegetables first. "You're a bad influence on the crew."

"I'm a bad influence on the crew?" I repeated, shocked. "What, for volunteering my free time to multiple other departments? You just mentioned fire drills and shore excursions. I also help out on the sports deck—"

"Were you there when Eddie nearly killed two passengers?" Emmet pressed, most cruelly. "Or were you too busy playing video games then, too?"

"What is with this video game shit?" I asked, utterly flabbergasted. I couldn't believe Emmet was laying into me like this.

"You sit comfortably in the lounge all day long, playing on your computer," the chief officer said in both explanation and rebuke.

"You think that just because I'm on the computer... I'm playing games?" I asked, incredulous. "Why on Earth... because I'm wearing headphones? That's a crazy assumption!"

"You're not working," Emmet calmly retorted. "Or you'd be sitting at your desk, selling art. I have serious difficulty with your contract, considering how much you work. I don't understand your role here."

"My role is to bring in revenue," I said firmly. "And I

do it without a desk. I bring in more revenue than the casino or the gift shop or the bar."

"Those are necessary ship systems," Emmet dismissed with a wave.

"And bringing in money isn't necessary? If you felt that way, why didn't you attack the previous auctioneer? He sold two thousand dollars worth of art last crossing. I've already sold over seventeen!"

But Emmet didn't seem to hear a word I said. He just continued irritably, "I don't want my hard working crew seeing you relaxing in the lounge all day and having drinks every night. Why don't you help me paint the rails? There's plenty to do."

"So my volunteering for three extra departments isn't good enough for you?" I retorted, now very much angry. "You need me to do manual labor as well? How 'bout old Gertie? You ask her to pitch in, too? Oh, that's right. She never made her goals even once in *years*. But there's that horrible Brian, exceeding sales goals and volunteering to give Barney's family a personal tour of Positano."

Emmet asked quietly, "Did you take them to a bar?"

I stared at him, mouth agape like a fish.

"Did you take them to a bar?" he repeated.

It was all clear after that, of course.

"I just don't get it, Emmet. We've had a great rapport —or so I thought. Just because I am an acquaintance of Rick doesn't mean—"

"Acquaintance?" Emmet scoffed. "Birds of a feather, more likely. You are dismissed."

Feeling unbalanced and hurt after the meeting with Emmet, I went to the bridge to talk to the second officer. I asked Barney to show me where I was to be stationed and what I was supposed to be doing during the boat drill I missed. He replied there hadn't been any boat drill and, even if there had been, auctioneers weren't involved.

***

It was a shame to have such a falling out with the chief officer. I really liked the guy. I resolved to work on our relationship when I returned from vacation. I didn't realize just how badly our relationship had torn, and that the loose threads were already unraveling. In fact, within just one day, everything would fall apart.

That afternoon I received a frantic message from my Sundance fleet manager. A surprise art swap was planned for *Wind Surf's* arrival in Barbados—*tomorrow*. That was the day I was signing off! Art swaps were major events that took a week of preparation. First and foremost, it required receiving a shipment of oversized boxes in advance. Safely boxing several thousand works of art for multinational shipping takes a long, long time. I hadn't received any such boxes.

Astoundingly, Sundance expected me to unload the boxes of fresh art and reload them with old art *simultaneously*. The logistics of that operation were staggering. It was clearly impossible to do safely without a large staff and amount of space. I had neither. But in true Sundance fashion, it was do it or be fired. Why they waited so late to inform me was a mystery. In order for thirty pallets of art to be waiting for me in Barbados, they would have to have been shipped out of Miami days ago.

In all my four years at sea—through all the trials and tribulations, all the slave labor and demeaning work, the crushing stress, the lies, the jealousies, the cheating—the next thirty-six hours were the worst. Just when I thought things were going so well!

Only one crane existed to load the pallets of fresh art onto *Wind Surf*. It did not drop loads into a hold, but instead onto a narrow, exposed strip of deck just behind the bridge. There was no staging area. I would have to work fifty feet away in a wide stairwell—a blatant violation of fire code, of course. I discussed the situation with Francois, who noted we'd need permission from the chief officer for any such action. After hearing of Emmet's and my blowout, Francois mercifully promised to run interference.

I began immediately. It was about six o'clock in the evening.

Because we were at sea, everybody I knew was working. No bodies were available to assist me except, perhaps, Yoyo. After careful consideration I decided he would just slow me down. So I transported my thousands of works of art up the two flights of stairs myself, one cart load at a time, load after load, hour after hour, all night long. The pile on the landing quickly grew too large and artwork had to be stacked outside on the deck. Of course there was no one to guard the artwork during any of this operation. I just had to hope nobody walking by stole anything.

Night fell. Darkness became a crippling issue. Because this was the bridge deck, no exterior lights were permitted. I began stacking more and more artwork outside —I had no choice—in the dark. The wind grew stronger and the night grew colder, but I'd long since been sweating from the labor.

Just after midnight I thought I'd catch a break. *Wind Surf* docked in Barbados. No longer did officers need to worry about a collision with anything in the dark. Emmet, however, refused to allow even a single damn lightbulb to be lit for me. Not one. Onward into the black night I labored.

The good news was that since we docked, the casino closed. Aurelia, now free, volunteered to help. Of course, I didn't even have enough muscle to haul a fully laden art cart, so what could little one hundred pound Aurelia do? Even so, her offer of help gave me hope. By 2 a.m., it looked like we were about halfway through.

Then came the squall.

Yes, as if I didn't have enough of a nightmare, a freakin' tropical storm blew in. Barbados was the easternmost island of the Caribbean, after all—outermost of the Windward Isles—and subject to the caprice of thousands of miles of open ocean.

The storm winds whipped artwork out of my hands, sent it skittering down the deck and nearly blew it overboard. As sheets of rain walloped the open deck, Aurelia frantically ran after fleeing, flying art again and again. There was no way to secure any of the hundreds of loose works of framed art stowed outside, no way to stop the wind from lashing, the rain from soaking. Even artwork inside the stairwell was wrecked, tumbling down the stairs with each swell, each list. Untold thousands of dollars in damage—much of it irreparable—was done. But then, Sundance was sloppy like that and used to paying such.

The storm was powerful but short. At about three o'clock it stopped. Having been hard at work since six, I needed to take a short break. Both Aurelia and I were soaked to the skin and shivering. A hot shower helped revive me. During that time Aurelia picked up the proverbial pieces of my livelihood. I thanked her and ordered her to bed. Onward I slogged, load after load, hour after hour. Only once did I stop, at 4:30 a.m., for a cup of coffee. The hard physical labor of transporting the old art to the crane took a whopping fifteen hours. It was finally completed at 9:30 a.m.—just in time for the hard part to begin.

Of course, I was supposed to sign off on vacation any minute. According to international law I was not allowed on the ship after 11 a.m. The new guy would have to finish. But he didn't show up.

Figures.

An hour of frantic paperwork shuffling was required to keep me legally aboard. Certainly it would take nothing short of being arrested to get me off the ship with the art in that condition. There was several million dollars worth of art spread out in the open all over the bridge deck, and I was liable for every penny!

Francois signed off on my immigration paperwork without issue, but Emmet was another matter. He refused to sign. He wanted me gone. He didn't think I was part of the family. Only after he personally verified with Francois that the new auctioneer would not arrive until tomorrow — apparently I was now a liar, as well — *only then* did he reluctantly sign the papers.

Quickly I had to cancel my taxi, cancel my flights from Barbados to Miami and Miami to Chicago and Chicago to Cedar Rapids. Then I had to rearrange a flight from St. Lucia all the way through to C.R. After that joyous hour of 'rest', it was time to start haulin' ass on the art swap.

Each crane load brought up one giant box of new art. I had to unload it, set the contents aside on the exposed deck in inclement weather, and reload the same box with old — now old and wet — art. Then I'd have it craned back down and repeat the whole procedure.

Loading huge, heavily framed art in those boxes meant bending entirely over and supporting all the weight with your lower back. There was no other way. It would have been brutal work even had I been fresh. But I was not fresh. I was already sixteen hours in. By six o'clock that evening — a full twenty-four hours of solid labor since I began, the second part of the job was complete.

Last came removing the new art from the raining, open deck and overloaded stairwell down to my art locker. That alone promised to take another fifteen hours. But I also had to remove the protective cardboard corners from each and every work of art. Otherwise they wouldn't fit in my locker!

Aurelia, despite my orders, stayed at my side the whole time. She wasn't a trooper; she was freakin' special forces. That second all-nighter was where she really saved me. She ripped off those corners hour after hour after hour, deep into the night. Her fingertips were a bloody wreck from ripping out all those staples. After ten p.m. Daniel, the fitness trainer, helped out, and after one a.m. Nigel and Neil did, too. With their help, by sunrise everything was stowed away.

The art swap had taken a nonstop thirty-six hours. All that was left to do was clean up the eight or so thousand cardboard corners and the tens of thousands of staples littering the stairwell.

"We did it," I said to Aurelia, giving her a heartfelt hug. My back was so sore I literally couldn't feel her slender arms around me. All I felt was one intense, throbbing ache. "It could have been a disaster. Instead it just sucked beyond belief. There's some killer art to sell when I return, though. That's good news."

"No, it was a disaster," Aurelia said firmly.

"What?"

"You didn't see the deck?"

"What?" I repeated, growing concerned.

She led me outside to the open deck. As the sun rose orange, warm rays highlighted dozens upon dozens of scratches in the teak deck. Many had been scraped and re-scraped so many times that they compounded into deep gouges. The entire area around the crane was absolutely trashed. Because I'd been working in the dark, in the storm, I hadn't known we were causing damage. I hadn't known to alter our procedure. I hadn't seen a thing.

You could bet your sweet ass Emmet would.

***

The handover to the new guy, Hugh, went smoothly. Because of the art swap there was no time-taxing inventory. Because the *Surf* was so small there was no tour. There was no staff. Obviously Sundance had sent a newbie to the

394

smallest ship in all the combined fleets. He was only a placeholder, after all, and we both understood this. Even so, the kid stared around with his mouth open, thinking the ship was a lot to handle. Poor kid had no clue.

No flights out of St. Lucia had been available on such short notice. I had been forced to book a room at a resort. Trying, I know. Aurelia joined me for the afternoon and evening, not having to return until 10 p.m. The vibe was sad, but not really. After all, I was already scheduled for a return in six weeks. Still, there were a lot of hugs and a few tears. And frogs.

After a lazy afternoon napping in each others' arms in a hammock, rocked gently by the warm, damp Caribbean wind, we took a walk. The grounds were lush with all manner of green things. As the sun set behind a screen of palms and a strip of beach, we found ourselves upon a wide, sloping lawn at the edge of a rainforest. We sat in the grass and were accosted by frogs. Lots and lots of frogs. Hordes of frogs. Big frogs, little frogs, pushy frogs. They were very demanding of our attention, like a house pet nudging your hand for a pat on the head. In this case, they jumped onto our bodies and wouldn't jump off. I had no idea frogs could be so tenacious. No wonder Kermit stuck with the exasperating Ms. Piggy all those years.

Darkness settled in. It was a wonderful, lingering moment in a place of charm, a place for a connection of hearts. The beautiful night and surroundings were a group hug. I didn't want to leave any of it. It was the first time I'd been anxious to return to a ship and pick back up right where I left off.

EPILOGUE

FROM THE VERY FIRST days of vacationing with my parents I received frantic emails from Hugh. He had no idea how to sell anything and was in a near panic. I offered him bits and pieces of advice, but mostly told him to just calm down. Nobody would judge him based on his performance on *Wind Surf*. Yet the emails got longer and longer, from days two through six. I heard nothing from Hugh on day seven. Then I get a call from Aurelia that changed my life.

"I heard Hugh talking to Francois," she said. "They were in the art locker by the casino. You know what he said? He said the guy walked up to him and asked, 'Are you the art seller?' He said 'yes,' and the guy said, 'I'll take that Picasso.' He didn't ask how much, just handed him an American Express card!"

My heart sank. In the new art load—sent at my request for *me* to sell, I might add—there had been three Picassos. Each was over $100,000. With the unique commission system in place on *Wind Surf*, that kid just made over $30,000.

He also got my job. Gene, the big dog from Sundance, called to personally inform me.

"You won't be returning to *Wind Surf* after all," his voice said over the phone. "The new guy is outperforming you."

"I heard all about his *one* sale," I told Gene with particular emphasis. "Do you even know the story of how it happened? One lucky sale and you are throwing out an entire contract of surpassing goals every cruise for almost a year?"

"Actually, it's not just that," Gene admitted. "*Wind Surf* has denied your return."

"But they all already signed off on me!"

"They *had*," Gene agreed, "but one officer changed his mind. I just got off the phone with the chief officer, who has initiated paperwork suing us for some damages. He claims your misconduct destroyed one hundred square feet of teak decking. He claims it will cost over twenty thousand dollars to fix. You better hope not, because we're not paying it. That will fall on you."

I was incensed. Further, I was sick of being bullied by ships and all their ilk.

"No way," I snapped into the receiver. "You pass that on to me and I'll go public. I'll lie through my teeth about Sundance selling fakes."

Gene was silent for a long, long while. Finally h
he'd get back to me.

A week later all was settled. Sundance at Sea failed
its effort to make money on the cruise ship gift shops an
was cutting losses. They sold everything at a loss across
multiple fleets. They settled the lawsuit with *Wind Surf* by
handing the gift shop back to them, inventory and all,
including $10,000 in improvements they made. So that was
all settled. What wasn't settled was my future with
Sundance. But that, too, was settled, as far as I was
concerned.

I told them to go to hell.

So what now? Aurelia was expecting me back on
Wind Surf. While we had made no commitment to each
other, we found great joy in each others' company. We
made a good couple. She was a curious blend of feisty and
shy, stubborn and aloof. She spoke four languages. I was...
tall, I guess. I wasn't sure I was happy with letting our time
together end so abruptly, so improperly. But my days at sea
were over. Hers were only just beginning. Then again, her
career wasn't about ships, but casinos. She'd worked a
casino in Morocco three years before switching to ship
casinos. If her goal was finding bigger and better casinos, I
had much to offer. I lived in Las Vegas, baby!

***

"He who hath known the bitterness of the Ocean shall
have its taste forever in his mouth."

I dwelt upon each of those words, turning them over
and over in my mind, thinking them particularly apt. They
were written by Joseph Conrad, who well knew of such
things. His time at sea had been filled with wonder—and
misfortune. I could relate. His further words, written after
leaving the sea forever, felt similarly relevant: "But one or
two of us, pampered by the life of the land, complained of

to swallow any of that stuff."

with a bitter taste but, unlike

a bite. The sea did, indeed,

.venture. If one could stand the

of salt, the sea provided a bountiful

ul.

gnt I went to sea chasing love, but in fact was chasing life. Yet there was nothing 'mere' about it. I didn't sustain my life in a cubicle any more than a fish in a cardboard box. It wasn't that I needed the sea, as the fish does. I hadn't known what I needed. I just knew something vital was missing. I had hunger, so I hunted. A glimmer of hope came in the form of Bianca, who led the way through the dark like a will o' the wisp: beautiful, entrancing, dangerous.

All the currents of the seven seas revolved around Bianca. Alas, she believed life was a destination. She worked her fingers to the bone to pay for future paradise. I lived it every day. I desperately wanted to share it with her, but for various reasons she did not accept. When pressed to commit, she said the words, but did not feel them. Eventually, regretfully, I realized she never would. Regardless of what set me down the path, I enjoyed the stroll.

I'd learned much in my four years at sea. I learned how to make time for important things when none seemed to exist. I learned to recognize a precious moment before it was gone forever. I learned my emotional limits. I pushed the boundaries of my physical limits and learned the durability of the body was greater than that of fear. I also learned the importance of self definition. Too often we think of ourselves in terms of our partners. I was no longer the guy who chased Bianca. I was not Mr. Bianca any more than she was Mrs. Brian.

Ultimately I learned that, despite our best intentions and most fervent hopes, happiness cannot be given, though it must be accepted. One would think accepting joy would come naturally, but it doesn't. Before you can accept happiness you have to feel worthy of it. I knew I was worthy not just because I'd been bloodied in the battle of life, but because I'd kept moving forward. Everybody who worked the sea was running, either from something or, sometimes, towards something. Perhaps the life aquatic wasn't so different from the life terrestrial, after all.

HE WHO HATH
KNOWN

the bitterness of the Ocean
shall have its taste
forever in his mouth.

— Joseph Conrad

BUT I NEVER WANTED

or tried to be anything else but a woman,
and I assure you,
no man coming to me is allowed to forget it,
even if he can find my brain answering his.
All the time I keep well awake in his mind
that he is having the pleasure
of talking with a woman,
that dreamed-of companion
of every man's soul.

— Queen Marie of Romania

Rogue's Gallery

Bianca (waitress) — still working at sea in the restaurants for Carnival Cruise Lines, providing her parents Piti and Lucky a comfortable and well-deserved retirement in beautiful Sighișoara.

Leo (asst. Maitre d') — married to an American lass and living in Kentucky; a Hyundai salesman and proud father to a host of pit bulls.

Calypso (waitress) — returned to her South Africa and a competition pole dancer. Yes, really! For fun, not vocation.

Rasa (waitress) — after happily reuniting with her daughter in Lithuania, now lives with a dalmatian the size of a pony.

Bill (auctioneer) — lost to the modern world after disappearing in Thailand in pursuit of cheap, prolific prostitutes.

Vela (spa) — living in Hungary with her husband, a professional soccer player, and their young son. Still running stronger than ever.

Marc (port guide) — after a rocky (surprise!) stint as an art auctioneer, now living in Ontario as a reiki healer and alternative medicine practitioner.

Laureen (singer) — still singing professionally and loving it, recently completed a months-long tour in Japan.

Ardin (photographer) — still a professional photographer, living with his Vietnamese wife and children in China.

Eddie (dive instructor) — in 2013 married the woman of his dreams (not Susie), and lives in Vancouver, British Columbia. He loves his new life as a teacher.

Nigel (musician) — took Nina (gift shop) back to England, where they lived several years together. They then split and he currently lives in Seattle.

Rick (spa) — fired from Wind Surf after missing the ship in a drunken stupor. Current whereabouts unknown.

Aurelia (casino) — married (happily, I hope!) to this author for the last seven years, as of 2014. She deals roulette at one of the Las Vegas Strip's premiere casinos.

AUTHOR'S NOTE

MANY THANKS GO to the following individuals for their enthusiasm, assistance, and acumen: Karen & Mike Gill of Florida (who gave me paper cuts from all those tabs), Amy Graziano of Virginia (proof I don't hate Italians), and Dobie Vasa of Arizona (who is not an oak).

This marks the end of my adventures at sea, but certainly not the end of my adventures! If you've enjoyed sailing with me all these years, I do hope you continue to hang out with me on land. Adventure is where you make it, after all! It's been a privilege to share my experiences with you all. I thank you very, very much.

CONQUER THE WORLD'S BIGGEST BIKE ride. Laugh the whole way. Finally enthusiasts, armchair cyclists, and adventure widows can live the full experience.

No sweat. No lube. Just laughs.

The rollicking, true story of two men rekindling an old friendship after twenty years. Foolishly, they choose to reconnect over a hometown tradition that just happens to be the world's biggest bike ride: RAGBRAI. 500 miles of biking during the hottest week of the year - humidity 100%, bugs 1000% - seemed like the ideal way to "get to know you" again. Their plans are waylaid by a last-minute addition: an outrageous, mysterious sailor named Cheek. His presence is not only intrusive, but utterly disastrous.

Enjoy the first two chapters!

RUMBLE YELL: THE CHALLENGES

WHY this place was chosen for 119 nuclear blasts was self-evident. Why I chose it for a bike ride was less clear. I was two hours away from the most revolting experience of my life, and I had no way of knowing it; a moment more awful than the 130° heat, more distressing than being alone in two million acres of utter waste. The nearest shade—a port-a-potty steaming in the sun—was twenty miles away. Getting there required a two-hour slog over desolate mountain ridges in unrelieved sun, on a bicycle so hot its metal burned any flesh unfortunate enough to touch it. My hands smarted even through gloves. No cars had passed this spot in days, barring a solitary DNR truck at 4AM. This I knew because I was already here in this horrible place. The truck's passage left a dead jackrabbit smashed upon the scalding asphalt at mile marker 33. Ravens circled above. They wanted me to leave. *I* wanted to leave.

But not before the most revolting experience of my life.

Training for the world's oldest, largest, and longest annual bike ride required some sacrifice. It was 500 miles of heat and hills and roadkill. Yet contrary to expectation, this greatest of Earth's bike touring tradition was not across the Sahara Desert, Australian Outback, or even somewhere in Europe. It was through America's heartland. I was training for RAGBRAI: *Register's Annual Great Bike Ride Across Iowa.* That's right: Iowa.

I wasn't doing this for glory—one rarely associates glory with Iowa—nor, as seemed more likely, was this some form of self-flagellation. This was to reconnect with an old friend I hadn't seen in twenty years. Aaron was a fascinating guy. Barring a penchant for wearing kilts and a need for corrective lenses, he was the living incarnation of Indiana Jones. Any opportunity to converse with such a man was worth some effort, and to rekindle an old friendship was even better.

I rubbed the grit from my eyes and squinted to the heat-wavering horizon. He better be worth it!

***

I am not a bicyclist by nature. I hadn't ridden one since my youth, which was a depressing number of decades ago. When Aaron suggested riding RAGBRAI, I said yes before actually thinking it through. Fortunately I was fit, but in other areas entirely, like running or dodging household objects occasionally thrown by my wife. If I was going to safely ride 500 miles, it required planning. Training. Oh, and a bike. I needed one of those.

How does one plan for such a monumental ride? Fortunately, RAGBRAI wasn't America's biggest bike ride without a great body of knowledge to draw upon. The official website was loaded with advice, including a calendar of recommended training rides. In fact, mercifully little thought would be required. Just follow directions to avoid injury. Being married, I was well versed in following directions to avoid injury.

So training I could do. 1,000 advance miles? Twas nothing. Buying all the gear from scratch? Ha! Credit cards. This was looking easier by the minute. But there was one great challenge I feared unsurmountable. No, not the heat of my home in Las Vegas, nor even finding *time* for 1,000 training miles therein. Something far, far more difficult awaited me: getting permission from my wife.

How to broach this adventure for the boys? Rare is the man who knows what women want to hear. This was compounded for me because my dear Aurelia was foreign. She grew up in the humble Romanian countryside but abandoned home for the action of the capital city. The result was a woman of ambition and self-reliance tempered by a natural shyness and her culture's enforced passivity in women. I just never knew when and where she would make a stand.

But what *really* made connection difficult, far more than her having lived under the Iron Curtain, was English. It was her third language and entirely self-taught by listening to hip hop music. Emigrating to Las Vegas did nothing to help get rid of her... colorful... phraseology. While I applauded Aurelia continually on this amazing feat of self-instruction, inwardly I cringed during even regular conversation. Her way of ordering me to the gym, for example, was by saying, "Junk in your trunk means no hoes 4 U."

Thus it was to this fitful little volcano I need explain my desire of riding RAGBRAI across my native state. Did I appeal to the fond pastoral memories of her youth, or work the 'everybody's doing it/hip today' angle? In the end I selected a different approach altogether. I decided to make it all about me. Dangerous? To be sure. Foolish? No doubt. But it was honest. That had to count for something.

Thus I expounded upon how completing RAGBRAI was every Iowan's rite of passage, a quantifiable method of proving our worthiness of that greatest of honors: being Iowan. We're a proud, hard-working folk, I exclaimed, getting positively worked up over the awesomeness of laboring 500 miles over 'amber waves of grain'—Iowa's lack of wheat fields notwithstanding—until I began singing the national anthem. This did not improve my argument.

"You want that for *vacation*?" Aurelia squeaked dubiously in her mousy voice. "Imma be in Hawaii. That's America, too."

"Come on, you've been to Iowa to see family..." I began.

"Chillaxin' with ya homies is different," she replied. "Doncha wanna go somewhere interesting?"

"So you think Iowa's not worthy?" I chided.

Alas, Aurelia had a point. Did I really want to spend my vacation in Iowa? I was *from* Iowa, what more was there to see? After twenty-five years there, surely I'd seen it all—or all I wanted to, anyway. Since this wasn't about family, what on Earth would take me there, after all the exotic places I'd seen as a travel writer? A friend, that's what.

"We went to Maui last year," I protested. "You forced me to drive all over the island so you could see each and every beach, each and every town, each and every palm tree! I chauffeured you ten hours a day, every day. It was the most exhausting vacation I've ever had."

"And biking 500 kilometers is chill?"

"Miles," I corrected reflexively. "They're a lot longer than kilometers."

She batted her pretty eyelashes at me, revealing to my slow wits that I had just blundered into a trap.

"But... but... old people do it!" I blurted, desperate. "I mean retirees and stuff."

"Then bag her when you're old," she said, wiggling figure settling into a firm stance.

"There's pie," I tried.

"No pie," she said. "Denied!"

Unfortunately Aurelia also loved Suze Orman's TV

show. She delighted in the long list of callers asking Suze's advice, such as, "I'm worth $1.3 Million. Can I buy a new Prius?" Suze's answer never varied: *denied!* Aurelia's tiny voice somehow only underscored the finality of the word. But I had an ace up my sleeve. One of Iowa's triumphs was Aurelia's Achilles heel.

"They have pork."

She paused.

"Old school pork," I pressed on, sensing my advantage. "Heaps of it. Iowa pork chops are over a pound each, baby."

Despite my dinky wife's utter lack of body fat, she consumed vast amounts of pork. One might say freakish amounts of pork. Her metabolism was hyperactive, like that of a small mammal, and she regularly snarfed down more food than I, an active man double her weight. Further, she went straight for the heavy stuff. No lean tenderloins for her, oh no. Growing up in rural Romania she learned to dunk hunks of pork into barrels of bubbling, rendered pork fat. With salt. They ate entire slabs of smoked fat called *slanina*, sometimes mixing it with eggs but more often popping it straight into their mouths. With salt. While American bacon was little meat and lots of fat, Romanian bacon abandoned the idea of meat altogether. But had lots of salt.

"Iowa has the best pork in the country," I continued. "It's glorious, I tell you, glorious! Our pigs live the high life. I can bring some home."

"When you leaving?"

***

Of course Aurelia encouraged rekindling my

417

friendship with an old high school buddy. Though Romanian, she wasn't a witch. But that didn't mean she gave me carte blanche, either. I was under strict orders to manage the budget such that Hawaii was still available later. I happily informed her that RAGBRAI meant camping, so the only cost was reasonably-priced vendor food all week. Oh, and transportation to Iowa. And buying a bike. And *its* transportation to Iowa. And, um, gear, like jerseys and bike shorts and a helmet. And a tire pump. And energy bars. Icy Hot? I was talking myself into a hole.

So my first task was to buy equipment under the intense scrutiny of an Iron Curtain Suze Orman. *Denied!* We had radically different views on the value of the US dollar. This was a good thing, because she kept me from frivolously wasting money on small items perhaps more expensive than need be. The downside was a complete denial of treats. "Snickers for $1.29? You know what that buys in Romania? Denied!"

I didn't know how much a new bike would cost, but figured it would surely cost more than the $200 Aurelia allocated for it. I protested, "I need to get something of fair quality. You expect me to ride safely for 1,500 miles on a bike that costs less than shoes you wear to a nightclub?"

"You said 500 miles," she countered.

"It's not just the ride," I pointed out, "it's also *training*. I'll probably need a grand for everything."

"*What?*" she squeaked in outrage. "You think I'm made of Benjamins?"

"You paid $500 for a leather coat you've never worn," I protested. "And never will, 'cause this is *Las Vegas*. Hello? It's hot here."

At least the leather coat made a good blanket for my night on the couch.

There were five bike shops in Las Vegas. We visited them all, with increasingly maddening results. Only two offered a 'cheap' bike for $3000. I refused to believe that bikes cost that much when something like 40% of Las Vegas homes had mortgages underwater. But compared to prices closer to the Strip, these were bargains.

Finally we went to the Schwinn dealer. I grew up with Schwinn bikes and knew they weren't titanium-alloy or whatever Schwarzenegger's *Terminator* was made of. The show floor was very wide and open, a refreshing change from the crowded boutique-style shops Vegas preferred. After having already wasted hours in fruitless searching, we wasted no more and marched right up to the counter. There waited a man of perhaps sixty, wearing a sweater and sporting a mustache. He looked very professorial.

"Good afternoon," I said. "I would like to see the bikes you have under $1,000."

"Certainly," he said, moving around the counter. We walked down row upon row of bicycles and he pointed out numerous delicate plastic and aluminum pink things with ribbons and stuff for little girls.

"I'm sorry," I clarified. "I meant for me. I'm doing a 500-mile ride."

He laughed. I couldn't believe it. He *laughed* at a customer!

"People in Vegas sure are dreamers," he said, snuffling back more chuckles, "But really, come on."

This from a sixty-something guy? Didn't he recall a different world than post-building nuthouse Vegas? I began to fear my visions of a perfect vacation by immersing myself into Midwestern wholesomeness as likely as meeting Elvis. OK, bad example.

Finally we found a mom and pop store we liked. The couple was extremely young, but the moniker still fit. Both were dubious of such a 'cheap' bike, but offered to try. Most likely they wanted to get their hooks into fresh meat. Using catalogues the lady helped me select a bike for a 'piddly' $800.

"This will be a good starter bike," she said, or rather grudgingly admitted. "But before the year is out you'll want to upgrade to a real bike."

Her comment was so offhand as to be honest.

"The price includes a custom fit to your gait when it comes in. And we generously give away a free water bottle."

The indicated water bottle was crammed with their logo, address, email address, and QR code.

"Do you need all the gear, too?"

"Yes," I said, grimacing. I was right to cringe because the list of necessaries was extensive. But I got moderately priced equipment in the form of a portable tire repair kit— imperative when biking alone through Nevada's desert wastes—a tire pump, a helmet, a bike rack for the Jeep, and other miscellaneous odds and ends. I also opted for the heavy-duty lock, since we had been robbed eight times in our three years in Vegas.

"Say, can I order a bike seat that's bigger? These are all so small and hard."

"The big ones are soft and squishy for short rides," she explained. "On long rides butts move around too much."

"But I have a little butt," I protested weakly. She looked dubious at this claim. Perhaps worse, Aurelia failed to contain a squeaking laugh.

"It's all about friction, you see," she continued.

"Smaller surface area means less friction. You don't want friction down there."

"No, I don't think I do," I agreed. "So a tiny, rock-hard seat guarantees no friction?"

"Oh, no," she scoffed, laughing at the absurdity of the idea. "There's no *guarantee* of anything. Why else do you think there's so many crotch lubes?"

"Crotch lubes?" Aurelia squawked. "Denied!"

The selection of crotch lubes was indeed impressive, not unlike the hair product aisle of a salon with dozens of tubes, tubs, and jars. I was mesmerized by the half-gallon vat of *Butt Butter*. I expected a broad selection of such things in this city, of course, but at the Adult Toy Emporium or any other of our 500-plus adult establishments.

Skipping the lubes for the moment, I instead loaded up on energy bars. Most were chocolate or yogurt-covered bars. At that early juncture, I didn't realize just how stupid it was to buy any of them. That would come back to haunt me. Like, four times a week for the next four months.

***

The morning after the arrival and fitting of my new bike, I pulled the Jeep into the garage and quietly unhitched the goods from the rear rack. Everything smelled of fresh rubber and crisp plastic. Aurelia tiptoed through the inside door wearing her robe. She looked tired but courteously pretended to be interested.

"I'm sorry I woke you," I apologized.

"Happy with your new toy?" she asked in a tiny, sleepy voice.

"My new *tool*, woman," I corrected with feigned

421

machismo. "I'm sure it pales in comparison with Aaron's bike, but that's OK. As long as it keeps me up with him."

Aurelia yawned. She worked nights as a roulette dealer on the Strip, so I didn't drain her further by expounding upon my excitement over the bike. I did, however, wax poetic over the reason for it.

"You'd like Aaron, you know," I said, leaning over the bike to engage her. "He and his wife Isabel are world travelers. Can you believe they just flew to Argentina to tour wineries and stay with friends? Yes, they somehow have friends in Argentina, unlike the rest of us mere mortals."

To my surprise, Aurelia groaned.

"What?" I asked, suddenly defensive.

"So they're bottles in the club?"

I just stared at her, waiting for an explanation of how people could be bottles in a club.

"You know, spending crazy money on bottle service just to show off. Who goes to Argentina to tour wineries? Go to California."

"Oh, it's nothing like that," I reassured her, "Aaron's a true traveler."

I launched into my best narrator's voice. "No mere collector of refrigerator magnets, he. Aaron is a man who takes the best of other cultures and integrates them into his life. To be sure, his latest example of cultural fusion was downright shocking. For he is a Portlander through and through, which means not only a love of coffee, but an obsession, a mania! He's a monster. Bereft of caffeine, he's the terror of co-workers and small children. Yet after spending a month in Hungary—yes, he's done that, too—he discovered that simple, strong peasant tea suited his stomach better. So back to America he went, and off of coffee he got. Now he drinks tea. His peers call him un-American, but I say it makes him the ultimate American: we're the Melting Pot, are we not? No, I declare Aaron Owen is no bottle on the shelf!"

Aurelia blinked and wavered, having apparently fallen asleep again during my droning. Rousing, she asked, "You done?"

"Yeah," I mumbled. "Sorry."

"It's bottle in the *club*," she corrected, stifling a giggle. "But really, you haven't seen him in twenty years. What are you hoping for?"

"That he doesn't wear a kilt," I said. "He's very proud of his English ancestry."

Aurelia giggled and sang, "Everybody in the house, *represent!*"

"You mean represent Las Vegas?" I said, aghast at the notion. "What, wear sequins and bushy sideburns? No way."

"So he's from England?"

"No, but both sides of his family are. His mother traced her lineage back to like the 1300s or something crazy like that. He did attend some college in Nottingham, though."

"Oh, wait," Aurelia exclaimed. "He's that Indiana Jones friend of yours!"

"That's right," I said. "He did an archeological dig in Israel during college. He's also toured the ruins of Machu Picchu and who knows what else."

"So they're rich."

"I don't think so," I said, frowning in thought. "Well, his *parents* are loaded. His dad's like some genius radiologist. I was always really impressed with how they handled their money. They refused to spoil their kids with stuff, but spared no expense for expanding their world-views. Aaron was smart enough to take advantage of the opportunities his parents gave him. True, he was lost in college for years trying to figure out what he wanted to do with his life. Too many options, I guess. His emails are more about being a Portlander than his job, so I don't know what he ended up doing. I think it has something to do with urban development."

"You'll find out in July."

"Indeed I will!" I exclaimed, patting the seat of my new bike. I frowned at how distressingly hard it felt.

***

Though very impressed with Aaron's world travels, I actually felt ever so slightly on par with them. Luckily, I had been around, too. When I neared thirty, fate stuck her nose into my life in the form of an exotic foreign woman. I was hopelessly—some would say pathetically—smitten and followed her everywhere. In her case that meant further afield than just her native Romania, but also the Caribbean, Mediterranean, and Baltic. Cruise ships were our vehicle, but not as passengers. Oh no: we worked on them, slaving ten months on, two months off. But those two months were free and clear, allowing travel to a variety of other cultures. It was an exciting life, but an exhausting one. After four years the time came to return to land. The question was where to make our fortune? Vegas, baby!

It was all about Aurelia, of course. She was a quad-lingual roulette dealer who had worked in multiple nations before joining ships, and she was pretty. That was a recipe for success. Within a year she had ascended to the best casino on the Las Vegas Strip. A good thing, too, because as a writer my income amounted to little more than a tax write-off. So Las Vegas was good to us, even if we didn't care for living there. But if there was anything I had learned in my travels, it was that every place was worthy unto itself. To think otherwise was simply ethnocentrism.

Thus, I was quite excited to return to Iowa and explore. Growing up in Cedar Rapids, one of the few *relatively* large cities in Iowa, I had seen no reason to visit tiny farming communities hours away in the far corners of the state. What starry-eyed teen would? So I did not necessarily know my own state. Now I had a chance to see it slowly, fully. Perhaps only now that I was older and wiser could I truly value the merits of small town USA. It was a shame Aurelia would not join me, but an athlete she most certainly was not, nor a camper.

Ah, but it turned out camping would not be so necessary! Aaron informed me that his father had volunteered to drive our support vehicle. This was more than just some guy driving a van full of tents and extra clothes: Doc was bringing a 42-foot RV!

While Aaron and his travels did not necessarily humble me, his father was another matter. Doc was a staggeringly intelligent and insightful man. Further, he was one of the bravest, yet most pragmatic men I knew. He asked the hard questions of life and the world and was not afraid of the answers he found, nor afraid to voice them. Yet this man was no dusty, boring intellect. Doc was a charming, patient conversationalist with a great sense of humor—and a 42-foot RV!

Doc was a world traveler, too, despite humble beginnings as a minister's son. He joined the Air Force and there became a doctor. Of immensely more importance, he also met his best friend and wife Barbara. After their military career they retired to Cedar Rapids, where Doc reinforced his already impressive medical credentials to become a leading radiologist in Eastern Iowa. They also started a family. Though I didn't even meet Aaron until our high school years, I was all but welcomed into their family as an honorary member. This made me exceedingly proud. Over the years their enthusiasm and support had never wavered.

It was shaping up to be a perfect vacation. A perfect opportunity to catch up with an old friend, with hours of quiet biking through gentle countryside. A perfect place to relax after a hard ride, with real showers instead of car washes and a perfect night's sleep in air-conditioned comfort. A perfect reunion. Perfect everything.

But one simply cannot just show up for a 500-mile ride. Training must come first. And my RAGBRAI training was far, far from perfect.

RUMBLE YELL: TRAINING ON PLANET Vegas

I don't know what normal is, but I know what normal is not. Normal is not Las Vegas. This is fundamental to the city, for who goes there to do what they normally do? Las Vegas exists to zipline naked over gyrating topless dancers throwing money at you. That just doesn't happen in normal life. At least not mine.

Nor is the location of Las Vegas normal. Humans were not meant to live there. Nor did they—until us foolish white folks, that is. The Native Americans of the area, the Southern Paiutes, Hualapai, and others, preferred the nearby rocks of Valley of Fire. Yes, they actually preferred living in a place called *Valley of Fire* to Las Vegas. That fact alone spoke volumes.

But live there I did, and training I needed. Aaron biked daily in Portland, and if our time together was going to be perfect, I needed to keep up with him! I began to obsess over training. First came rides around my neighborhood. It seemed an excellent way to start because I could keep the rides short but worthy, because we lived in mountain foothills with some tough inclines. But I had to do a lot more than just thirty minutes during lunch, or an hour after work. I had to do some pretty big rides. I needed rides over fifty miles, even up to eighty. That meant exiting the city, and that meant hostile terrain.

For my first trip into the wild I selected the Red Rock Canyon Scenic Byway. This was actually right next to the city sprawl—beginning at Red Rock Casino and Spa, of course—so I was not too terribly far from civilization should things go awry. I was excited to see how my new bike handled the untamed undulations of tectonic madness

that created the candy-striped Rainbow Escarpment and
cherry-red upthrusts of Red Rock Canyon. Lonely country,
indeed, but simply gorgeous. The bike worked great for
being so 'cheap'. I began hitting that route several times a
week, gleefully inching up the mileage each time. A month
passed and the heat level rose. It soon became the defining
issue of each ride. But I persevered for adventure, for
Aaron, for me.

The time came for a big ride. A thirty miler on the
Scenic Byway would max out the loop. I was eager to
conquer that road. But most of all, I was eager to plumb
that greatest biking mystery of all. For, unbeknownst to my
dear Aurelia, I had secretly bought some crotch lube. Even
more secretly—so secret I didn't dare admit it even to
myself—I was excited to try it. I didn't exactly know why
chamois cream intrigued me so, but I was eager to find out.

A chamois was simply the name for the cushion built
into biking-specific shorts: a big, smooth pad in the crotch.
Somehow, somewhere, lubricant was involved. I'd never
before devoted time to exploration of this uniquely biking
ritual. Though I had worn some pretty outlandish stuff—
generally in the privacy of my own bedroom—this was a
new one.

Chamois creams had exciting names. Vegas names.
Most were anatomically-minded—as if deep down we
aren't all anatomically-minded—like *Assos, DZ Nuts*, or
Butt Paste. Others were playfully animalistic, such as
Udderly S-MOO-th. Some combined both, a la *Bag Balm*.
I'm not afraid to admit that *Beljum Hard Core Budder*
intimidated me, as did the description for *Friction
Freedom*: 'helps heal and manage existing saddle sores,
while preventing chafing, and bacterial and fungal
infections that cause hot spots and infections.' Did I really

want to risk all *that* for Aaron, or any reason whatsoever? In the end I opted for the apparent leader of the pack, *Chamois Butt'r*. Even then I was scared because it came in little portable containers that looked distressingly like a suppository.

My first dilemma was figuring out if I wore underwear with the bike shorts or not. I decided in true American fashion that more is better, which meant if one layer was safe, two was safer. I wore underwear. Feeling exceedingly self-conscious, I squirted a bunch of *Chamois Butt'r* down there. Chafing even as I walked around the Jeep did not bode well.

Things immediately took a turn for the worse.

By mile six, I had to stop. This was a common turn around point for day-trippers as it was the location of a beautiful scenic overlook. I didn't stop to enjoy the gaping views of tectonic splendor and wildly diverse color, but rather to adjust my smarting crotch and answer nature.

It was hot outside, of course. Though only March, the sun already burned a good hundred degrees in the Mojave Desert. Heat waves bounced off the hard earth with more intensity than even from the highway's black asphalt. Crazy anything could grow in that dirt. Few things did, actually, and all were ornery as Hell. If something grew, it had spikes. If it didn't have spikes, it had hide thick as an elephant's. Supposedly, animals lived out there, burrowing things like lizards, kangaroo rats or jackrabbits. A rather vocal non-profit organization insisted this was the habitat of the endangered desert tortoise, but I didn't believe it. I had been hiking these wastes for years and hadn't seen a thing, including tracks. To this day I maintain that tortoises don't exist.

So, sweating and panting, I eased my aching ass off

the bike and unbuckled my helmet. The straps dangled down my cheeks to scratch off the sunblock, but breathing came more easily. I stiffly proceeded to the toilets, keenly aware of suffering some sort of diaper rash. I couldn't remember the last time I had that, but was pretty sure it sucked then, too.

The facilities were merely pit latrines, if immaculately maintained. The concrete structure provided a measure of relief from the heat, but it was still more than hot enough to keep the pit's contents fresher than I cared to smell. I stood before the latrine and looked down to deal with the rather intimidating bike shorts. There was no fly in the chamois, of course, just soggy cloth and spandex stretched perversely across my privates, smashing them into forms no man ever wants to see. True, people probably paid for that in Vegas, but I was not one of them. I tried not to dwell on the fact that I was doing it to myself, for free, for Aaron. I leaned forward to get a better look at my brutalized package.

Mistake.

My helmet tumbled from my head, dropping directly into the latrine. The fall was a clean one, missing the rim entirely to plummet directly into the pit. It landed with a sickening, squishy thump. I blinked in disbelief, staring down at my new $65 helmet perched neatly atop a rising mound of feces. This was not good. This was distinctly bad. And I had twenty-four more miles to go!

Turns out head safety wasn't the problem. The problem was a wild burro attack. Yes, a wild burro attack. I sensed that maybe, just maybe, Aaron's training in Oregon presented less challenges for him. Bigfoot, maybe.

It happened at mile twenty. I had reached the end of the Scenic Byway and already turned back, pausing at a

430

rather enchanting notch between mountains that obviously had a hidden water source somewhere. A few lonely willow trees rose up, but, confused and defeated, drooped back down to the rocky earth and rough scrub. It was the only roadside shade on the entire Scenic Byway, other than the manufactured overlook back at mile six.

Severely stiff and crotch blazing, I eased off my bike. Groaning, I awkwardly squatted to remove a snack from a seat bag on the bike. Progress was even more painfully slow than slogging up miles-long hills against thirty mile per hour winds. Finally I retrieved my treasure and grinned through sun-cracked lips.

The euphoria was short-lived. The energy bar was nothing more than a gooey mess, like a cookie pulled too soon from the oven. Grunting and still squatting like some sort of animal, I licked the hot gunk from the wrapper. I carefully forced out of my mind worries about training rides when summer hit. This was only early spring, after all.

I spied the burro half a mile away through the scrub brush, nuzzling a cholla. He spied me, too, and began noisily honking. The sound carried easily over the dead, scorched earth. He began trotting towards me until perhaps a hundred feet away. Then he charged.

Panic flashed through me. The burro moved incredibly fast. I could never outrun him—certainly not with a funky diaper rash—and I doubted I could start on my bike with anything approaching alacrity. I wasn't sure what to do. I considered briefly sitting down and crying, but sitting would hurt worse than anything the burro would do. So I frantically hobbled to a desert-willow and peeked around the trunk. At least that would break the wild beast's charge.

I never underestimated wild animals in Nevada, for I had been attacked by some pretty benign-seeming beasts. Once a horde of bunnies nearly ended my life. Yes, really. The worst, though, was being attacked by an angry stallion who thought I was chasing his fillies. That had been absolutely terrifying, seeing such a huge, magnificent animal overtly displaying aggressive behavior and me being several miles of cross-country running from my Jeep. I survived that, so there was nothing to worry about in a lousy mule, right?

Wrong.

The charging burro was easily an eight hundred pound wild animal. Many reached a thousand pounds. All were hardened survivors of the worst land nature had to offer. I had seen cute, fuzzy youngsters placidly snacking on cactus thorns the size of my fingers. I didn't want to mess with *anything* that had a mouth that tough. He could have bitten right through my helmet, if I still had one. I didn't even want to imagine a kick from those hooves.

The burro got about twenty feet away and slowed. Finally he stopped and eyed me. I eyed him back from behind the relative safety of the tree.

He appeared young because his coat was pretty and trim and he was slender. Most wild burros I'd seen had barrel chests and shaggy coats. His neck had a rough spot, as if something had tried to take him down. It looked exactly like a predator's mark, and it gleamed. Yes, that was blood. For sure it was. I didn't know what could take a chunk out of an animal that big, and I didn't want to find out. There were no big predators in the Mojave, unless you counted the aggregate mass of a coyote pack. That was unlikely, but not impossible.

The burro seemed content to just observe. Then he

became vocal. He honked at me. Presumably he associated humans with food. I told him I didn't have anything to eat, which was true. He didn't believe me. Nor would he shut up about it. It's rare to find someone who talks more than me. And in the animal kingdom? You have to look for screaming monkeys and stuff. A long time passed, and he seemed in no hurry to leave. I, on the other hand, thought leaving most prudent.

But, simply put, I couldn't take any more chafing. I just couldn't. Squatting beneath the desert-willow, I stripped off my loathsome chamois. Decency was irrelevant as it was just the burro and me.

If only.

Suddenly, and for the first time in *hours*, cars appeared on the Scenic Byway. What were the odds they would pass at this one and only moment? But life could be mean like that. The cars whizzed by as my white, über-lubed butt glowed brilliantly from the shade of the tree. But removing my soggy underwear provided instant relief, and that mattered more than anything else. I smashed the squishy underwear into the bike satchel and oh-so-carefully remounted. I delicately rubbed my tender privates atop the bike saddle. Everything slid properly over the lubricated chamois. I sighed. The burro approved with a honk. I was glad he couldn't speak English.

All that was just a single thirty-mile ride! Of course, it got worse. Much, much worse.

***

But I learned. I learned that the proper and generous application of *Chamois Butt'r* prevented saddle sores. I learned that, as I've always maintained, underwear is just in the way. I also learned that sometimes Mom was right.

Like so many rebellious youths, I had scoffed when Mom told me drinking from the garden hose would cause a bacterial invasion that would devour my flesh and eat my brains. I did it anyway. I'm fine. I also scoffed when Mom told me that not wearing a hat would cause frost bite that would destroy my flesh and freeze my brains. Soon as she wasn't looking, off came the hat. Mom also told me to wear a helmet when riding my bike. Really, Mom. Just how uncool do you want your son to be?

But I learned that helmets *were* necessary. Very, very necessary.

I was beginning at the Red Rock Canyon Scenic Byway. A traffic light separated the parking lot from the desert road. I neared the traffic signal and slowed on the sidewalk, waiting for a green light. My bike wavered a bit, but my balance was good. My distance calibration needed some work, though. The handlebar met a pole and jerked the front wheel perpendicular to my forward momentum. In a blink I was falling backwards to the pavement. My head smacked onto the sidewalk with a thunderous CRACK!

I lay there a moment, seeing stars. I had never seen stars like that before. It defied credulity that my head hit so brutally hard. Damn you, physics! Whiplash... at three miles per hour! But while my bike was only moving slowly, my body had fallen much faster, with my head whipping down with crushing force. Had I not been wearing a helmet I would have been really and truly damaged. What followed was a rare moment of sobriety. And, of course, yet another trip to the store to buy yet another helmet.

So I learned to give it up to Mom on that one.

I also learned to hate Vegas cyclists.

***

Red Rock Canyon Scenic Byway. Saturday morning. 7AM. The parking lot was full. A long line of men and women in brilliant spandex jerseys snaked out of the Starbucks. Small clusters talked to each other, but that rarely meant meaningful conversation. Most merely waited for the other to stop talking so they could brag about their bike and gear.

I generally avoided the Scenic Byway on weekends because it was a favorite cruising destination for Las Vegans and tourists. The road rumbled with speeding Lamborghinis, Ferraris, and Harleys. Staying alive in all that meant sticking to the shoulder. After half an hour I passed the scenic stop with its helmet-eating latrine. The area was brimming with bicyclists already turning back. Go on, little riders, shell out $3000 worth of bike, and another $1,000 worth of clothing, just to stop and turn around for only an hour ride. Go on, I say! These bikers were all show and no substance. I had faced a wild burro and survived! Go ahead, little people, discuss your expensive doodads at Starbucks. I'm busy being awesome.

Enter: rude awakening.

A block of riders overtook me, dominating the shoulder by riding double-wide, handlebar to handlebar. A single cyclist rode at the fore, like Death himself on a pale bike, leading the Riders of the Apocalypse. They numbered not four, but eleven: leader crying havoc before ten instruments of Armageddon, crushing and casting aside all in their path.

Exit: stage right.

Forced off the shoulder at top speed, I was nearly

435

hurled into a rugged washout twenty feet deep. By sheer luck—and adrenaline—I managed to collapse instead of fly. Pain blasted through me as I hit the crumbling bank of rocks, sliding right up to the very edge. I felt each and every rock, but it was better than a similar crunch after a twenty-foot fall. The Hell riders zoomed past my head, a blur of snapping yellow jerseys and disdain, their cadence booming into desert, crossing the wastes and echoing off distant mountains.

"Who's Lance?"
"WE'RE LANCE!"
"Who's Lance?"
"WE'RE LANCE!"
"How many?"
"SEVEN!"
"How many?"
"SEVEN!"

Surely this wasn't what I was going to encounter on RAGBRAI: herds of Lance Armstrong wanna-bes? Only then did it occur to me I would be one of a *minimum* of 10,000 simultaneous riders. My vision blurred, only to refocus on recollections of one Tour de France rider falling and dozens of poor, following riders tumbling into him. I wasn't prepared for that at all!

***

But when things don't go your way in Vegas, nobody calls it quits. We double down. In my case, I swapped the Scenic Byway's thirty miles of all but lonely desert for the unlimited milage of freakin' aliens-only desert. Literally. I chose the wastes north of Las Vegas, mere miles from Area 51 and its supposed UFO sightings. This was a place so God-forsaken that the U.S. military continued to test top-secret stuff out there, knowing no normal human would ever dare go there. So for Aaron I risked getting abducted by aliens. Fortunately, no anal probes occurred. At that point my butt was so numb I probably wouldn't have noticed anyway. But something particularly loathsome did occur.

It was on my longest training ride, an eighty-five miler. I started the ride at 3:40AM. That didn't mean I woke up at 3:40, oh no. It was an hour drive just to get to my starting point. So up at 2:30 I was, knowing how bad the heat would get. Or I thought I did. You never really prepare yourself for heat pushing 130°, you just think you do.

I parked the Jeep on the side of the road at mile marker 1. It was still dark. Stars were visible to the north and west, but already fading into the rosy glow of the east. To the south lay Las Vegas, source of enough light to make the cosmos squint. This place was so awful that after 119 nuclear blasts the landscape hadn't noticeably changed. So they set off 500 more underground.

By flashlight I readied my hydration backpack with a forty-ounce bladder. Two ice packs were tucked within to keep it all relatively cool, for after a few hours in *that* heat water could brew tea. I brought some gel-like globules called Gu-Chomps, hoping to swallow the scalding hot mass they would inevitably become. For lunch I had a Pemmican-brand energy bar. This was carefully devoid of chocolate or yogurt or anything else that would melt. Thus my reward at halfway—43 miles!—was basically a sack of oats, fat, and sugar compressed into a bar. For you, Aaron.

I sprayed myself liberally with half a can of 50 SPF

sunblock—an odd thing to do in the blackness of night—
wet my lips with 50 SPF Chapstick, and was ready to go.
Out there nature provided no shade whatsoever. Well, that
wasn't entirely true. At mile fifty-something—beyond the
turn-around point—was a stagnant oasis of crusty water
laden with violent amoebas. There rose three sorry-looking
trees and five signs warning the water was toxic.

Though starting in darkness, I wasn't worried about
being struck by a car. My bike had been haphazardly
painted Day-Glo green and would easily catch headlights.
Who would drive out there at this hour anyway? At *any*
hour? Only a single DNR truck forced to do so. I
considered the solitude. The quiet of the desert was
awesome, humbling, frightening. This was a rare place
where man held no sway, but only left evidence of passage
to elsewhere. Yet the silence was deeper than merely the
absence of man. It was the rarified silence of no life at all.
No plants to rustle, no crickets to chirp, no birds to cry. The
ribbon of asphalt undulated alone across bone-dry washes
and through barren mountains of exposed rock upthrust to
reveal literally four billion years of past life. *Past* life.

Such a profound record of life's fecundity surrounded
me. Where had it all gone? Why?

The answer rose presently. Sunlight crawled over the
'cool' 85° landscape with destroying heat, stirred brutally
hot winds and lethal aridity. Out there people had been
found dead with water still in their possession. The severe
dryness sucked all moisture from their bodies faster than
drinking could replenish it.

Another hour or so the thermometer registered 115°.
Heat rebounding off the dead earth added uncharted
degrees. Surprising, then, was encountering the first sight
of life. Buzzards circled up ahead. No, not buzzards, but

ravens: huge, black, and bigger than my fourteen-pound cats. I rode towards them, wondering for what they were waiting to die. But do not ask for whom the bell tolls: it tolls for thee. At mile marker 33 I passed a dead jackrabbit the size of a beagle. The poor creature was smashed, innards steaming in the sun. It freaked me out.

Just two hours later it would freak me out far, far more. But more on that later.

***

Over the course of four months of nearly constant riding, I discovered that I hated biking. It wasn't just the Vegas riders, though that was a big part of it. It wasn't even the heat, though that was an even bigger part of it. No, I loathed biking because my rides had almost universally been in winds ranging from twenty to thirty miles per hour —on a *good* day. Nothing broke the wind for hundreds of miles in all directions of Vegas, so gusts fanned out over the wastes to push you off the road and belittle your puniness of size and effort. When mountains interfered they made it worse, channeling the winds into tunnels that roared through the barren passes I labored through. Biking was not fun. It was torture.

But all that was done. The time had come to pack away the hateful skin-searing, crotch-killer. Dismembering the bike was a surprisingly satisfying experience. My victory was ultimately denied, however. The last pedal refused to come off. I struggled so mightily that I broke the ratchet! After a trip to the store and much profanity I resumed my effort, only to be continually defeated. Finally I just shoved the frame into the slender box, scraping the pedal down the side. It burst through the cardboard. With devilish glee I drew a band-aid over the area and added a cartoon-style bubble caption shouting "$@&%!"

But the drama wasn't done. The shipping company failed to arrive and pick up the wounded box. Because timing was critical in this step, I called them in a panic.

"You didn't pick up my parcel!" I cried into the phone. "It's gotta be shipped by today or it won't make it on time."

"Our apologies," replied a nasally man through the phone. "What is the address?"

"Shiny Skies Drive," I replied hastily.

"Chinese Guys Drive," the voice repeated. "Yes, my notes say they went there yesterday and found no package."

"Shiny Skies," I repeated with emphasis.

"Chinese Guys."

"*Skies*, man!" I burst out. "Isn't this Las Vegas? Clear *skies*, as in no clouds. The sun *shines* here all the damn time. *Shiny skies*."

"Of course, sir. Our apologies. We will send a truck to pick up your parcel at Chinese Guys Drive, in sunny Las Vegas. Thank you for your business."

Irrationally angry, I shoved the box into the Jeep and hauled it straight to the transport company's office. I was thrilled to get rid of the thing. I never wanted to see it again. But boy, would I. A week's worth of loathsome riding awaited.

Aaron better be worth it.

But rid of the toil of actual riding, and with the assistance of much rum, happy dreams of biking bubbled to the surface. I grew enthusiastic anew and began scouring the internet for bits and pieces of trivia or advice. Eventually I clicked on the official map of elevation. My jaw dropped.

RAGBRAI claimed that Day 1 had 4,298 feet of elevation gain over 59.5 miles. According to the source I had been training with, MapMyRIDE.com, the route only climbed 1,400 feet. RAGBRAI was going to be *66% harder* than I thought. In fact, Day 1 and Day 2 were *both* harder than *any* single day of Colorado's famed Ride the Rockies! Though the latter crested several mountain passes, its total elevation gain only beat RAGBRAI by 400 measly feet.

I tried to calm myself. I knew this. I was raised in Iowa. Everyone not from Iowa stereotyped it as flat as a pancake. Such riders faced one hell of a learning curve! There are easily eighty rivers in Iowa, with each and every one carving its own valley—a valley to pedal out of. Then, of course, there were the two monsters bordering the state: the Muddy Missouri and the Mighty Mississippi. 10,000 years ago the glaciers receded and let those bad boys loose. Since then they've wreaked havoc unchecked, carving and moving and carving again. And carving power did they have: the Mississippi alone tapped a whopping thirty-two American states and two Canadian provinces to make the fourth greatest drainage on the planet.

None of it mattered. It was too late to chicken out. Like it or not, I was going to Iowa!

***

Saturday, July 23rd. Glenwood, Iowa. Such was the date and place, one day prior to the celebrated tire dip. The Midwest's largest bike expo—take *that*, Chicago—was set up in the parking lot of the Glenwood Community High School. After goodbye hugs from my shuttling parents— and Mom's last minute check that I had a helmet—I said goodbye, shouldered my week's worth of gear, and strode down to the sprawling series of tents, canopies, and kiosks.

Aaron had texted me to meet him at the bike delivery area. For some reason cell phone reception was spotty in Glenwood, but the message squeaked through. Finding the appropriate tents among the many presented no challenge, as the dozens of slender boxes stacked fifty yards deep demanded attention. Perfectly easy.

I worked my way through the milling crowd towards the bike delivery. Hundreds of people had already arrived despite the early hour and the rain. The clouds above were thick and twisted, like a giant nebulous towel being wrung over yonder. Fortunately, above us directly it was only drizzling. It was delightful to this desert rat. Perfectly refreshing.

A surprisingly small tent was allocated for the organizing and distribution of all the shipped bikes. Several enthusiastic men and women waited with clipboards, ready to check off names and send the eager young men into the piles of boxes to muscle out specific parcels. Not seeing Aaron anywhere nearby, I went ahead with the process. Because the expo had only officially opened thirty minutes ago, there was no wait. Perfect timing.

Yes, it was all going as planned. After months of slaving and sweating, planning and stressing, it was all going to be as perfect as I had imagined.

A stranger approached. He was of average height but much bigger build. His huge shoulders and arms said bodybuilder, but his equally huge belly admitted those were days past. The man's dress and manner were rather slovenly, his face unshaven. All his hair was shot with grey, be it on his head, on his face, or protruding from his nose. A spandex biking jersey strained ludicrously over his paunch, the pattern of Vincent Van Gogh's *Starry Night* stretching stars into large, furry comets around a moon bloated to a white super giant. He seemed oddly intent on me.

He moved through the crowd, snarfing down a cheap microwave burrito. Under one armpit was the smashed wrapper of another. He finally made eye contact with me. His gaze was bold and handsome, intense beneath a strong brow. He quickly crammed the remains of the meal into his mouth—meaning the entire second half of the burrito—swallowing it in a painfully forced gulp. The stranger beamed at me and offered his hand. His vice-like grip made me squirm.

"I'm Cheek!" he said enthusiastically. "I'll be riding with you!"

Who the Hell was this?

Don't miss the ride of your life—get *Rumble Yell* today!
Available everywhere books are sold.

Mediterranean Sea & featured ports

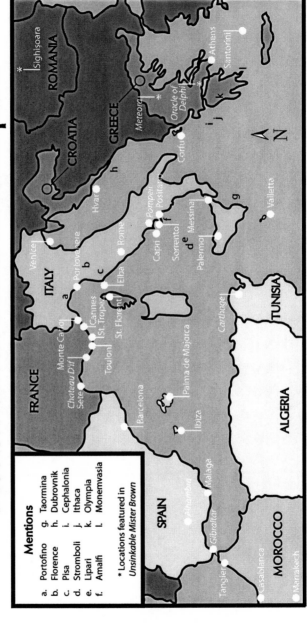

Mentions

a. Portofino
b. Florence
c. Pisa
d. Stromboli
e. Lipari
f. Amalfi

g. Taormina
h. Dubrovnik
i. Cephalonia
j. Ithaca
k. Olympia
l. Monemvasia

* Locations featured in
Unsinkable Mister Brown

Don't miss my new paranormal series, American Gothic!

"Reminiscent of classic Gothic horror stories by the likes of Edgar Allan Poe, it is B.D. Bruns' style of writing that is most pleasing. Rather than the too often used jump-out-and-scare-you or shock effect writing that so many 'horror' writers create, he instead allows the story to build gradually, making the whole experience that much more enjoyable.
"Bruns has the science of tension building down to an art form. *As I read each of these stories, I was squirming in my seat to find out what would happen in the end. I highly recommend The Gothic Shift to anyone looking for a good scare, and I can't want for volume 2 to come out in this collection."*
—Reader's Favorite Reviews

Worried it's too scary? Follow me on Twitter (@LoveBruns) and tweet the message below. I'll send you a free ebook! That's how convinced I am you'll love it.

Send my free #ebook of The Gothic Shift
@LoveBruns #amreading #goodreads
#giveaway

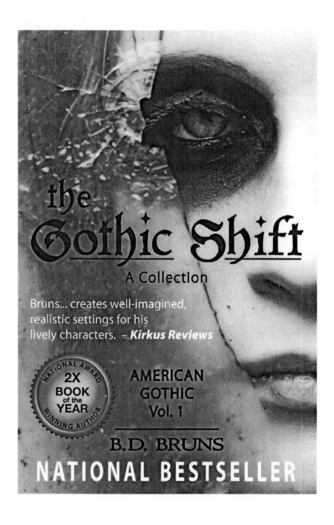

CPSIA information can be obtained at www.ICGtesting.com
Printed in the USA
LVOW08s2037060414

380542LV00004B/773/P